ROBERT WIGHT AND THE
BOTANICAL DRAWINGS OF RUNGIAH & GOVINDOO
BOOK 2

Robert Wight and the
Botanical Drawings of Rungiah & Govindoo

BOOK 2

BOTANICAL DRAWINGS
BY RUNGIAH & GOVINDOO
THE WIGHT COLLECTION

H. J. NOLTIE

Royal Botanic Garden Edinburgh

MMVII

First published 2007
by the Royal Botanic Garden Edinburgh
© all rights reserved

ISBN 978 1 906129 00 2

Designed and typeset in Verdigris by Dalrymple
Printed in Belgium by Die Keure

Frontispiece: detail at actual
size from plate 41b

Introduction

The original intention of the Robert Wight project was to research the collection of drawings by Rungiah and Govindoo at the Royal Botanic Garden Edinburgh (RBGE), which he commissioned, and to reproduce a selection in a volume similar to the *Dapuri Drawings*.[1] However, even preliminary research revealed complex and intimate links between these drawings and with Wight's vast collections of herbarium specimens at RBGE, and also with substantial collections of drawings at Kew (RBGK), the Natural History Museum (NHM) and Edinburgh University (EU). To do adequate justice to Wight's enormous lifework it was therefore necessary to document these interconnected collections of drawings and dried plants, to draw up a detailed account of his life and work, and to experience at first hand the landscapes in which his great achievements were undertaken – the results thus grew into four volumes.[2]

The most important part of the present volume will be the pictures themselves, but while these to some extent 'speak for themselves', a fuller appreciation will be gained by an attempt to explain their context – the reason for Wight's commissioning them, the little that it has been possible to find out about Rungiah, Govindoo, and the other artists represented in his collection, the collections in which these paintings are now located, and the use Wight made of the drawings, especially through the medium of lithography.

2717
1023*

R.K.G. delt.   November 1st 1831

Fig. 1. *Astragalus alpinus*, hand-coloured copper engraving after a drawing
by R.K. Greville, from the second Supplement to *English Botany* (ed. W.J.
Hooker, 1837).

CHAPTER ONE

The Validity of Botanical Art as a Scientific Tool

The insufficiency of language alone to convey just ideas of the forms of natural objects, has led naturalists …
to have recourse to pictorial delineation to assist the mind through the medium of the senses. ROBERT WIGHT[1]

As an observational classificatory science, botany had come [by 1838] *to rely heavily on pictures,*
the inspection of which provided both sensory enjoyment and rational pleasure. ANNE SECORD[2]

From early on in Wight's time in India he had been frustrated by the number, quality and accessibility of the published illustrations of Indian plants then existing, dating from the period 1678 to 1820 – copper engravings, from the relatively simple ones in the works of the Burmans (Johannes and Nicolaas) [fig.2] and Leonard Plukenet, to the lavish ones in the publications of Hendrik van Rheede and William Roxburgh, but all united in their scarcity and inaccessibility. That Wight passionately believed in the value of illustration was shown when in 1828 he started to send drawings by his artist Rungiah, amassed over a period of several years, to Professor William Jackson Hooker for publication in Glasgow.

The admissibility of using 'the medium of the senses' as a way of 'assisting the mind', and as a way of gaining scientific knowledge, had, however, been a contentious issue as far back as the second-century Graeco-Roman doctor Galen.[3] While the Renaissance European herbal tradition, starting with Leonhart Fuchs and Otto Brunfels, placed great importance on accurate pictures, and used new technology to reproduce drawings of plants, others, most notably Linnaeus, could (at least on occasion) be positively scornful of their value:

> I do not recommend the use of images for the determination of genera. I absolutely reject them – although I confess that they are more pleasing to children and those who have more of a head than a brain. I admit that they offer something to the illiterate … But who ever derived a firm argument from a picture?[4]

In 1838, at the very time Wight embarked on his major illustrated publications, discussions on the validity of illustration once again became a live issue in Britain, as illuminatingly written about by Anne Secord.[5] The effect of these discussions outwith Britain has been little considered, but it is in this context that Wight's vast contribution to the corpus of scientific botanical illustration is to be seen and understood. It should be pointed out that there are direct links between Wight and many of the key players (including W.J. Hooker, R.K. Greville and H.C. Watson) in the debate as discussed by Secord. Of these the most important was Wight's close connection with W.J. Hooker, the supreme exponent both of the use of illustration in the Scottish university lecturing tradition, and of illustration in the encouragement of the *philosophical* study of little-known floras,[6] and also of exotics grown in British gardens. There is also a less direct, but interesting, link with Henry Brougham, who slightly earlier (in 1827) had discussed the popularisation of science, and its appropriate methods, in his widely read and influential work *The Objects, Advantages and Pleasures of Science*. Brougham, like Wight, was a product of the late Scottish Enlightenment, had passed through exactly the same educational system (though a decade and a half earlier), and had honed his debating skills in the Speculative Society founded by Wight's cousin Allan Maconochie, whose biography Brougham wrote; Brougham's wife was a niece of William Robertson who had baptised Wight's mother. Furthermore Brougham was married to the niece of R.K. Greville's wife, Greville being another important believer of the importance of illustration – both in the lecture room and in his scientific floras (notably his outstandingly fine *Scottish Cryptogamic Flora* illustrated by himself, and see also fig.1).

Nothing, unfortunately, is known of the use (if any) that Daniel Rutherford, Wight's first teacher of botany, made of illustrations in his lectures. But, because his illustrations collection has miraculously survived, we do know the extensive use made by his predecessor John Hope, and the influence this had in India through his pupils. Hope had no reservations about use of the senses (particular taste and smell) for analytical purposes, used large teaching diagrams to illustrate his lectures, and commissioned analytical botanical drawings for taxonomic purposes, for example from James Robertson.[7] Hope was a major influence on William Roxburgh and Francis Buchanan who carried this belief in the value of illustration, along with other aspects of his teaching, to India.[8] Roxburgh's and Buchanan's extensive commissioning of botanical drawings from Indian artists is well known, and the influence of especially the former on Wight in such matters is clearly demonstrated by Wight's dedication of his own monumental *Icones* to the memory of Roxburgh, his predecessor as Madras Naturalist.

Fig.2. 'Filix zeylanica', copper engraving from Johannes Burman's *Thesaurus Zeylanicus* (1737). Not a fern, but a flowering plant, Wight & Arnott based their *Rhus decipiens* (now *Filicium decipiens*) on this plate.

Of Wight's contemporaries Hooker and Greville both made extensive use of large scale illustrations in their lectures, and Hooker later sold the collection he had made and used at Glasgow (after 1834 these were painted by W.H. Fitch) to Wight's great collaborator George Walker-Arnott. Most of this collection has unfortunately not survived, but one that has, of *Vallisneria spiralis*, turns out to be partly based on a drawing by Rungiah (Book 3 fig.8) – the fascinating topic of copying and recycling will be returned to in Chapter 4. To accompany his lectures and practical classes Hooker, as early as 1821, also used a book of *Botanical Illustrations* compiled by himself, made up of composite (lithographed) plates of minute analyses of vegetative and floral structures. When Wight visited Hooker in Glasgow between 1831 and 1834, at a time when Hooker was still publishing Rungiah's drawings in the *Botanical Miscellany*, they discussed illustration and publication at length.[9] It was at this very time that Hooker was contemplating a more extensive use of lithography, and of publishing uncoloured analytical drawings of plants of primarily botanical (rather than horticultural) interest, which emerged as his long running periodical *Icones Plantarum* first published in 1836.

The debate about the admissibility of illustration into didactic and popular scientific works touched on notions of amateur/professional, of social class, and the role of the senses in acquisition of scientific knowledge. There was concern about the role of pleasure and, in particular, as expressed earlier by Linnaeus, a worry that use of the senses made things 'too easy' and that knowledge obtained in such a way would be superficial.[10] Brougham had taken a high moral tone in promoting the diffusion of scientific knowledge and in his work stated that 'no figures will be at present used to assist the imagination; the appeal is made to reason, without help from the senses'.[11] So, despite their similarities in background, Wight took a contrary position to Brougham, but one should bear in mind the different audience each had in mind (Wight's will be discussed below: Brougham's was largely the English middle and lower classes). Similarly contrary views were aired in a debate conducted in the pages of the *Naturalist* in 1838, in which the amateur botanist Edwin Lees took the Wightian view that readers: 'must be charmed into the path of science by pictures'. Lees had no time for those who thought it 'almost criminal in recognizing a bird by its figure in a good plate' and, rather, that 'a figure often gives information where language is found quite inadequate'. Peter Rylands responded in an article with the self-explanatory title 'On the abuse of prints in works on Natural History' and believed that 'cognition governed by the senses and not by the intellect could only be "superficial"'. In fairness, Rylands did allow the use of plates showing magnified analytical details, so would probably have approved of Wight's works – at least up to a point.

It is worth noting that when Wight embarked on his own illustrated works he cited *English Botany* as a model. The text of this multi-volume work, consisting of plant descriptions, was written by James Edward Smith (significantly, another Hope pupil) and the illustrations are hand-coloured engravings by James Sowerby. However, what came to be universally known as 'Sowerby's English Botany' could be seen to have been an unfortunate precedent. The author, Smith:

had come to the "mortifying conclusion" that his descriptions were ignored … [and] feared that this work had not produced as wide "a taste

for correct and scientific botany" as he had hoped but instead may have fostered "the great facility with which a trivial and superficial knowledge of plants is now gained, by turning over books of coloured figures".[12]

By contrast Wight's illustrated publications were, perhaps, a more seamless whole: he personally and closely supervised the plates in which the analytical details are much more prominent than in Sowerby's plates. In the case of the *Icones* both from the title of the work and the physical space occupied, there is no doubt that Wight intended the plates to be the more important part, being accompanied by the briefest of written descriptions. Though this is by no means to suggest that the latter were not seen as important, and Wight specifically cautioned against identification by merely looking at plates and not reading descriptions: there was 'no royal road to science' and users of his work 'need never expect through an inspection of plates or specimens of medical plants to become a medical Botanist'.[13] Wight must have been fully aware that there were 'tensions between pleasure and work, entertainment and intellectualism, sensuality and reason'.[14] In fact the plates of the *Icones* are so extremely abstract that it is almost impossible to use them to identify plants by superficial means – they force inspection of the all-important analytical details and Wight specifically drew attention to Indian artists' excellence at outline, but lack of ability to show (what he probably took to be much less important) features of habit. Wight's hand-coloured works, the *Illustrations* and *Spicilegium*, were coloured specifically to appeal to a broader audience. But it was not enough for them to look attractive, they must also be didactic – as a means of recruiting members to the body botanic (especially in India) who would take its study seriously and be able to distinguish plant families. It is not, therefore, accidental that these two works have vastly more extensive texts than the *Icones*.

The use of illustration made by Wight's collaborator Arnott both in his own publications, and in his deployment of Wight's drawings, is of some interest, and the following statement in one of his letters to Hooker is revealing:

I perfectly agree with you that engravings are ruinous jobs: and it is on that account that although I sometimes happen to have drawings from Wight of new genera of plants that I have described, I neither offer them to you nor others with my papers. With regard to *Torreya* [a new genus of conifer Arnott was describing], it would please me equally well, if not better, that there should be no plate, but my difficulty lies in this, that Torrey asked it.[15]

Although Hooker was extremely generous in paying for the lavish illustration of his own publications it seems that Arnott had scruples about encouraging such extravagance, and witheld from Hooker the temptation to use many of Wight's drawings after the close of the series published in the *Botanical Miscellany*. Arnott certainly had Wight's drawings in his possession as early as January 1834,[16] and many are annotated in his hand. However, there was one case [fig.25], which he evidently thought particularly outstanding, where he threw caution to the wind and even offered to pay for some coloured copies:

As to the *Loranthus* I fear that the uncoloured plate will not do justice to it but could a few separate copies of the plate not be coloured for me to send to Wight, DeLessert, Jussieu, Torrey, Esenbeck, DeCandolle, say 10 or a dozen at most – I will pay for the colouring – unless *very* expensive. It is a splendid plant.[17]

Hooker & Arnott's *Botany of the Beechey Voyage* is extensively illustrated (with 99 plates), but this was due to the influence of Hooker who drew the plates himself, and Arnott's own later scientific papers in periodicals are entirely unillustrated. As might perhaps be expected from his legal and mathematical training, he would appear to have inclined towards the stern Brougham school and, though his finances were chronically challenged, Arnott's use of expense as a reason for not reproducing illustrations seems more like an excuse. For his single popular publication, and in teaching, the case was different. The 1831 *Encyclopaedia Britannica* article is lavishly illustrated,[18] but this was doubtless specified by the work's editor Macvey Napier. As already noted, Arnott bought Hooker's collection of teaching diagrams for use in his lectures when he eventually obtained the Glasgow chair in 1845.

The question of audience is also highly relevant in the case of Wight's illustrated publications. These consisted of at least two major groups – one in India, the other in Europe. The European consisted of (more or less) professional, practising botanists, and it was to these whom Wight felt it necessary (repeatedly) to apologise on account of the difficulties of production of his works and the resulting production quality and errors. The Indian audience must have consisted largely of Company officials (there being virtually no other British colonists other than a small merchant community). The only information about these is in the form of the lists of subscribers given in the *Icones* and *Illustrations*. Of these, an extensive one (but including some obvious errors) covering both the *Icones* and *Illustrations* is included in the RBGE copy of the *Illustrations*; and the author's own copy of vol. 1 of the *Icones* has an evidently more accurate list for that work. It is worth giving a preliminary analysis of the longer list (corrected where possible from the shorter one). This shows the expected, but nonetheless striking, difference in popularity between the coloured and plain works:

Subscribers to *Illustrations*: 165
Subscribers to *Icones*: 53
Subscribers to both works: 44

From the titles and designations given the lists also reveal something of the social status of the readers. The military are denoted by rank and/or name of regiment. What might be termed 'gentlefolk' are distinguished by titles (from the Governor General downwards), or as 'Esq.' or 'Mrs', though the 'Esq.' category includes at least three known to be medics.[19] It might be possible to discover more about some of this category (for example, which part of the service or merchant community they belonged) from the Madras Almanacs. Those denoted 'Mr' include Apothecary Bertie, and must therefore include those in humbler ranks of the Company's service.

Employment/Status of individuals in combined list:[20]

Military: 69
Medics: 17
Veterinary surgeon: 1
Ecclesiastics: 7
'Esq.' and titled: 76
'Mrs': 2
'Mr': 5

Gloriosa superba

Fig.3. *Gloriosa superba*: an early drawing by Rungiah, showing his characteristic filling of the page, which in this case happens perfectly to suit the position of the reflexed style (top left) characteristic of this genus (RBGE W508).

CHAPTER TWO

The Artists

Unfortunately little is recorded in Wight's letters or publications of what he sought in an artist, a conspicuous exception being a comment about a drawing sent from Bangalore by William Munro:

> The *Volkameria* is a pretty drawing and finely coloured, but still is not such a one as pleases my eye. There is a want of outline I think which takes from its vigour and gives it a half inaccurate appearance. I may perhaps have assigned a wrong cause for the imperfection which strikes my eye, but be that as it may, it is not the style which pleases my eye, though I acknowledge its beauty.[1]

This shows Wight's emphasis on the importance of line, and that mere beauty was not enough. In the NHM collection are some paintings by a native artist done for Munro in the Nilgiris and sent to Wight. These might perhaps be from the same series as the one referred to, but if so Wight was being excessively generous, probably not wanting to discourage the young Munro – they are certainly lacking in 'outline' of the sort so expertly drawn by Rungiah, but are the crudest of daubs and neither pretty nor finely coloured.

Another revealing criticism of Wight's, applied specifically to Govindoo, but showing what he thought generally about strengths and weaknesses of Indian botanical drawings, is to be found in the *Icones*:

> owing to want of room they often fail in conveying a correct idea of the habit, a point on which native artists are apt to fail, their drawings being usually deficient in ease, but so far as correct outline can compensate for deficiency of grace, I believe the accompanying [illustrations of the *Pouzolzia* monograph] may generally be depended on.[2]

Although Wight might have believed the problem to be 'want of room', it is more likely that Govindoo was merely following traditional Indian practice of filling all available space [fig.3]. In fact this would have been seen as a strength by critics of the use of illustration for diagnosis: users would have to concentrate on the 'line', and details of form – such as leaf shape, and floral and fruit structure, rather than being distracted by superficial 'jizz'. It should also be noted that, even if they could be accurately represented, field characters such as habit were viewed with suspicion by botanists such as Joseph Hooker.[3]

Neither can much be told about how Wight regarded the drawings he commissioned as 'works of art', though from the liberal sprinkling of annotations, they would seem to have been regarded more in the light of scientific specimens, or at least as supplements to such. That Wight was proud of them, however, and saw them as something slightly more than this, is suggested by a comment in the Preface to the *Spicilegium*. From this it is apparent that at least on occasion he showed them to appreciative friends who considered it 'a pity to throw away so much labour and skill of the painter by pub-lishing them as uncoloured outlines'. The thought that these same drawings would one day be framed for a temporary exhibition and put on the walls of Inverleith House (for a time the residence of J.H. Balfour, a friend of Wight's later years), now turned into a public art gallery, would doubtless have surprised Wight, Rungiah and Govindoo, but one can hope that it would have given them all pleasure.

Because of the rules and conventions of Linnaean taxonomic practice, and before the establishment of public herbaria and libraries in India, or of a publishing tradition open to them, it was virtually impossible for Indians to contribute to taxonomic botanical literature in the Western scientific tradition. But this was not the case with art, which (*contra* Linnaeus) has always played an important role in the taxonomic process, and one to which skilled Indians could contribute on equal terms – at which point we enter a subject known as 'subaltern science'. David Arnold has briefly discussed botanical illustrations made by Indian artists from this point of view,[4] but the contribution of Rungiah and Govindoo to the field is truly outstanding. While Wight may have been suspicious of indigenous plant knowledge – as regards vernacular plant names and medical practice ('polypharmacy') – he was particularly aware of the validity and quality of the contribution his Indian artists could make to his grand taxonomic project. This is proved by the unusual scrupulousness in individually crediting the drawings when they were published. The *Icones* especially can be seen as a joint British-Indian enterprise – the botanical descriptions are minimal and the letterpress occupies only a tiny proportion of the total bulk, and while the artists' names are not given on the title page, they appear on every single plate except for a few cases where it was doubtless the lithographer who forgot it.[5] Wight also testified to Rungiah's objectivity, and the value of empirical observation:

> the Draftsman … knows nothing of Botanical opinions or theories, but sets down what he sees.[6]

The benefits of the unbiassed eye will be attested to by any botanist who has collaborated with a skilled artist: it is not uncommon for an artist to notice details overlooked by the botanist, and to be more objective, in some cases shattering a botanist's preconceptions or wishful thinking.

Until now nothing has been known of Wight's artists or their backgrounds other than their names, Rungiah and Govindoo. Two small shreds of evidence, however, have recently come to light – one indirect, the other direct – that links at least Rungiah with the Tanjore school of painters. The indirect evidence is a comment from Wight's own time on likely places to find an artist capable of undertaking botanical work in South India. The Rev Bernhard Schmid had been sending botanical specimens from the Nilgiris to his cousin J.C. Zenker in Jena, who apparently made (or had made) drawings there for publication. However, Schmid evidently came to realise that it might be better if he sent drawings with the specimens (as Wight had already done to his European collaborator Hooker) and informed Wallich that:

> Dr Lane, who has just returned from the Hills to Madras … has also been so generous as to offer to engage a Native Painter at Tritchinopoly or Tanjore, to come up and to paint any plant for me which I may wish to send to my Cousin Dr Zenker, as a pattern. I have not yet heard of Dr Lane's success in finding a suitable one.[7]

This shows that in the 1830s it was Tanjore and Trichy, rather than Madras, that were thought of as the likely places to recruit botanical painters, both being well known as centres for South Indian religious art. Further confirmation of Tanjore as a source of botanical artists was eventually found by following a garbled reference cited by Mildred Archer.[8] This led to the published diaries of Mountstuart Elphinstone Grant Duff, Governor of Madras 1881–6, extraordinary and sustained feats of polyglot, literary showing-off and name-dropping. Although he was knowledgeable about botany,[9] this was not the place one would expect to find a reference to a mere artisan, but this would be to do Grant Duff an injustice, for it is here that some further information about Rungiah is to be found:

> [8 April 1886] Mr. Rungiah Raju, who has been in my service as a flower-painter since the beginning of 1884, took leave to-day. He has produced during that time between a hundred and fifty and a hundred and sixty pictures of flowers with which one is most familiar here, at Madras, and at Ootacamund. Two volumes of these have been despatched to York House [GD's house at Twickenham later sold to the Duc d'Orleans] and some fifty more pictures are now being sent to be bound. He is connected with an artist who was much employed by Wight, and whose name is perpetuated by the Acanthoid genus *Rungia*.[10]

These three volumes of drawings were sold at Sotheby's on 29 March 1982 by Grant Duff's descendents for the astonishing sum of £42,000 but it has not been possible to trace their present whereabouts, and it is likely that they have been broken up and dispersed – the fate of most such collections that have remained in private hands. From the single example illustrated in the sale catalogue, however, the drawings can be seen to have been of extremely fine quality, though rather more Western in composition than the works of the artist's earlier namesake.

That Grant Duff was wrong about the etymology of the genus *Rungia* is neither here nor there – it gives us the family name of Wight's Rungiah, and also links him with a botanical painter working at the Lal Bagh in Bangalore at exactly the same time. In 1887 the garden's Superintendent, John Cameron, obtained the services of an artist called 'K. Chelviah Rajoo, son of K. Ramanjooloo Rajoo' to draw botanical specimens, and recorded that he was 'descended from a family of Tanjore artists of the Kshatriya caste … formerly in the service of the Rajahs of Tanjore'.[11] According to James White, Cheluviah (sic) worked at the Lal Bagh from 1884 to 1923.[12] Another member of this family, J. Chengalvarayam Raju, is known to have been at the Madras School of Arts in 1862. His name appears on works in the two volumes of botanical watercolours still surviving in

what is now the Government College of Fine Arts, one of which contains 13 magnificent drawings of cotton species by three artists, made in 1862–3.[13]

Mrs Archer provided further information about the origin of the Tanjore painters known as 'moochys', and the style in which they worked:

> There is an oral tradition still current in Hyderabad that a number of Indian artists migrated from there to Tanjore in the late eighteenth century in search of work … By about 1830 a most delicate and realistic style had developed … which is unrivalled by any other school of Company painting. It may well have been the ultimate response to Sarabhoji's [i.e., Serfoji II] resurrection of Tanjore culture.[14]

This geographical origin would explain Rungiah's and Govindoo's names and the Telugu annotations on their drawings. Rao & Sastri have described how artists from the same background had also moved to Seringapatam in the seventeenth century to work under the patronage of the Wodyear dynasty of Mysore, where they had 'a temple dedicated to the goddess Nimishamba, the family deity of the Chandravamshi Kshatriya Raju community'.[15] This temple still exists, but has been completely refurbished and sadly contains no old records;[16] curiously it is on the island in the Cavery to the east of Tipu's summer palace, and must have been close to the Public Cattle Depot where Wight was stationed in 1825. It was perhaps this Seringapatam branch that provided the Lal Bagh with its artists.

These Telugu-speaking Tanjore artists were primarily painters of religious subjects:

> Tanjore paintings on wood were commissioned by patrons whose wealth decided the quality of art work … [decorated with] gold leaf or gems. The artists were Kshatriyas of the Raju community, for whom art was a ritual expression rather than a creative one. In fact, paintings followed prescribed themes and it was only on the lowest part that the artist was allowed to exercise his own imagination. The commonest themes for Tanjore paintings are the ones portraying Krishna, or the coronation of Rama, called the Rampattabhishekam. The Navnita Krishna, or Krishna holding a ball of butter, is an oft-repeated theme, as is the Darbar Krishna, Radha Krishna or Krishna with Rukmini and Satyabhama. Other popular themes are the Sreeranganatha or sleeping Vishnu, gajalakshmi and Vishnu with his consort Bhudevi and Sridevi. Uncommon themes are subjects like Markandaya, Dasavatar, Ashtadipala or the secular company school portraits and Sikh themes using the Tanjore technique.[17]

In the nineteenth century, other major subjects depicted by Tanjore (and Trichy) artists were Indian castes and trades, and Hindu deities, produced in often extensive series, either on paper or mica, for British patrons; but some of the artists clearly also turned their hand to natural history. It was not only the British who commissioned natural history paintings and, while unique both in terms of his outlook and the sorts of work he commissioned, mention must be made here of the exceptional Raja of Tanjore, Serfoji II (1777–1832), who had close connections with the Tranquebar missionaries.[18] Serfoji, as did many British EIC employees, used painters to record natural history subjects, and sent a collection of drawings of 'various fish, Birds, Plants, Buildings etc. of Hindustan' to Benjamin Torin, who from 1800 to 1803 had been British Resident at his court. Torin had returned to London, and in acknowledging the drawings told Serfoji that his 'Moochy has been so careful and correct in his representations, that I thought these paintings deserving Public notice', which resulted in the presentation to the Court of Directors of two bound volumes of drawings.[19] These were unfortunately later disbound before being reassembled, but 117 superb animal drawings, including some denizens of Serfoji's menagerie – birds-of-prey and an improbable cassowary – have survived in the India Office Collections.[20] Three related volumes of botanical drawings are still to be seen in the Sarasvati Mahal library in Tanjore; these were apparently referred to as an 'hortus siccus' and may have been the work of artists called Venkataperumal, Venkatanarayana and Gopalkrishna Naik.[21] Another reference to Tanjore moochys of this period is in a fascinating publication illustrated with hand-coloured aquatints of mainly South Indian subjects based almost entirely on drawings by Captain Charles Gold of the Royal Artillery. Plate 40 of this work, depicting an unfortunate member of the 'Collary' caste punished for theft by having had one leg amputated below the knee, however, is different in style:

> The accompanying is the *fac-simile* of a painting done by one of their ablest *artists*, well known by the title of the Tanjore *Moochy*, and famed throughout the country, not so much for the specimens of his own invention, as for his great skill and ingenuity in imitating the finest miniatures from the European pencil, so as to deceive persons of good taste, if not the connoisseur. The Moochys, or Artists of India, usually paint in the stile represented in the present drawing, but in body colour, and sometimes finish their pictures in the delicate and laboured manner of a miniature; though they at the same time are entirely devoid of truth in colouring and perspective.[22]

Benjamin Heyne as Madras Naturalist from 1802 to 1819 is known to have used artists to draw natural history subjects, and, with his Tranquebar connections, these are most likely to have been from Tanjore.[23] On an excursion between Samulcottah and Hyderabad Heyne recorded using a time-saving technique later adopted by Wight, Cleghorn and others: 'as plants were daily brought in, I ordered the painter to draw only the outlines with Indian Ink; and colour only one flower, fruit, and leaf'.[24] 44 bird drawings made for Heyne survive in the India Office Collections, but none of his plant drawings are known (or, rather, have been so attributed).

WIGHT'S EMPLOYMENT OF ARTISTS

In using South Indian artists to depict plants Wight was following a tradition started by William Roxburgh. Almost nothing is known of Roxburgh's artists, though the one who became head painter at Calcutta had worked for Roxburgh for 'nearly five years' on the Coromandel Coast before being taken to Calcutta when Roxburgh became Superintendent in 1793.[25] This artist died around 1814, and must therefore have been responsible for many of the Roxburgh Icones. Is it coincidental that at Samulcottah in the Northern Circars Roxburgh was close to chintz painting country? Might his painters have been chintz painters accustomed to drawing stylised vegetative forms? This is by way of an aside, for although undoubtedly inspired by Roxburgh's example, there is no evidence that Wight employed a painter while he was based in the Northern Circars in 1819–22. It is worth noting that after 1828 Wight paid his artists, as he did his collectors, entirely from his own pocket, so there was no question of the Company trying to claim ownership of the drawings and specimens such as had caused such anguish both to Buchanan and Roxburgh in Calcutta and after they retired.[26]

The first record of Wight's using an artist was during his brief episode in the Public Cattle Depot of Mysore. Here Wight had requested the employment of a draftsman, though for what purpose was not stated. This was duly authorised by Sir Thomas Munro, Governor of Madras, in November 1824:

> with reference to the resolution dated the 22d June last, that they have sanctioned the entertainment of a Native Draftsman or painter for the Medical department of the Cattle Depot in Mysore at the monthly pay of Rupees fifty. This rate of pay has been fixed after submitting specimens of the artist's work to competent judges & who have public establishments of draftsmen under their charge.[27]

A bill for the materials used by this artist has survived:[28]

> Indent on the Superintendent of Stationery for drawing Materials &ca. for the use of the Draftsman attached to the Public Cattle Depot in Mysore for the probable consumption of one year

Newman's Colour Box of 4 rows	No	1
Hair Pencils	Dozens	No 4
Drawing Pencils	Dozens	No 1
Indian Rubbers (whole)		1
Drawing Paper of sizes (1st Sort)	Sheets	60
Mathematical Instruments	Case	1
Sponge	No	1
Blotting Paper	Quires	1
Parallel Ruler	No	1
Penknife	No	1
Steel Drawing Pen	No	1

This may be a red herring, the nature of the equipment suggesting technical drawing rather than a medical artist recording dissections of diseased cattle. However, it appears that this draftsman was still there in 1826 working for A.E. Blest,[29] Wight's successor after he had fled the malarial swamps of Seringapatam, and this artist therefore cannot have been taken with him to Madras.

RUNGIAH

Early work for the Madras Naturalist's collection

It seems almost certain that Wight first used Rungiah in the period 1826–8, while he held the post of Madras Naturalist, and it is known that he took a draftsman with him on the great excursion of 1826–7.[30] It is entirely possible that Rungiah could already have been working for Wight's predecessor James Shuter, or, conceivably even earlier, for Benjamin Heyne. These early drawings [fig.5 and plate 36] were sent back to London with the scrapping of the Naturalist's post in 1828 and will be described in Chapter 3 under the Kew collections.[31] On the grounds of stylistic continuity with drawings made at Negapatam it seems beyond doubt that these are Rungiah's work. Although not named, it was certainly Rungiah who in October 1829 had been 'long in my service'.[32] This shows not only that at this point he was Wight's servant, rather than on the payroll of the Company, and while the 'long' is distressingly vague, it surely takes the date of his first employment by Wight back at least to 1826. Further proof that these early drawings are by Rungiah is that the drawing of *Gardneria* at Kew, which is in the same style, is attributed to him on the lithograph in Wallich's *Plantae Asiaticae Rariores* [fig.6].

Until recently, practically all that was known about Rungiah was that his name is a Telugu form of a name for Krishna with the honorific suffix '-iah'.[33] Unfortunately Wight recorded no patronymic, or name associated with his birthplace, so nothing further was known until Grant Duff's comment came to light and proved that he belonged to the Raju community. Rungiah's name, either as a signature or an annotation, has not been found on a single drawing.

Fragments of Rungiah's progress from the Negapatam period onwards can be gleaned from remarks in Wight's correspondence with Hooker, starting in October 1828 when Wight first sent five of his drawings to Glasgow.[34] There is the occasional anecdotal comment – for example in January 1830 'my painter's sickness … for some time was very severe';[35] but more interesting are details of the artist's working method. Initially Wight worried about how the drawings would stand comparison with the European illustrations Hooker was then publishing in works such as his *Exotic Flora*, but Wight admitted that improvement would be partly his own responsibility – 'by greater attention on my part, particularly to the Dissections'.[36]

At this stage at least some of the paintings were actually made in the field, and in October 1829 Wight was about to set off with 'the painter' to accustom him to 'the drawing of plants on the outline plan; only filling up [i.e., colouring] the dissections' – a method used earlier by Heyne. The earlier works had been fully coloured, but this new method would 'probably enable him [Rungiah] to finish enough of 1 or perhaps 2 species per day to admit of his completing them when more at leisure'. Wight evidently trusted Rungiah a good deal, as he put his plant collectors 'under the direction of the painter'.[37] As Wight was not present when these drawings were made identifications of the plants depicted had to be made subsequently. At this point the majority of the related herbarium specimens were also still unidentified, and it was only back in Britain that names could be added to the drawings and specimens, which is why so many of these early drawings are annotated by Arnott. It is a tribute to Rungiah's accuracy that such identifications were possible, as has been confirmed when checking them for the present project.

Rungiah was certainly prolific and, given the complexity of the drawings, surprisingly fast working – in 1829 Wight assured Hooker that the 'artist could easily supply 10 or 12 drawings monthly',[38] and the 31 drawings sent in June 1830 completed 'the hundred now sent' in under two years.[39] Despite this Wight was still able to take a further 'nearly two hundred drawings, I think, many of them of new plants' back with him when he returned to London on furlough in 1831.[40] That the drawings published by Hooker as engravings by Joseph Swan [fig.16] in the *Illustrations of Indian Botany* were all by Rungiah (though uncredited on the plates) can fortunately be firmly established, as when Wight saw them for the first time in Glasgow he wrote 'how proud my friend Rungiah will be when he sees them'.[41]

Wight has left an interesting description of Rungiah's method of drawing by 'laying the plant on the paper and then marking it off – a sure way to secure the accuracy, but not to save room in a limited space'.[42] The plants were thus drawn life-size, which meant that some of the early drawings were large, and Hooker asked for them to be produced in octavo format,[43] the size they were to be reproduced, presumably in order to avoid the need for an additional stage of reduction (either by an artist or the engraver) in Glasgow.

Although some of the drawings were made (or at least started) in the field, it is clear from comments in the *Icones* that many were made from herbarium specimens. No doubt as the *Icones* progressed and taxonomic gaps needed to be filled, the herbarium had to be resorted to. British artists, notably Hooker's artist Walter Hood Fitch, have been given special praise for the ability to reconstruct an illusion of three dimensionality from two dimensional specimens. The ability of Indian artists to draw from herbarium specimens has not previously been noted, but should not necessarily come as a surprise given their traditional reliance on line, love of pattern and lack of interest in perspective. The recently dried specimens would have retained a good deal of original colour, but in any case Rungiah and Govindoo's use of colour was not particularly subtle or naturalistic even when presumably drawing from life.

By an extraordinarily fortunate coincidence when William Griffith first went out to Madras in 1833 he met Rungiah and 'being himself an artist was able to give R[ungiah] some lessons particularly on the use of the microscope & in the delineation of Microscopic views from which I hope he will derive much benefit'.[44] Wight reported this tutelage in a letter to Hooker, in which he expressed the thrill of receiving his first-ever botanical letter from India, written by Griffith. In fact the previous year Wight had received a letter from Rungiah himself, which shows him to have been educated, and (even if Wight gently mocked his grammar) able to write in English:

> Rungiah writes me that he has "much plants in Trichinopoly" though expects more things to be got there.[45]

It is pleasing to note that Griffith did not forget Rungiah – five years later, in a letter from Assam, congratulating Wight on the first part of his *Illustrations*, 'especially on some of the dissections', he asked Wight to 'give my best salam to Rungia[h] your native painter'.[46]

Publication of Rungiah's drawings in the *Illustrations* and *Icones* ceased abruptly in 1846, when Govindoo took over. As Govindoo's early works are indistinguishable in style, this suggests an apprenticeship under Rungiah, and from a fortunate remark of George Gardner we know that in February 1845 Wight had 'two native artists … constantly employed', which gives a date for this training.[47] At this point Rungiah had been working for Wight for about 20 years, and the instruction of a successor suggests that he was getting old, and that the retirement was planned rather than due to illness.

It is sad that Rungiah was cheated of a printed eulogy such as Wight was later able to pay to Govindoo – the reason being the rule of nomenclatural priority, there already being a genus *Rungia* in the family Acanthaceae named by Nees after the German analytical chemist Ferdinand Runge (1795–1867).[48]

Rungiah's style

Rungiah's style changed over the long period that he worked for Wight, both in terms of composition and technique. Always a consummate draftsman, the early works show him closer to traditional styles both in terms of composition (for example the spectacularly asymmetric *Parkinsonia*, Plate 36), and the complete colouring of the image in thick bodycolour. Among the earlier works there is a tendency to take the image to the edges of the sheet (e.g., Plate 97), and he clearly revelled in the opportunity for sinuous arrangements that climbing plants such as members of the families Convolvulaceae and Cucurbitaceae allowed him (e.g., Plates 55, 91). Perhaps under Wight's direction Rungiah's composition became a little more Westernised, especially in the 1840s in the drawings for the *Icones* and

Fig.4. The mature styles of Rungiah and Govindoo compared.
Left: *Schefflera venulosa* (Wight & Arnott) Harms, by Rungiah, *c*.1834
Right: *Strophanthus boivinii* Baillon, by Govindoo, for H.F.C. Cleghorn, 1859.

Spicilegium where the plants tend to be more centrally placed (e.g., Plate 22).

It is in this context that Rungiah's use of 'frames' should be mentioned. In the earliest drawings (Series A) he simply filled the page, but in the period 1828–31 (Series C) and in the 'Large Dissection' series (D), some of which were done around 1834, the image does not occupy the whole page and pencil lines have been drawn to form tight 'frames' around the image [fig.4]. It seems likely that these lines were added when it was later decided to make prints from these drawings – as guides for the lithographer. Later on, in the 1840s, in the drawings made especially for the *Icones* (Series E), the boxes seem to have been drawn first, as frames for the composition, though parts of the plant often stray beyond their confines. This method was carried on by Govindoo and, interestingly, by the Lal Bagh artist Cheluviah Raju. While the latter could be merely the result of copying the style from the printed *Icones*, it could also confirm the family connection.

Wight described how drawings made in the field were only partly coloured for reasons of speed. However, in works of the 1830s and '40s (Series D, E) although the coloured areas are smaller than in Rungiah's early work, these drawings are by no means unfinished. This was clearly the result of a conscious design decision on the part of Rungiah, and not merely a labour saving device, as the non-coloured areas (whether ink or pencil) are as heavily worked as the coloured. This technique is useful in making the drawings balanced compositions, but is also functional in allowing parts such as painted flowers or fruits to be shown against non-coloured backgrounds such as leaves. Such a technique had, of course, long been used in Western botanical illustration, as seen in the hand-coloured plates of the *Botanical Magazine*, and in the drawings of Rungiah published by Hooker. It also gives the drawings a sense of depth independent of perspective, with a coloured 'foreground', and uncoloured 'background'.

Rungiah's Technique

Rungiah started his drawings with pencil and then gradually built them up to varying degrees of finish. If intended to be heavily worked on with either opaque bodycolour, ink, or a combination of the two, then the pencil work consisted merely of sketchy lines. However, sometimes the pencil work was highly finished, for example in some of the floral analyses for the *Icones*, either drawn more or less at the same time as the habit study (e.g., Plates 78, 80), or in some cases done much later to supplement an earlier drawing (e.g., Plates 77, 79). The next stage was to apply ink (or sometimes further pencil work) and bodycolour over the initial sketch. The relative proportions of ink and paint varied, for example in the earliest drawings the thickly applied bodycolour almost completely obliterates the pencil work and sometimes there is no ink outlining. In later drawings, areas of the under-drawing were worked over in great detail with ink or pencil, and only a portion of the leaves and flowers 'coloured in'. Ink was sometimes used for outlining coloured areas to help with definition. In some drawings veins have been added on top of the green ground of the leaves, either in pencil or bodycolour, and highlights in opaque white. The final stage was the application of a varnish – gum arabic, or perhaps some local substitute – to give a gloss to selected areas, either whole leaves, or highlights such as leaf midribs or the centres of petals. In the 1840s, when major production on the *Icones* started, and the floral analyses

were made on small, supplementary fragments of paper, these were commonly done in pencil and water- or body-colour. It should be noted that even the ink was applied by means of fine brushes, rather than with a pen.

Publication of Rungiah's Work

When Rungiah started to work for Wight, it was probably largely as a visual record to supplement herbarium specimens, but very early on Wight must have thought of the possibility of publishing the drawings to make them more widely available. The first fruits of the publishing project took place in distant Glasgow, where they were engraved by Joseph Swan under Hooker's direction. 67 of these were hand-coloured for publication in the *Botanical Miscellany* [fig.16] and other later Hooker publications, and Hooker reproduced a further 19 (though uncredited) in vols 2 and 3 of his periodical *Icones Plantarum* as uncoloured lithographs made by Allan & Ferguson [fig.24].

The vast proportion of Rungiah's published output, however, was in the form of lithographs in the works Wight produced in Madras: in the first volume and first part of the second of the *Illustrations*, and the majority of the first three volumes of the *Icones* (in the fourth are only ten of Rungiah's plates). However, two other botanists published prints based on Rungiah's drawings – one in Britain, the other in India. The only use in Britain, other than by Hooker, was in 1831 when Nathaniel Wallich published Rungiah's drawing of *Gardneria wallichii* as plate 281 of his *Plantae Asiaticae Rariores* [fig.6].[49] This lithograph is by the Maltese born artist Maxim Gauci and in its layout (centrally placed, with wide margins around the image), and lithographic technique (with careful shading visible beneath the hand colouring), makes an interesting contrast with the simple outline lithographs produced in Madras. In 1844 Wight sent copies of drawings of two South Indian palms (*Calamus wightii* and *Arenga wightii*) to William Griffith in Calcutta, at a time when he was working on the family.[50] From their date these drawings are almost certain to have been Rungiah's work, and they were reproduced (unattributed) as simple, unshaded, line lithographs in the posthumously published illustrations to Griffith's *Palms of British East India*;[51] these are probably the work of Lachman Singh or Ishwarchander Paulit who worked on the lithography for this project for McClelland.[52] What are probably the original drawings of the *Arenga* are at the Natural History Museum (NHM 649, 650.1 & 2), but the versions sent to Griffith may well survive in the collection of palm drawings at the Calcutta Botanic Garden.

GOVINDOO

Even less is known about Govindoo than of Rungiah, and no associated patronymic or name associated with his birthplace was recorded by Wight. He did, however, sign his name in Telugu script on nine of the surviving drawings:

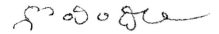

His presumed training under Rungiah has been noted, and, given the strength of Indian tradition, it seems highly likely that he belonged to the same community, or even the same family, as Rungiah. None of Govindoo's drawings for Wight is dated, and the first appearance of his work in published form is in a part of the *Icones* dating from September 1846 (t. 1148). At this point Rungiah completely disappears from the record, and Govindoo was the artist for the final three volumes of the *Icones* and from the second part to the end of the *Illustrations*. However, far less of Govindoo's work for Wight has survived – only about 75 published drawing pairs at Edinburgh and about 170 individuals or pairs at NHM that can be attributed to him on stylistic grounds. Almost 1000 of his published drawings are therefore missing. Although literally nothing else about Govindoo is known, we know roughly what he was paid by Wight, although the two figures mentioned in letters to Hooker are inconsistent. In August 1849 Wight stated that his draftsman's pay was £30 per annum,[53] but seven months later it was given as £25,[54] though the discrepancy seems likely to be due to vagueness on Wight's part rather than to what would have been a substantial wage cut. The lower amount is about 1/30th of Wight's salary at the same time, and is equivalent to about £1250 per annum in today's values.

After Wight's retirement Govindoo continued to work for Hugh Cleghorn and Richard Beddome. Govindoo's style seems to have become ever bolder, and there are many drawings in the Cleghorn collection at Edinburgh that can be attributed to Govindoo, some of which bear his name written in Roman script [fig.4],[55] and Beddome published many of Govindoo's drawings as lithographs in his own *Icones*, published in Madras up to 1874. It is hoped that some references to Govindoo might eventually be found hidden away in the correspondence of these, or other, Madras botanists.

It has been said that Govindoo was Wight's 'favourite artist',[56] but this is probably only because Wight commemorated him in the generic name *Govindooia*. The reason for there being no genus named for Rungiah has already been explained, and there is no reason, at least on that account, to think that Wight rated Govindoo the more highly. The dedication did, however, allow Wight to write an appreciation of Govindoo's talents:

> I have dedicated it to the artist [Govindoo] whose facile pencil produced the drawings for the greater part of the plates of the last three volumes of this work [the *Icones*], and whose skill in analytical delineation is, I believe, as yet quite unrivalled among his countrymen, and, but for his imperfect knowledge of perspective, rarely excelled by European artists.[57]

At the time Wight was concerned that of only three previous attempts to commemorate an Indian in a generic name none was likely to persist,[58] and while these were discouraging precedents Wight was keen to make another attempt 'on account of the great merit of the man', being sure that this time he had a good genus – though in this hope he was sadly wrong.

Govindoo's style and technique

Initially close to Rungiah's, no doubt as result of his apprenticeship, Govindoo's style rapidly diverged to become bolder [fig.4], perhaps because he realised that subtle details would not be translated into the line lithographs of the *Icones*, which by now was the driving force for his work. Neither are Govindoo's plates nearly so skilled in terms of composition as Rungiah's, and there is a feeling of a more random filling of space with the habit drawing and the floral details. Govindoo did not use ink in the same way as Rungiah for uncoloured areas, which he left in pencil, only occasionally using ink (or a very dark bodycolour) to sharpen up outlines on some of the floral details. With Govindoo larger areas of the drawing tend to be coloured, and these colours are rather harsh: in short Govindoo's style shows a tendency towards abstraction verging on caricature. Despite this there are places where Govindoo attempted to be naturalistic, as seen in his free use of watercolour brushwork to convey fragments of (micro-)habitat, for example lichens growing on aerial roots, or a mossy branch supporting an epiphytic orchid. The only attempt at a naturalistic drawing to show the habit of a tree in the combined output of Rungiah and Govindoo is by the latter, that of *Artocarpus hirsutus* (*Icones* t. 1957, NHM 440), though this too is heavily stylised.

THE ANNOTATIONS

One of the most interesting features of the drawings in the various Wight collections is the annotations they bear. While these may somewhat reduce the aesthetic impact, they add greatly to the documentary and taxonomic value of the drawings. As already noted these were not regarded as fine-art objects, but rather as scientific specimens, as supplementary sources of information to Wight's dried herbarium material. They were treated as such by Wight and his contemporary collaborators Hooker and Arnott, as they have by botanists at Kew and Edinburgh up to the present day.

Much of this supplementary information is written in English and Latin – for example cross references to specimens in Wight's herbarium (mainly added by Arnott), and changing opinions as to the identity of the plant depicted – by Wight, Arnott and later generations of taxonomists. The annotations in Telugu and Tamil scripts are, in a way, even more interesting, being contemporary with the making of the drawings, and written by Rungiah and Govindoo, and, where decipherable, could potentially add to our pitifully small knowledge of the artists, and the context in which the drawings were made. These annotations are written in faint pencil, but most have turned out to be legible to those familiar with the scripts, though among the seven people to whom they have been shown, all native speakers either of Telugu or Tamil, there has been much disagreement over their exact transliteration, let alone their meaning.

The Tamil annotations, relatively small in number, are straightforward, usually representing simply the native name of the plant, often also given in contemporary Roman characters, and often reproduced by Wight on the corresponding plate in the *Icones*. These names must have been recorded from locals at the time the drawing was made and related specimens collected. The Telugu inscriptions are more problematic. Both Rungiah and Govindoo were clearly primarily Telugu speaking and wrote their notes in Telugu script, but they must also have been fluent in Tamil, the predominant language in the areas where Wight and his collectors worked. For this reason the language of the inscriptions is often Tamil, but written in Telugu script! In one case a Malayali local name is written in Telugu script. Many of these extensive annotations are not comprehensible to modern native speakers, and it seems to be difficult even to distinguish which words represent localities, which local plant names, and which descriptive matter now obscure in meaning. Nonetheless some headway has been made, though further linguistic study is required, and would seem worthwhile given that these represent a curious and previously untapped source of vernacular information about the plants and ethnobotany of Southern India, and even on printing techniques, dating from the period 1825–53.

Plant names

Some of the plant names are still in use, others agree with names given on plates in the *Icones*. Those still in use today are of useful plants, such as the Tamil names for radish and tobacco given in Telugu script on drawings in the N H M collection. However, many of the drawings depict obscure plants, with no uses, so it is reassuring to find the occasional 'name not known' ('perutheriyadu'). Some names are descriptive, for example 'little rattler' on *Crotalaria willdenowiana*. The suffixes *maram* for tree, *kodi* for climber, and *shedi* for shrub all make frequent appearances.

Localities

Dr Lakshmi Subramanian identified about 23 place names on the Edinburgh drawings, but almost all are impossible to locate on modern maps, doubtless referring to small villages, even if still in use. Some are, however, recognisable: though given the vast number of plants Wight's collectors found at Kuttalam, its appearance on drawings is surprisingly rare; Kunnivadi is known from herbarium specimens as 'Cunnewady'. Most of the place names, however, are unknown either from herbarium specimens or from the text of the *Icones* suggesting that Wight either did not or could not read these annotations, or, as we know in other ways, seems not to have been interested in precise details of where his drawings were made or specimens collected.

Personal Names

None of the translators who have looked at the annotations has found even a single signature of Rungiah, but Govindoo's name appears on nine of the drawings. The name of Wight's factotum Ramasami, is written on the back of three – perhaps it was he who delivered them to or collected them from the Lithographic Office.

'new February month'

This enigmatic annotation appears on several of the 'Large Dissection' drawings (Series D), along with various dates in February 1834. The plants are varied and cannot all have been in flower at this time, suggesting that this might have been a period of copying of earlier drawings, perhaps the occasion when the large floral analyses were added.

Printing instructions

'367 required' (Tam: vendiyada) and '367 pulled off' (Tam: vuchu pottadi) give the edition size of plates reproduced only in the *Icones*, and '467 required' for the ones also included in the *Spicilegium*. On *Sophora velutina* (EW 211) is a reference to a fruit being upside down, and when one compares the drawing with the print in the *Icones*, finds that its position relative to the habit drawing has been corrected in the transfer process. The lengthy annotations on the Roxburgh tracings have so far proved unintelligible, though are probably instructions to the lithographer from Rungiah.

Graffiti

In addition to botanical notes, or technical ones relating to printing, some of the drawings bear other sorts of graffiti. The most interesting is a faint pencil profile of a handsome young Indian man wearing a turban and ear-ring on the verso of a drawing that is probably by Govindoo (N H M 464). The identity of the subject is an enigma – the ear-ring, doubtless gold, suggests someone of an upper caste, and there is the tantalising possibility that it could be a self portrait. Perhaps more likely is that it shows one of the other Indian members of Wight's household sketched in an idle moment and providing an intimate glimpse of Coimbatore 150 years ago.

On the back of a pencil sketch drawn on a scrap of blue paper, almost certainly by Govindoo (of the orchid *Agrostophyllum planicaule* RBGE W448), is to be found a list of materials for a puja ceremony to a goddess, but of a very un-Brahminical sort that might be performed in a simple local temple. This includes an expensive goat (price Rs 10), a cock (3 annas), 6 coconuts, fruit, rice, milk, sugar, honey, incense, camphor, curd, ghee, lemon, flowers, betle leaf and nut, and the services of a pujari (priest). Here again is a fascinating, if disembodied, relic of an historical event that must have taken place in Coimbatore around 1850, but whether it was Govindoo who arranged the ceremony (and therefore revealing something about his religious practice), or the piece of paper was a reused one can never be known.

PAPERS AND WATERMARKS

Botanists are great users of paper – for drying and mounting plants, for writing manuscripts (notes, plant descriptions, etc.), and supplying to their artists and printers. The supply of high quality Western papers was a constant concern in India, and one raised by Wight in some of his early letters to Hooker. Native papers were adequate for purposes such as drying plants, and in his earliest days in the Northern Circars Wight used a very fine one for mounting specimens. The portion of his drawing collection at N H M is still stored in its original folders of such a native paper, which have stood the test of time better than some of the drawings on Western papers they enclose. The drawings themselves, however, are all on British papers, and represent a wide assortment, doubtless in part due to the long period over which they were made – more than a quarter of a century. This diversity is far greater, for example, than that of the Roxburgh Icones or the Dapuri drawings. As already noted, the drawings were paid for from his own pocket and Wight exhibited a certain Scottish parsimony: he seems to have bought supplies at various points which he proceeded to use over a considerable period. This parsimony is also reflected in another characteristic of the collections – the drawings are almost entirely on very much smaller sheets than the folio sheets used at Calcutta and Dapuri. However, an advantage of this diversity is that a study of the papers and their watermarks reveals something about the chronology of the drawings and of Wight's projects. Given the climate of South India the keeping of paper for long periods is a particularly bad idea in terms of conservation, and it is all the more surprising that the original drawings are in as good condition as they are, given that they must have spent the first several decades of their life in India. In the Preface to the first volume of the *Illustrations*, written in 1840, Wight wrote that the paper for the plates (a heavy wove paper similar to that used by Rungiah for the 'Large Dissection' series) was 'much deteriorated by age' until a new supply came in time for the 11th number.[59] For example, in the Edinburgh copy of the book, plate 42 printed in 1838 is on Ruse & Turner paper with an 1829 watermark, and the watermark on plate 46 is for 1828 – these two dates appear on other plates, and demonstrate Wight's stockpiling of paper, which he was forced to use a decade later. The situation is similar with the original drawings – many with 1819 watermarks must have been made long after this date.

At the start of Wight's great illustrated publications project he applied to the Public Department of the Madras Government for help in obtaining paper (and other supplies – that paints are not included is significant and will be discussed later), but for which he paid himself. The Court agreed to this request:

> We have also received your Indent of the 23rd March 1838 for a supply of [20 reams of] Lithographic Demy Paper, and [3 gross of] Camel Hair Brushes required for Dr Wight's Botanical Work, with which we have complied upon the understanding that it is to be issued on payment.[60]

The papers used by Wight merit further study, but at this stage it is worth simply listing the watermarks to give an idea of the diversity involved (see Appendix 1). With the exception of the Jones & Mather paper from Wales, the other identified ones used by Rungiah and Govindoo (Wilmot, Hollingworth, Ruse & Turners and Balston) were all made in Kentish paper mills.[61]

PAINTS

As will be noted below, Wight experienced difficulty obtaining good paints. It was only when a selection of the paintings was framed and hung on the gallery walls of Inverleith House in April 2006 that the limited palette used by Wight's artists became apparent. This was especially obvious for the green of the leaves, for which Rungiah relied almost exclusively on a single (rather strong) shade. This, coupled with the fact that there is no mention of paints in Wight's request to London for brushes and paper, suggests that Rungiah and Govindoo used local paints, also suggested by Cleghorn's observation that he saw Wight's colourists 'mixing their own colours'.[62] No chemical analysis has yet been undertaken to support or refute this, though such an investigation would clearly be of great interest.

The only information so far discovered on pigments used in South India occurs in Francis Buchanan's *Journey*,[63] and in Benjamin Heyne's *Tracts*.[64] Both of these refer specifically to mural paintings, and their relevance to works on paper is therefore questionable. However, from the oxidation of the white on some of Rungiah's drawings (e.g., Plate 18), it is clear that he used lead white, the preparation of which was described by Heyne. Other pigments mentioned by Heyne were cinnabar (i.e., mercuric sulphide) for red, and orpiment (i.e., arsenic sulphide) for yellow, though the green used on the botanical drawings does not appear to be verdigris, the only source of this colour that he cited. It is likely that some of the pigments used by Wight's artists came from vegetable sources, such as those recently investigated by Christine Mackay and Aditi Nath Sarkar used by the *chitrakars* (scroll or *patua* painters) of the Medinipur district of West Bengal:

> although admitting to the occasional use of manufactured pigments like vermilion or zinc white, mostly they continue to use traditional pigments: powdered burnt rice or the burnt ground roots of the *Gaab* tree (*Diospyros peregrina*) for black, scrapings from the interior of terracotta ovens for browns, powdered turmeric for yellow, the extract of bean leaf (either *Dolichos lablab* or *hinche*) for green. The blues come from the *nilmoni* flower or *aparajita* berries and occasionally indigo, reds are prepared from the hibiscus or the *palash* [*Butea*] flowers, while purple is the result of mixing mud from the Ganges with the ground seeds of *pui saag*, a member of the spinach family, the flowers of this plant

> providing a very delicate pink. They make the colours opaque with the addition of ground conch shell, and for the binder they usually use gum from the *Acacia catechu* … Another binder is made from the strained, pressed fruits of the *Bael* tree, *Aegle marmelos*.[65]

Although this reference applies to current practice in Bengal, similar methods, using locally available plants, must surely have been used by South Indian painters in Wight's era.

WIGHT'S COLOURISTS

A lowlier grade of artist was also used by Wight in his publishing projects, for colouring the plates of the *Illustrations* and *Spicilegium*. In October 1837 he referred to:

> my Colourists 8 of whom are now engaged on monthly pay and will no doubt after a little steady practice greatly improve in the application of colours if we can only get good colours to apply – a most difficult business in this country & my absolute privation of Books treating of such matters leaves me without any assistance from those who have travelled the same road before me.[66]

It seems that the colourists did not improve, and in a 'Notice' issued with one of the fascicles of the first volume of the *Illustrations* (one is bound into the RBGE copy), and therefore likely to date from between 1838 and 1840, Wight had to offer an apology for inconsistencies in the 'style of coloring'. He explained that:

> a number of my best painters having struck work, and that not [for] the first time, on grounds so frivolous, as left me no other alternative than to dispense with their future services. The fresh hands not having yet attained the perfection of the old ones, will satisfactorily account for any falling off that may be observed. They are now, however, improving so rapidly, that I have not fear of any deficiency in the future.

Cleghorn must have witnessed the colourists at work as he recorded that at one point (and it must almost certainly have been at Coimbatore) Wight had 'about twenty natives employed in a large room of his house, colouring the plates for his "Illustrations"'. [67] This technique, using a master copy, was widely used in the West for colouring runs of publications, but Wight's colourists occasionally made mistakes, for example some copies (including both of those at RBGE) of plate 59 of the *Illustrations*, depicting *Geranium affine*, have the flowers coloured yellow (perhaps it was mistaken for a buttercup?). Wight's own copy, still in the possession of his family, however, has the flowers correctly coloured purplish-pink.

The name E.A. Rodrigues is recorded as colourist on the plate of floral analyses of Cucurbitaceae, and on four of the plates of the Compositae part of Wight's *Illustrations*, probably published in October 1848. Etienne Alexander Rodrigues (or Rodriguez) is a fascinating character who, on the title page of his remarkable book *The Hindoo Pantheon*, is given as the 'Honorable Company's Head Draftsman' working in the Survey Department, and 'son of the late Captain Francis Rodrigues of L'Esperance, &c'. As Winchester was the Company's lithographer, and Wight's lithographs were printed in Fort St George, presumably Rodrigues was brought in during some hiatus to help with what must have been seen as a semi-official publication. Rodrigues will be discussed further in the chapter on lithography.

Fig.5. *Hibiscus tiliaceus* and *Sesbania grandiflora*, an early plate (RBGE W403), probably by Rungiah,
from the Madras Naturalist's Collection.

CHAPTER THREE

The Wight Collections

Although only drawings from the Edinburgh collection are reproduced in this book, the closely related material at the Royal Botanic Gardens Kew, the Natural History Museum in London, and a collection at Edinburgh University (found during the course of the research), has been studied and catalogued, as this clearly all once formed part of a single collection assembled by Wight. Together these collections contain 2118 individual items, representing some 1809 'works' (many of the species being depicted on two sheets). This wealth of material initially proved somewhat confusing, but gradually a picture emerged of how Wight built up a collection of drawings as raw material for his illustrated publications – using not only the two artists he (sequentially) employed and whose development it is possible at least roughly to plot, using style and paper types. But there was also, though far less well known (as, in the end, little of it was used by him), a large body of drawings and tracings sent by various botanists from other parts of India – in many cases of rather lower artistic quality than Rungiah's and Govindoo's work, some by ('amateur') Westerners, some by other Indian artists. It should be pointed out that this surviving corpus represents less than half of the drawings that Wight must originally have had – no originals have yet been discovered for about 1445 of the prints in the *Illustrations* and *Icones*,[1] and in the last part of the *Icones* Wight stated that he still had 'materials … so ample, that I could easily have continued this work through 1500 or 2000 additional plates'.[2] While this does not necessarily mean that he had plates of all these there are about 740 such unpublished ones at the NHM (see below) and a similar number could easily have followed the fate of the missing published drawings; it would therefore appear that Wight's original collection amounted to over 4000 drawings (and actually many more individual items, as many of these would have been pairs). This must be one of the largest such collections ever made, significantly larger than, for example, Roxburgh's 2500 drawings;[3] Cleghorn's collection was probably larger, but this will not be known until it is studied in detail and catalogued.

The bulk of these works can be divided into five major groups or series, which have been given the initials A–E in the Plates section. However, by no means all of the drawings fit neatly into these groupings. There is much miscellaneous material, and some drawings belong to more than one category, e.g., an early sheet to which details were later added for publication in the *Icones*, either drawn on the original sheet, or on a smaller supplementary one, the latter method of 'drawing pairs' being the method developed during the 1840s the time of greatest production of the *Icones*. Most of the series are split between Edinburgh, Kew and the Natural History Museum, though each of these collections has a predominant character in terms of the major series represented.

ROYAL BOTANIC GARDENS KEW (RBGK)
The earliest drawings made for Wight, and also the first to reach Britain (though by two different routes), are now at Kew and will be described first. The drawings have been mounted on herbarium sheets, and up to the time of the present project were distributed taxonomically among the Illustrations Collection scattered through the Kew herbarium.

Series A: the Madras Naturalist's Collection
The earliest series in the Kew collection comprises the drawings from the Madras Naturalist's collection sent back to East India House in 1828. These remained in the India Museum (where they were blind-stamped 'Secretary of State for India Library') until 1879–82 when the 3359 botanical drawings that remained in this collection were sent to Kew, of which 150 were attributed to Wight.[4] It was doubtless at this point that Wight's name was added to the drawings in pencil, having been annotated in his own time on the verso with two numbers and the initials 'RW'. Because of this attribution the drawings had been catalogued under Wight's name in the partial card index to the Kew Illustrations Collection and were thus easily located and extracted; one of this collection (Plate 36) was at some stage given to Edinburgh. These drawings are on small sheets of heavy paper: 94 have been located, but 12 in the card index probably belonging to this series remain to be found.

At Edinburgh are 47 drawings from this series not marked 'RW' or with any EIC stamps that were evidently retained by Wight personally, some of which bear an 1824 watermark (e.g., Plates 2, 6, 11). Two plates in one of the Wellesley albums (NHD 22) in the India Office collection of the British Library, tentatively ascribed to Wight by Mildred Archer,[5] are also from this collection. They show two renowned Indian plants, the banyan and the pipul, and were doubtless removed from the Madras Naturalist's collection when still in the India Museum, for comparison with Wellesley drawings, and subsequently bound in with them by mistake.

Also from the Madras Naturalist's collection (annotated 'RW') is an intriguing series of six drawings (five at Kew; one at Edinburgh – fig.5) showing comparative floral dissections of several different species on a single sheet. These were made with the aid of a hand lens or simple microscope, but reveal Wight's earliest interest in the floral characteristics of families that would later result in the magnificent drawings of series D and the *Illustrations*.

This collection is of interest not only in showing Rungiah's early style, but also in terms of the plants depicted. These include many of the common and conspicuous plants to be found in and around Madras, including useful and ornamental species that Wight would largely exclude from his publications. The two figs have been mentioned; examples of ornamentals include *Canna speciosa*, frangipani and oleander; and of medicinal plants *Calotropis gigantea* and the Tinnevelly senna (*Senna alexandrina*).

Series B: drawings for W.J. Hooker

Not being annotated with Wight's name, the second major series at Kew had not previously been recognised as having any connection with him. These are the drawings sent by Wight to W.J. Hooker, and were among the vast collections taken to Kew by Hooker from Glasgow in 1841 and purchased for the nation after his death in 1865. As Hooker published many of these drawings it was possible to seek them in the herbarium Illustrations Collection under the name of the plant depicted.

Wight sent illustrations and plant descriptions to Glasgow from Negapatam between 1828 and 1831, from which Hooker chose the most taxonomically interesting for publication in (sequentially) the *Botanical Miscellany*, *Journal of Botany*, *Annals and Magazine of Natural History* and his *Icones Plantarum*. 188 of these have been found, though 25 of those published are still unlocated (probably being on sheets bearing other drawings that have been refiled for taxonomic or other reasons). This series is heterogeneous in terms of paper type, size and date, as Wight by this time clearly had a varied stock of paintings on which to draw, selecting the most interesting (many of which were unidentifiable to Wight in India), though it is worth recognising these drawings as a distinct series, given the purpose to which they were put, and being the first works by which Wight (and, though uncredited, Rungiah) became known to European botanists. Hooker evidently returned to Wight the drawings he did not publish, as at Edinburgh are a number that form part of this series (e.g., Plates 84, 96, 104, 136) – some annotated by Hooker, and some fortunately still associated with their long and detailed descriptions in Wight's hand that have been lost from the Kew examples.

Miscellanea at Kew not referable to Series A or B include four early drawings from the Madras Naturalist's Collection, the most interesting of which is Rungiah's drawing of *Gardneria ovata* published by Wallich [fig.6]; ten late works that went to Kew with Wight's Herbarium in 1871 related to series E (i.e., associated with the *Icones*, most of which are at RBGE and NHM); some reduced outline copies of *Hortus Malabaricus* plates; and a single drawing by M.P. Edgeworth belonging to a series mainly at NHM.

Fig.6. *Gardneria ovata*, hand-coloured lithograph by Maxim Gauci after a drawing by Rungiah, from Wallich's *Plantae Asiaticae Rariores* (1831).

Fig.7. *Passiflora walkeriae* (now *P. suberosa*), drawing (RBGE W362.1) by Ann Maria Walker, published in Wight's *Illustrations* 2, t. 108 (1841).

Fig.8. *Acanthophippium bicolor*, watercolour 'tracing' (RBGE W412) by Ann Maria Walker of one of her own drawings.

ROYAL BOTANIC GARDEN EDINBURGH (RBGE)

The second largest of the collections, with 710 individual items (505 'works') is at RBGE. The majority of the drawings in this collection were published by Wight, about three quarters being by Rungiah and a quarter (almost all orchids) by Govindoo, but there are also smaller numbers of unpublished drawings by other artists – both Indian and European. The earliest have already been described, belonging to series mainly at Kew. The largest proportion of the Edinburgh drawings falls into three major groups, though these overlap to a great extent with the slightly larger collection at NHM.

Series C: the 'small drawings on thin paper'

These drawings by Rungiah are characterised by their paper size and type, being smaller and on lighter paper than those of Series A; many bear an 1819 watermark. Another characteristic is that they are extensively annotated (with names, and cross references to the numbers in Wight's herbarium *Catalogue*). Although from letters to Hooker it is known that Arnott retained some of Wight's drawings, and was doubtless sent new ones after Wight returned to India in 1834, from the style of the drawings and the watermark, the drawings of this series appear to have been made before Wight returned home in 1831 and were used in Wight & Arnott's work on the *Prodromus* and Wight's *Catalogue* (e.g., Plates 1, 4, 5).

Series D: the 'large dissections'

Rungiah's finest drawings are characterised by the exceptional magnified floral details on the verso of larger sheets (of varying size) of heavy paper, with the plant habit on the recto. Some of these are dated 1834, which perhaps refers to the date when earlier drawings were copied and the details (which are much larger and clearer than Rungiah's earlier dissections) added. It seems likely that these large details are the result of Rungiah's instruction in the use of the microscope by William Griffith in 1833 (e.g., Plates 3, 7, 10). The details are especially useful in showing family characteristics, and the series is associated with the *Illustrations*, which Wight began to publish in 1838. However, when it came to lithography the floral details were squashed into odd gaps and corners, giving no idea of the exceptional quality of the original drawings.

Series E: the 'Icones series'

The format that evolved for Wight's most extensive publication, the *Icones*, was that of a pair of drawings (e.g., Plates 74, 78, 124). This method was started by Rungiah, and, after 1845, continued by Govindoo. The plant habit (which is only partly coloured) is shown on a larger sheet and the floral details on a much smaller one. Sometimes the habit drawing represents an earlier drawing from Series A or C, but the majority appear to have been made specially for publication, and are on rather poor quality machine-made paper, with the floral details on supplementary fragments of laid writing paper of various shades of blue and grey. From the attributions in the *Icones* most of such drawing pairs at Edinburgh are attributable to Rungiah, with the exception of the orchids, which are mostly by Govindoo.

Other material

Also at Edinburgh are a small number of drawings by other artists, generally of much lower quality, though nonetheless of great interest. When Wight started publishing illustrations his interests became public and, as hoped for, several amateur botanists with an artistic bent sent him material from various parts of India. Wight in

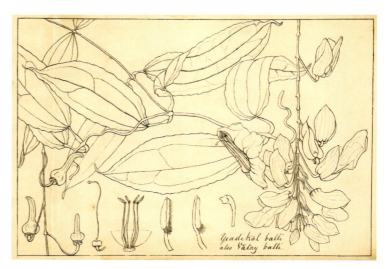

Fig.9. *Lichinora jerdoniana* (now *Porpax jerdoniana*), collaged drawings (RBGE W339) – details 1 & 2 by Flora Jerdon (others details by Govindoo), reproduced in Wight's *Icones*, t. 1738 (1851).

Fig.10. *Thunbergia mysorensis*, ink drawing (RBGE W464) by Alphonso Bertie, c.1835.

fact published very few of these, probably because he was not confident about their identification, having little or no supporting herbarium material. The most prolific of these botanical-artist correspondents were Michael Pakenham Edgeworth from northern India and Ann Maria Walker from Ceylon. Mrs Walker sent Wight at least one finished watercolour [fig.7], but what she mainly sent were partly coloured tracings of her orchid drawings [fig.8], of which there are six at RBGE and 51 at NHM.

Also in this category is Flora Jerdon, who also specialised in orchids: two of her works are at RBGE, one of which has been cut up and collaged onto a sheet by Govindoo [fig.9], and about 20 are at NHM.

Wight was keen to encourage Indian artists, as shown not only by his long continued support of Rungiah and Govindoo, but in the encouraging remarks he published about a Portuguese- or Anglo-Indian apothecary called Alphonso Bertie.[6] Bertie's work is represented by some relatively unsophisticated ink outline drawings of which there are probably eleven (certainly seven) at RBGE [fig.10] and five at NHM. There are two other works at Edinburgh belonging to this category: one orchid watercolour initialled 'JS' is possibly by J. Suares, and an anonymous highly skilled pencil drawing, which, from the identity of the two species depicted, is possibly by the Singhalese artist Harmanis de Alwis (also represented by a single work at NHM). Biographical details of these other artists can be found in Appendix 2.

Taxonomic range

Whereas the earliest collections at Kew show a rather general range of species of the sort that a botanist just starting to get to know a new flora might choose to have painted, and the Hooker series was chosen deliberately for their taxonomic interest, the Edinburgh collection is the fruit of Wight's mature labours, representing the entire taxonomic gamut, with the exception of a conspicuous blind-spot when it came to monocotyledons other than orchids. Representing almost entirely the works Wight chose to publish in the *Illustrations* and *Icones* it shows his increasing interest in using these publications to produce partial monographs of some of the more important and species-rich South Indian families – for example orchids, and more obscure groups such as Euphorbiaceae and Urticaceae.

Rosa Wight's album

The final series in the Edinburgh collection consists of fourteen sheets that bear signs of removal from an album of the sort compiled by young Victorian ladies of the middle and upper classes. These were discovered among a pile of miscellaneous drawings and prints that had evidently been laid aside as (taxonomically) unworthy of mounting and incorporation into the Cuttings Collection. The album pages are varied in subject matter and style, including paintings of exotic fruits (rambutan, mango, guava, cacao and nutmeg – among others), one shows two species of cotton (Book 3 fig.65), and there is also a delicate watercolour of a yellow rose [fig.11]. The proof that this album belonged to Rosa Wight is found in an annotation 'Miss Ford' on the back of the rose, referring to Rosa's maiden name; the connection with Wight is confirmed by a sheet bearing a flowering sprig of the rose apple, and an exotic spider and its web – the former is annotated 'copied by Goindoo', the latter 'from the guaver tree Coimbatore' [fig.12]. Also in this collection is a lithographed still-life to be discussed later [fig.20].

Fig.11. Rose of unknown variety (probably heavily stylised) (RBGE W504), probably by Rosa Wight.

Fig.12. Rose apple (*Syzygium malaccense*) and spider (RBGE W492), by Govindoo, from Rosa Wight's album.

In the University Library at Edinburgh are two portfolios of extremely fine pencil drawings of Indian plants, catalogued under the name of William Roxburgh [fig.13]. On both covers is a note reading: 'sent by Nathaniel Wallich to Robert Wight for inclusion in his "Icones Plantarum Indiae Orientalis"'. This is indeed what the drawings are. It has long been known, for they are superscribed 'Roxburghiana', that Wight reproduced 419 previously unpublished 'Roxburgh Icones' in his own *Icones* (mainly in the first three volumes), and William Griffith contemporaneously paid credit to Wallich for making these drawings available to Wight.[7] What was unknown was the format in which the Roxburgh images were sent to Wight – far less that the 'originals' of the Wight prints had survived. Copies of seven of the letters that accompanied these drawings from Calcutta to Madras, dating from 1839–40, have also been found in the Wallich correspondence at Calcutta, shedding further light on this project. It seems likely that these 'copies' of the Roxburgh drawings ('originals' of the Wight prints), are the work of Lachman Singh, one of the best and longest serving of the Calcutta Botanic Garden artists. It was Wallich who chose the taxonomically most important species for publication, and Wight followed his suggestions, except for species already depicted in the *Icones*. Three hundred and eighty one of these drawings are at Edinburgh, and another 52 from this series are in the Wight collection at NHM.

Wallich's selection had the incidental effect of adding greatly to the geographical and taxonomic scope of the *Icones*, not least for the large number of monocots (especially of the family Araceae) otherwise largely neglected by Wight in his vast published output.

The largest single part of Wight's surviving 'illustrations collection' is in the library of the Botany Department of the Natural History Museum. Amounting to 840 individual items (741 composite 'works') it is also the most heterogeneous and clearly represents the remains of a 'reserve collection' on which Wight drew when choosing material for publication in his *Icones*; unlike the Edinburgh collection, by far the majority of these drawings is unpublished. It is also distinguished from the Kew and Edinburgh collections in never having been mounted, and the drawings are still stored in Wight's original folders (*c*.230 × 290 mm) made of native paper and annotated with the family name. Of the drawings by Rungiah and Govindoo, the majority can be assigned to the various series already described from Kew and Edinburgh (e.g., a fine one of the tomato (NHM 373) is from series D; a pair of delphiniums (NHM 5, 6) is from series C, and a large number are from series E, of the 1840s, though it is not always possible to be certain which of these are by Rungiah, and which by Govindoo. As already mentioned, 52 of the shaded tracings of Roxburgh Icones, made under Wallich's direction, are also here.

Elements unique to the NHM collection

There is, however, much, and extremely interesting, material of types not represented at Kew or Edinburgh. Of works by Rungiah and Govindoo unrepresented elsewhere is a small series of economic plants, and a collection of cryptogams. There are also works by a range of other artists both European and Indian (for further biographical details see Appendix 2).

Economic Plants

As part of Wight's 1836 economic botany commission, he was specifically asked to produce 'outlines' of the most valuable economic plants (see Book I p.72). In the end, and rather curiously, illustrations of no such plants were published in the *Icones*. However, in the NHM collection is a series of very beautiful line drawings, safely attributable to Rungiah, clearly made with these instructions in mind. These include three native cereals, with notes on how the grains were prepared for eating: *Pennisetum americanum* (Tam: cumboo, NHM 682), *Brachiaria ramosa* (Tam: sethay vayr pilloo, dated 2d February 1836, NHM 683) and *Paspalum scrobiculatum* (Tam: worrugoo, NHM 684). Among the drawings of cultivated and introduced plants are Indian mustard (NHM 20), radish (NHM 21), grape vine (NHM 90), strawberry (NHM 171), chili (NHM 380), cannabis (NHM 433) and *Rumex vesicarius* (NHM 476). Related to these is a series of drawings of four fig species dating from Wight's days in the garden at Bangalore in 1841 (NHM 427–30), with notes on their habit and suitability as roadside trees.

Taxonomic Groups

Of drawings by Rungiah and Govindoo showing taxonomic groups unrepresented at Edinburgh or Kew are drawings of some 16 grasses and 4 sedges, and some fine palms. There is also a beautiful drawing of the strange climbing gymnosperm *Gnetum ula*. The cryptogams include 29 ferns and clubmosses, and four extraordinary fungi.

Indian artists

In the NHM collection are works by two Indian artists not represented at Edinburgh. The first is Walter Abraham who worked for J.E. Stocks in Sind. Stocks sent some of his drawings to Wight, who reproduced five in vol. 4 of the *Icones*. The whereabouts of the originals of these published plates is unknown, but at NHM is a single drawing by Abraham, of *Lycium edgworthii* (NHM 383). A second Indian artist, though an extremely poor one, is represented by five extremely crude drawings of Nilgiri plants, sent to Wight by William Munro; it seems doubtful that these are by either of the two artists employed by Munro whose names are known, but one (NHM 287) is annotated by Munro 'Drawn by my native draftsman'.

European artists

In addition to drawings by Mrs Walker and Mrs Jerdon, already described under the Edinburgh collection, at NHM are ones by three identifiable Western botanist/artists (in addition to one or two unidentified ones). These are: E.A. McCurdy, better known as a topographical artist, who supplied Wight with three rather sketchy watercolours of *Caralluma adscendens* in 1838; F.N. Maltby, a Madras civil servant, is represented by possibly two watercolours of orchids similar in style to Mrs Jerdon's. By far the largest series of such material is that sent from the Western Himalaya by the Bengal civil servant M.P. Edgeworth, consisting of 76 delicate ink tracings (on which only a few details are coloured), of which there is also a single example at Kew.

While the provenance of the Kew collections is clear, that of those at RBGE, EU and NHM, which clearly once formed a single collection that remained in Wight's hands, possibly up to the time of his death, remains a mystery. It cannot be coincidental that the majority of the material in Edinburgh represents published work, while that at NHM is largely unpublished. Wight himself could well have made this division, realising the importance of the published drawings (which often represent original material of his new species), but, as already noted, the drawings of at least 1445 of the *Icones* and *Illustrations* are still missing, and who split the collection between London and Edinburgh, and when? There are three main possibilities as to how the drawings came to Edinburgh.

The first is through George Walker-Arnott. He was Wight's greatest taxonomic collaborator, and the earlier of the drawings at RBGE bear copious annotations in his hand, so were clearly used in the writing of the *Prodromus*. Arnott's herbarium came to RBGE in 1966 from the University of Glasgow, but with an almost complete lack of accompanying documentation. There is, however, no oral history at Edinburgh of any drawings coming with the herbarium specimens and this seems, on the whole, the least likely possible source.

The largest proportion of Indian drawings at RBGE is from the collection of H.F.C. Cleghorn, and, although there is no specific mention of them, it seems certain that these came with the Cleghorn Memorial Library and other botanical collections transferred from the Royal Scottish Museum in 1941.[8] There were very close connections between Wight and Cleghorn: Cleghorn had access to Wight's papers and quoted from unpublished ones when writing his obituary; he also stayed at Grazeley shortly before Wight's death (see Book 1 p.175). One of the drawings (RBGE W97), which is undoubtedly part of the Wight collection, bears an ambiguous note 'drawn by Govindoo my native artist' in what is definitely Cleghorn's hand, but this could conceivably have been copied by Cleghorn from an annotation originally made by Wight. This is

certainly a possible route, but why the published/unpublished split, and why send some to London, when Cleghorn was based almost exclusively in Scotland after his retirement?

The most likely explanation seems to be that the distribution of the collection was done by Wight's executors. In his will, written in 1861, Wight bequeathed his:

> Library of Books and my Collections in Natural History unto my said Wife and to my Brother in Law James Dorward … and Octavius Adolphus Field … my Trustees … [and] that they shall sell, call in, and convert into money my personal estate.

The resulting funds were to be invested for the benefit of his wife and, after her death, to go to his children. This shows that it was up to Rosa, Dorward and Field to sell the remaining collections, though by the time of Wight's death eleven years later the valuable herbarium had already been given to Kew. Wight's books were doubtless then worth even more, at least financially, than the herbarium, but it is questionable if the heavily annotated botanical drawings would at that time have been considered of any value whatever,[9] and could well have been given away at the discretion of the trustees.

Although at the time Wight's will was made Dorward was still in Madras, by 1872 he had retired to Haddington, perhaps explaining why the most important part of the drawings collection came to Edinburgh University, Wight's *alma mater*. It is possible that the Roxburgh 'tracings' were thought to be of merely bibliographic interest and retained in the University Library, while the coloured drawings were clearly of greater taxonomic value and sent to the Botanic Garden, at that time effectively the botany department of Edinburgh University. The dismemberment of Rosa's album is also suggestive. Clearly the botanical material was preserved, and ephemeral material, such as the autographs and sentimental verse it must also have contained, discarded. This preservation of Wight's artistic-botanical relics, no matter how trivial, seems a considered act such as might have been performed by conscientious executors.

Fig.13. Pencil 'tracing', possibly by Lachman Singh, of *Cassia bacillus* (now *C. javanica*). Edinburgh University Library.

Fig.14. *Cassia bacillus* (now *C. javanica*), by an unknown Calcutta artist, one of the set of Roxburgh Icones sent to the EIC in London. Royal Botanic Gardens Kew.

CHAPTER FOUR

Copying and the Hybridity of Indian Botanical Art

The extensive use made by Wight of copies of the unpublished Roxburgh Icones raises the subject of the copying tradition in Indian art. The ability of the 'moochy' as a copyist in Tanjore around 1806 has already been noted (see p.15), and copying continues to play an important role in Indian art. The extraordinary school of painters in Kutch between about 1720 and 1820 might be cited as a historical example. These Kutch artists copied eighteenth century English mezzotint portraits using the technique of Chinese reverse paintings on glass, and European topographical and architectural prints in traditional gouache on cloth.[1] While some of the paintings produced were facsimiles of European originals, the latter could be taken as starting points for bizarre architectural capriccios, and on occasion original portraits of Indian subjects, or even Hindu gods, were painted on glass in the Chinese style.[2] The technique of copying and the concept of hybridity are two that seem to merit further investigation, but will be raised here with respect to botanical art.

The earliest recorded Indian examples of the copying of Western botanical illustrations appear to have been in Mughal art of the seventeenth century, as discussed by Ray Desmond.[3] As Mughal artists are known to have copied European religious engravings, so did they copy botanical ones, and Vivian Rich traced the source of some paintings in the 'Dara Shukoh Album' in the British Library (dating at latest to 1641–2), and the later 'Small Clive Album' at the Victoria and Albert Museum, to their late sixteenth- and early seventeenth-century European prototypes.[4] Such copying for artistic purposes was correspondingly free, and has relatively little in common with copies made for 'scientific' purposes such as plant identification. The latter is a fascinating subject, but one on that has been little studied. In the West it was, of course, the only means by which illustrations could be reproduced and transmitted until the late fifteenth century. By the end of this period, due to a process of visual 'Chinese whispers', drawings dating originally from the Classical period, ended up as the Lear-esque apparitions (they can scarcely be called plants) of the Latin *Herbarius* or the *Ortus Sanitatis*. It was such distorted images, completely useless for identification, that led Leonhart Fuchs and Otto Brunfels to get artists to draw plants from nature. However, the succession of large, finely illustrated books that originated with this Renaissance tradition and produced over the next 300 years, were always rare, expensive and bulky, and, especially with eighteenth century travel urges, a renewed interest in copying developed, before photography, xeroxing or digitisation became options. Desmond noted William Hooker's copying of the Roxburgh Icones (the set then at East India House and now at Kew [fig.14], itself a copy set from the Calcutta 'originals') in anticipation of a voyage to Ceylon.[5] Many such works have doubtless been destroyed as being 'mere' copies, and it was only with the discovery of the huge body of such work in the Cleghorn collection at RBGE that the importance of this as a genre was recognised, and the interest of

it as a possible art form in its own right noted.[6] Cleghorn, in fact, got the idea of copying botanical prints from Wight, but in the end did so on a far more extensive scale. Such copies vary greatly in terms of style, depending on the medium both of the original and the copy – from simple uncoloured tracings to coloured facsimiles, or, at other times, what amount to free translations. While the botanical liberties taken by the Mughal artists (such as extra petals) were avoided, rearrangements in terms of layout, and/or reductions in size, were nearly always required for practical reasons.

However, it was not enough for Wight to copy rare and expensive illustrations for his own use – he wanted to share these works. Thus at one point he intended reproducing Rheede's large engraved plates on a reduced scale using the relatively simple and direct technique of lithography. In a letter to Hooker in October 1837, when discussing his forthcoming *Illustrations* he wrote:

> I also contemplate the publication of portions of all Rheede's plates abridged in the manner of your copy of Roxburgh's, but 4to size to allow room to give a better idea of his gigantic figures, but that of course cannot be undertaken until I have become a proficient in Lithography.[7]

Nothing came of this project of Wight's, but it might be the origin of some simple, small format Rheede copies in the Kew collection.

The Rheede plates were not the only ones that Wight had copied, and according to Cleghorn, around 1834 he:

> had tracings made of Roxburgh's Coromandel plants, and of his unpublished drawings at the Calcutta Gardens. These he arranged systematically in portfolios, and carried them about for reference on his tours.[8]

This might well be a confusion on Cleghorn's part with the copies that Wallich slightly later supplied to Wight, to be described below, but it could be the origin of some reduced copies of Roxburgh plates (similar in format to the Rheede ones at Kew) in the Edinburgh collection.

COPIES OF ROXBURGH ICONES SENT BY WALLICH

The original intention, when Rungiah's drawings were all that Wight had available, was to confine the *Icones* to depictions of 'Peninsular plants', but, as his ambition and botanical contacts expanded, the work evolved to cover other material, including the occasional reproduction of an already published illustration.[9] The opportunity to broaden the scope came as early as the second part, with Wallich's generous, and greatly appreciated, offer to send copies of Roxburgh's unpublished Icones from the Calcutta Botanic Garden.[10] The story of the 2542 'Roxburgh Icones' and their repeated copying has been told elsewhere,[11] and by 1838, when Wight started publishing his own *Icones*, only a small fraction of Roxburgh's drawings had been published – chiefly the 300 in the

Plants of the Coast of Coromandel. In the 'Notice' Wight referred to the problems of reducing Roxburgh's large drawings to the smaller format of the *Icones*, and he was aware of the resulting danger of 'misrepresentation', intending to use only 'portions ... when that can be done without injuring the character of the figure', or by spreading one Roxburgh drawing across two plates. The surviving copies at EU and NHM have already been briefly described, and provide a particularly fascinating manifestation of the Indian copying tradition.

Roxburgh's fully coloured original drawings are on folio sized sheets, and were frequently copied for a variety of different patrons with differing purposes in mind,[12] – highly finished coloured ones for noblemen and amateurs, largely uncoloured ones for scientists. What Wallich sent Wight were skillfully shaded graphite tracings [fig.13], folded into four for ease of postage between Calcutta and Madras. They are the work of a highly competent artist, and in some ways finer than the, often rather crudely coloured, originals. It is known that Lachman Singh was still working at the Calcutta Botanic Garden in 1845,[13] and a comparison with the shading on a lithograph he based on a drawing by William Griffith [fig.21] suggests the strong possibility that these 'copies' are in his hand.

Carbon copies of seven of the covering letters sent with these 'tracings' to Wight in 1839 and 1840 have survived at Calcutta, and in one of these Wallich described at least something of the process:

Here are six tracings from Roxburgh's drawings; I copy, as always, from the back of the drawings.[14]

The 'I', which should be read as 'my artist', is revealing and notably different from Wight's integrity in such matters. The shading was redundant for Wight's simple line lithographs, but the question remained as to how to reduce these large drawings to the Royal Octavo format of the *Icones* without 'misrepresentation'. How Wight and Rungiah set about this can be seen on the 'copies', and their annotations. Some of the latter are in Wallich's hand, including the Roxburghian plant name, but sometimes he wrote other details, as on the drawing of *Quercus ferox*:

"when copied cut off this spike" – Thus on the drawing in Roxburgh's own handwriting, from whence I infer that the same must be done by my friend Wight in transferring this to stone. NW.

More interesting are the annotations by Wight and Rungiah (in English and Telugu) – instructions to the lithographer in Madras as to which parts of the drawing were to be reproduced. On a plate showing two species of *Colocasia* Rungiah has amusingly written to the lithographer:

Sir, you should write the word "Fig." near the number, otherwise Dr Wight will get angry.

Fig.15. *Cochlospermum gossypium* (now *C. religiosum*), copy by unknown Indian artist of an engraving by Joseph Swan, made for H.F.C. Cleghorn in Madras c.1850.

Fig.16. *Cochlospermum gossypium*, hand-coloured copper engraving by Joseph Swan made for W.J. Hooker after a drawing by Rungiah, published in the *Botanical Miscellany* (1831).

Sometimes boxes are drawn around the part to be reproduced, in other cases the instructions are written out, such as 'make a double plate of this'. The resulting cramped prints fit uniformly into the series of lithographs of the *Icones*, betraying nothing of the elegant layout and shading of their 'originals' – at either one or two removes – and are captioned 'Roxburghianae', following Hooker's method of identifying particular collections within his own *Icones Plantarum*.

In total 419 of these Roxburgh tracings were published by Wight in his *Icones*: 88 in vol. 1 (1838–40); 259 in vol. 2 (1840–3); 63 in vol. 3 (1844–5). They came at a particularly useful time, representing a ready made source of illustrations to keep the *Icones* going when Wight was heavily preoccupied with the demands of his cotton work in Coimbatore. This source dried up when Wallich left Calcutta in 1846 and the very few printed after this (four in vol. 5, and five in vol. 6) had doubtless been kept in reserve by Wight.

COPIES AFTER RUNGIAH

Reference has already been made to Cleghorn's extensive illustrations collection, which contains vast numbers of copies in various styles and hands from a large range of rare botanical works, both historical and contemporary. Being a close personal friend, Cleghorn owned his own copies of most of Wight's publications, but it would appear that he did not have a copy of the rare *Illustrations of Indian Botany* brought out by Hooker in Glasgow in 1831, illustrated with engravings by Joseph Swan after drawings by Rungiah. Cleghorn therefore got an artist to copy the plates: 18 of these are at RBGE, extraordinary examples of what might be called photo-realism, with even the copper-plate script of the titles copied [fig.15]. These are therefore Indian watercolours made by an unknown artist around 1850, based on hand-coloured Scottish engravings of 1831, based on Indian watercolours by Rungiah made 1826–31. These must have been used by Cleghorn for his own researches, and perhaps also for teaching purposes at the Madras Medical College, where he was Professor of Botany.

Another example of copying for teaching purposes has come to light – behind which lies an even more convoluted, and trans-continental story. It was not only in India that copies of botanical drawings were made, and Hooker in Glasgow quarried many published and unpublished sources when getting W.H. Fitch to make large teaching diagrams to illustrate his hugely popular lectures. Only a handful of these diagrams has survived, but among them is one based on Rungiah's drawing of *Vallisneria spiralis*, though it is not known if Fitch copied the original drawing or Swan's engraving based on it. As already described this collection was sold to Arnott, and used for teaching generations of Glasgow medical and botanical undergraduates, but Arnott probably had no idea of the history of this particular image.

COPYING TODAY – A LIVING TRADITION

The copying tradition continues in India to this day, but inventively adapted to new ends. I first became aware of one of these in 2000, on a visit to a touristy antique/craft boutique at Sundar Nagar in New Delhi. Here were some extraordinary artefacts – meticulously painted in the Mughal miniature style in Jaipur, but showing images of birds, dogs, butterflies, shells – all brand new, copied from books, and painted on pages removed from nineteenth-century manuscript books of Quranic commentaries and Islamic devotions written in Naskh calligraphy.[15] These pages provide a smooth, almost polished, surface for the gouache; lines of the original calligraphy have been left above and below the image, and ruled lines and cloud-shaped areas of gilding added, to make them look like Mughal miniatures – an extraordinary form of hybridity and cultural appropriation. One of these sets of paintings that particularly interested me showed the bulbs of a variety of monocots – highly abstract images, as there were no backgrounds, shadows, or any other visual distractions. Not wanting to condone the vandalism of devotional manuscripts I did not buy these at the time, but, perhaps unsurprisingly, given their rather stark subject, they were still there when I visited the shop two years later. This time their interest as examples of latter day copying and cultural hybridity overcame my scruples [fig.17]. At least one turns out to have been copied from a photographically illustrated book on bulbs by Martyn Rix and Roger Phillips. Curiously the leaves and flowers have been removed from most of them, the bulbs enlarged, and the papery bulb tunics so beautifully rendered in paint that the original source took some finding. Much more obvious and instantly recognisable were some ornithological paintings copied from Archibald Thorburn's classic *British Birds*, but again vastly improved over the rather crude offset litho reproductions of the modern reprint (edited by James Fisher) from which they must have been 'copied'.

An even more surprising example of botanical copying in contemporary India has come to light. On visiting a friend in Edinburgh about three years ago I noticed a handsome waste paper bin made of sheet metal. It was painted all over, and on each of the four faces was an image of the extremely rare tree *Bauhinia foveolata*. Although slightly altered (a leaf had been lost, and two inflorescences gained), this could only have been taken from one of the plates in the *Dapuri Drawings*. The source of the WPB was traced, via an Edinburgh importer of ethnic objects, to a workshop in Jaipur that had bought a copy of the book and was copying images from it on to a range of household goods! It is wonderful that such living traditions and inventiveness continue, and one can only wonder what Gibson or his anonymous Portuguese-Indian artist would have made of it – an Indian watercolour made in Maharashtra in 1848, translated (via the medium of a photographic transparency) into an offset litho print in Belgium in 2002, and translated into oil paint on steel in Jaipur very shortly thereafter.

HYBRIDITY – REASONS FOR NEGLECT IN EAST AND WEST

The question of whether copies can be works of art in their own right raises the issue of hybridity, and a broader consideration of the nature of Indian botanical illustration. Whereas a certain amount of attention has been paid to Western botanical art both from an artistic and scientific point of view, almost no critical scholarly attention has been paid to the botanical drawings of the 'Company School' by professional art historians either Indian or Western. A notable exception was the pioneering work of Mildred Archer, but this really provided no more than an introduction, is outdated, and was done without any technical knowledge of the subjects depicted.

The lack of interest in precise identification of the subjects also applied to the dealers and cataloguers working for the London salerooms who presided over the sale (and unfortunate subsequent dispersal) of so many collections of Indian botanical drawings from the 1970s onwards. There seems to have been no realisation that accurate identification of the plants, or critical examination of annotations, could help resolve questions such as where in India particular collections were made, and that while the artists might be anonymous, it might well be possible to discover something about who commissioned them. They were merely denoted 'Company School', bolstering the myth that there was a single school, with an origin in the dying embers of the Mughal miniature tradition. The true diversity of the 'School' is only now becoming apparent. William Chubb's catalogue of another regrettable and recent dispersal,[16] an album of Calcutta drawings from the Earl of Derby's collection, with botanical information supplied by the present author, shows (I hope) the benefits of a joint botanical/art historical approach. It should be stressed that such an approach is only likely to work with entire collections since vitally informative annotations might be limited to just one or two drawings in a whole collection, or only a few might be informative by virtue of depicting highly localised, species. Once a collection is split up, the chance of finding such informative

images is remote, and in any case by this stage there is little point as it would be impossible to reassemble the collection and restore it to its botanically meaningful whole. The work on the Wight and Dapuri collections only became possible when the individual works were brought back together, which was possible because they were still (more or less) in one place.

One reason for scholarly neglect is at least partly because drawings such as those in the Wight collection fall between various deeply entrenched, though artificial, art-historical taxonomic categories; the most notable being East/West, art/illustration, original/copy, and art/science. They have been invisible to art historians for various reasons – to Indians perhaps in part because of Nationalist agendas, and to Europeans because of snobberies over definitions of 'art', the legitimacy of categories of objects as subjects for study, and long shadows cast by, especially nineteenth-century, art historians.

Fig.18. Photographic plate (page 106) from *The Bulb Book*, by Rix & Phillips (1981). By kind permission of Roger Phillips.

Fig.17. Bulb of *Narcissus minor*, gouache by unknown artist, Jaipur, *c*.2000, executed on nineteenth-century paper taken from an Arabic manuscript, based on a photograph in *The Bulb Book*, by Rix & Phillips (1981).

Partha Mitter has illuminatingly discussed the problems that Western art historians have had, over many centuries, with the understanding and appreciation of Indian art,[17] and the ghost of 'monsters' still hovers in the background. While Mitter dealt only with Indian religious art and architecture, this blindness applies to all work produced by Indian artists, including that strongly influenced by the West – either in terms of technique or choice of subject matter. One of the critics discussed by Mitter was John Ruskin and his role in Western debates on Indian art. One of Ruskin's major criticisms (over and above what he took, implicitly, as unsatisfactory underlying moral and religious motivation) was that Indian artists failed to draw from nature:

> It is quite true that the art of India is delicate and refined. But it has one curious character distinguishing it from all other art of equal merit in design – it never represents a natural fact. It either forms its compositions out of meaningless fragments of colour and flowings of line; or if it represents any living creature, it represents that creature under some distorted or monstrous form.[18]

Even someone as dogmatic and inconsistent as Ruskin could hardly have written this had he seen examples of Rungiah's virtuosity, but at the time he wrote the drawings were locked in a Naturalist's cabinet at Grazeley and not considered as art. However, have things changed so much today? Drawings such as Govindoo's and Rungiah's are commonly referred to as 'botanical illustrations'. Personally I have never seen much point in the distinction between art (by which is meant 'fine' or 'high' art) and illustration, or even design (which, by extension, must therefore be 'low' art). Given the development of the former in the twentieth century (post-Duchamp), and the variety and extremities to which it has diverged (to the point where a helter skelter can be presented in Tate Modern as a work of 'physical art'), there seems no option today but to accept John Carey's definition of a work of art as:

> anything that anyone has ever considered a work of art, though it may be a work of art only for that one person.[19]

Although no public art gallery to my knowledge has a permanent exhibition of botanical drawings displayed as works of 'fine art', many individuals do in their own homes, and they are certainly sold as 'art' by salerooms and commercial galleries. On these criteria, the Indian botanical drawing undoubtedly represents an art form, and a particularly fascinating one that crosses several traditions and categories – cultural, artistic and scientific.

There has, however, and unfortunately, been a reluctance on the part of Indian scholars to admit that Company School painting has anything to do with Indian art. However, Rungiah's control of line and sense of design in his botanical drawings would not have been possible unless he had been brought up in a traditional Indian school of drawing and painting that paid great attention to such matters,

regardless of what the subject depicted. What could perhaps (from a botanical point of view) be seen as defects, for example, lack of range of colours and inability to render subtle surface textures, can also be explained by this background, as can the much-vaunted lack of skill in rendering perspective (though in fact both Rungiah and Govindoo could do so when they wished – see, for example Plate 20A).

For these reasons it seems to me that these Indian botanical drawings are legitimate subjects of study by both Western and Eastern art historians. The case of Lachman Singh is of particular importance in this context, and the discovery that the pencil Roxburgh 'copies' commissioned by Wallich are most probably his work makes this a matter of relevance to the Wight collection, though a tangential one and their story belongs with that of the Calcutta Botanic Garden painters.[20] Here boundaries completely break down – they are copies of Roxburgh's artists' work, but 'originals' of Wight's lithographs, but surely, above all, works of art in their own right. It is known that when Singh was working for Royle at Saharunpore (while Wallich was on leave from Calcutta in 1828–32) he decamped for a spell to work as a Court painter in one of the Punjab Hill states.[21] What is more one of his works in this style has survived, a portrait of George Potter, head nurseryman at the Calcutta Garden, reproduced by Desmond.[22] Did Rungiah, when not working for Wight, also work in a traditional style, perhaps for his local temple, or making pictures of gods and goddesses for sale to Indian pilgrims? If so was this work influenced by his naturalistic work? Can someone with the necessary skills in Tamil and Telugu, the collecting of oral histories, and examining temple records please go to Tanjore and try to find out more! Only in this way can individual biographies and details of schools, influences, patronage and chronologies be built up.

Botanical drawings have already been noted as a particularly valuable contribution by Indians to Western descriptive science, and another way to see this body of work is as a result of artistic and scientific globalisation. There are many reasons to be suspicious of globalisation – for example, in this context, if it has been responsible for the death of indigenous artistic traditions, which have either had to be artificially revived or else disappeared for ever. However, there are also reasons to celebrate it, and there is such a thing as hybrid vigour – novel, syncretic styles are not necessarily or inherently, inferior. Perhaps regrets about loss are merely the result of stultifying taxonomies of 'pure' artistic schools? The vigour of Rungiah's and Govindoo's drawings, the work of the Portuguese-Indian artist at Dapuri, and the 'copies' by Lachman Singh and those after Rheede possibly by Govindoo,[23] seem worthy of celebration as highly individual contribution, and not merely as part of some generic 'Company School'. As had been hoped the three Edinburgh exhibitions of the work have been acknowledged as sources of inspiration by some of Scotland's leading contemporary artists and art students, and also, through reproduction, by 'craftsmen' in India.

Fig. 19. *Arum costatum* (now *Arisaema costatum*), lithograph made at the Government Lithographic Press, Calcutta, after a drawing by Vishnupersaud, published (t. 19) in Wallich's *Tentamen Florae Napalensis Illustratae* (1824).

CHAPTER FIVE

Wight and Lithography

It can be argued quite forcefully that the introduction of lithography to India in the 1820s had a far more significant impact on the history of printing in South Asia than the arrival of typography in the 1550s.[1]

The establishment and improvement of the art of botanical drawing on stone in the peninsula of India is wholly due [to Wight].[2]

Copying is all very well if an artist is to hand, but two of Wight's greatest concerns were to make botanical illustrations more widely available in India (to assist with identification), but equally importantly, to make these as accessible and cheap as possible. These concerns lie behind his espousal of lithography, which had a major impact not only in reproducing text – in both English and the vernacular languages – but in revolutionising the relatively cheap and easy reproduction of maps and drawings, not least of natural history subjects.

Reproduction of botanical illustrations changed with developing technology over the centuries, starting from the woodcuts in herbals of the sixteenth century. By the late eighteenth century the commonest method was by means of copper engravings of great sophistication, usually coloured by hand and correspondingly expensive to produce. Lithography was invented in Germany by Aloys Senefelder in 1798 (as a means of reproducing music manuscript), and introduced to London as early as 1803; in Scotland experiments were probably first made around 1815 and a description of the process was published in *Blackwood's Magazine* in May 1817.[3] Perhaps its earliest use for reproducing drawings of Indian natural history subjects in Britain was for two hand-coloured plates (tt. IX, X) of 'the Baya or Bottle nested sparrow [i.e., weaver bird]' lithographed by James Forbes in 1811 and included in his diversely illustrated *Oriental Memoirs*.[4] An early use in Britain for botanical purposes was a print made from a plate of orchids drawn by a Dutch soldier at the Cape of Good Hope for Francis Masson. This lithograph was made by the London firm of Moser & Harris and included in volume 4 of the *Journal of Science and the Arts* in 1818.[5] The horticultural taxonomist John Bellenden Ker wrote the accompanying text, but a major purpose of the exercise was to promote the new printing technique:

> When it is considered that by this art, drawings are multiplied to any extent, without either the expense or the labour of engraving, there can be little doubt but that it will in a short time be much more generally adopted in this country. Although the process is simple, yet much care and delicacy are requisite, in order to procure perfect and distinct impressions.[6]

There were disadvantages: for example, as Wight pointed out copper plates could be stored and 'run off when needed: for lithographs the whole edition has to be run off at once'.[7] The reason being that the large stones used for printing were polished after each job and reused. Fortunately in South India there was a local source of suitable porous limestone, which had been discovered at Kurnool in the Bellary district in 1826. This was said by W. Garrad, Chief Engineer at Fort St George, to be:

> obtained in any quantity, it is denser and of finer grain than any I have yet seen from Europe, and may be considered as so far superior for manuscript copies, and every description of fine work where clearness and minuteness of character are required.[8]

With lithography there was no problem with the size of the edition and it was common for 1000 prints to be taken from a lithographic stone,[9] and the greatest number of copies Wight ever needed was 467 in the case of prints required both for the *Icones* and *Spicilegium*, and 367 for those issued only in the *Icones* or *Illustrations*.

As noted above, one of Wight's greatest concerns was accessibility, which he knew to have been a problem in the case of earlier, lavish, botanical works. When he first heard that Wallich intended to produce folio-sized plates he wrote, horrified, to Hooker:

> What could have induced Wallich to publish the plates in folio? The immense expense of engraving plates of that size must place an almost impossible bar in the way of their sale. Roxburgh did the same and now it is next to impossible to get his work at any price, whereas by publishing it in a cheaper form … he might have doubled both the sales and the number of copies, thus having a useful work & one occasionally, even at this distance of time, to be met with – in place of one only known by report. For my part I never saw a plate of it until I met with the work [the Coromandel Plants] in the Literary Society's library at Madras. The same must necessarily be the case with Wallich's splendid work.[10]

At this point, in 1829, Wight did not know that Wallich would use lithography for his *Plantae Asiaticae Rariores*, but this does not invalidate the point about the expense of large plates, and the only botanical lithographs Wight could then have known were the unsophisticated ones produced in Calcutta for Wallich's *Tentamen* (1824, 1826) [fig.19].

When the first part of *Plantae Asiaticae Rariores* reached Wight in Negapatam in 1830, lithographed in London by Maxim Gauci [fig.6], the plates therefore came as a revelation as to the possibilities of the process:

> the plates considering that they are Lithographic uncommonly fine. I had not the most distant idea that that kind of printing could ever be brought to such a high state of perfection … as good as the Copper plate engravings of the Coromandel Plants and I fancy not half the price.[11]

With the same post came 59 sheets of Wallich's *Numerical List* of the specimens in the EIC herbarium, which demonstrated the possibilities of another, more plebian, use of the process.

LITHOGRAPHY IN SCOTLAND

Wight's furlough between 1831 and 1834 coincided with a great expansion of lithography in Scotland, as related by Schenck.[12]

LITHOGRAPHIC BUSINESSES IN EDINBURGH AND GLASGOW

	1820	1826	1830	1835	1870
Edinburgh	1	6	6	11	60
Glasgow	0	5	6	15	122

Scotland's first lithographic printer, in 1820, was John Robertson, who operated from South Union Place, Edinburgh. At this time most lithographers 'confined their activities to commercial jobbing works such as circulars, business forms, invitations, display cards, and funeral notices etc.',[13] or, as Shaw more picturesquely put it, 'in its lowest *avatar* as the early nineteenth-century precursor of photocopying'.[14] As noted above, Wallich had used the process for such a purpose in London, for reproducing the EIC herbarium catalogue, and this example was followed by Wight for the *Catalogue* of his own herbarium. The first part of this work was printed lithographically in Edinburgh in May 1833, for which Wight & Arnott must have gone to one of the eleven firms then extant, such as Forrester & Nichol of George Street, or William Burness of St James's Square.

Wight was already aware of the possibility of lithography for illustrative purposes, and Robertson had used the process to reproduce David Octavius Hill's drawings, being responsible for the first 15 plates of *Sketches of Scenery in Perthshire* in 1821–2. Wight could well have known these – they include several scenes around Blair Atholl, such as Loch Tummel, Blair Castle (Book 1 fig.15) and the Falls of Bruar, and it is not impossible that his sister and brother-in-law, the Stewarts, might have had a copy of the work, or at least seen it in the Duke's library.

Glasgow was also a great centre for lithography, and Hooker recorded that, while staying with him (and this must refer to 1833), Wight:

> with characteristic energy visited the lithographic establishments in Glasgow, made himself thoroughly acquainted with the machinery, tools, and manipulations, purchased at large expense, from his own resources, the necessary materials, and took them out to India.[15]

A botanical connection exists in the early history of lithography in Glasgow in the person of Thomas Hopkirk.[16] Hopkirk was a keen botanist, and well known to Hooker, being involved with the botanic garden to which he donated a large number of plants. He published *Flora Anomoia* a pioneering work on plant teratology,[17] which includes no lithographs, but an interesting early example of a nature print by 'J. Hardie Junr.', the other plates being engravings by 'R. Gray'. However, it was Hopkirk's 'interest in botanical illustration [that] may have stimulated a curiosity in lithography for he was known to be an excellent lithographic writer'.[18] Hopkirk's exact role as a lithographer is uncertain, and it may have been largely as a backer of the printer John Watson; he moved to Ireland 'after 1830', and died in Belfast in 1841.[19] By 1835 fifteen lithographers were active in Glasgow, and there was also extensive use of the technique in the calico trade. It should be noted that Hooker recruited Walter Hood Fitch from drawing designs for calico, so he must have been aware of the process, though he would not use it himself for high quality botanical illustrations until slightly later, and at the time of Wight's visit, Hooker was still using the engraver Joseph Swan (1796–1872) to reproduce drawings for his botanical periodicals. At this time 'Swan was already well established as a top-class and highly successful engraver and copperplate printer',[20] but in the Glasgow Herald of 10 October 1834 appeared the following advertisement:

NEW LITHOGRAPHIC PRINTING OFFICE,
17, TRONGATE, (OPPOSITE TONTINE,) GLASGOW

J. SWAN respectfully informs the Public, that he has commenced Business at the above place. Being regularly brought up to the writing department in one of the principal establishments in this city, and from the knowledge acquired for the last two years in Belfast, he is enabled to furnish Lithographic Printing in all its departments, with the greatest *neatness*, *cheapness* and *despatch*, and therefore assures those who will be kind enough to make a trial of his workmanship, that nothing shall be wanting on his part to give every satisfaction.

Swan himself cannot have gone to Belfast to learn the trade, and he presumably sent an employee, but could there be a connection here with Hopkirk? What is more remarkable is the date, for at this very time Wight was actually staying with Hooker in Glasgow and they could have read this advertisement together over the breakfast table at 7 West Bath Street. An amateurish lithographed still-life from Rosa Wight's album might, [fig.20] perhaps represents one of her husband's exercises from this period, an image possibly copied from a drawing manual, kept for sentimental reasons, and later given to his wife.

Hooker's own first use of lithography had been in September 1821, for the plates of the first edition (landscape format: 'quarto oblique') of his *Botanical Illustrations*, a series of 21 plates illustrating botanical terms produced for his students. The letterpress was printed by Archibald Constable in Edinburgh, but the unattributed plates are lithographed. This must be one of the earliest, but previously un-noticed, uses of the technique in Scotland for illustrative purposes, but it is unfortunately impossible to say if they were made in Glasgow or Edinburgh. In 1837 the work was republished in 'portrait' format, with new plates by Fitch, lithographed by Allan & Ferguson. Hooker's first use in a more 'serious' publication appears

Fig.20. Still-life with oysters and shrimps, lithograph, possibly by Wight.

Fig.21. *Podostemon wallichii* (now *Polypleurum wallichii*) and *P. griffithii* (now *Hydrobryum griffithii*), lithograph by Lachman Singh after drawings by William Griffith, published in *Asiatic Researches* vol. 19, by J.-B. Tassin's Oriental Lithographic Press (1836). Royal Botanic Gardens Kew.

to have been to reproduce a drawing by Mrs Walker of Adam's Peak in Ceylon, which was made by Allan & Ferguson and appeared as the frontispiece of the *Companion to the Botanical Magazine* in August 1835. Hooker later used this same firm for reproducing the illustrations in his *Icones Plantarum* (from 1836) and *Journal of Botany* (from 1840).[21]

Scotland was also of significance in the technology of printing presses used for lithography in India. John Ruthven, a printer and 'patent printing press manufacturer' in Edinburgh patented several innovative designs.[22] The presses used by Rind in Calcutta in 1824 were made according to 'Ruthven's construction', and Shaw reproduced an illustration of one such Ruthven 'iron press' from the *Gentleman's Magazine* of 1820.[23] Andrew Cook gave further details of these Ruthven presses exported to Calcutta from Edinburgh – one of their 'Foolscap Lithographic' presses cost £22, and their 'Folio Lithographic Presses for Maps Charts &ca' cost £36. At this time the stones also had to be imported into India from Germany via Britain – these were 2½ inches thick and available in three sizes: 30 × 30 inches (£5), 20 × 16 inches (£2 5s) and 16 × 11 inches (£1 5s).[24]

LITHOGRAPHY IN INDIA
Calcutta

There are several reasons for Shaw's statement on the importance of lithography in India quoted at the head of this chapter. Especially important were its advantages for reproducing Indian scripts and as a simple way of reproducing the mass of official reports, maps and diagrams required by the EIC bureaucracy. Despite some slightly earlier experiments by two Frenchmen, a Monsieur Belnos and Philippe de Savighnac, the first practical introduction into Calcutta was by a Scottish Surgeon, Dr James Nathaniel Rind, who in a pre-echo of Wight, had learned the process while on furlough, but in his case in Edinburgh, from Alexander Forrester.[25] Rind became Superintendent of the Government Lithographic Press in Calcutta, which was established in 1823, and he provided illuminating advice on the setting up a similar establishment in Bombay in 1824.

Significantly, as a background to Wight's important contribution in Madras, one of the earliest uses of the Government Press in Calcutta was for a botanical purpose. Wallich's first use of printing

Podostemon Wallichii. Podostemon Griffithii.

techniques to reproduce drawings made by his Indian artists had been copper engraving.[26] These unsophisticated plates were made by two Indian engravers 'Ramnaut' and 'Kasinaut'. For his pioneering illustrated work on the flora of Nepal Wallich, however, turned to lithography [fig.19]. Only two fascicles (each containing 25 plates) were produced, in 1824 (at the Government Lithographic Press) and 1826 (at the Asiatic Lithographic Press), but these are the earliest botanical lithographs made in India.

As already mentioned the French had an important role in the early development of lithography in Calcutta, and in this context should be mentioned the three botanical plates in Robert Baikie's *Observations on the Neilgherries* of 1834,[27] which have a somewhat complicated history. The book was edited by W.H. Smoult who must have undertaken to produce the book while based in Madras. The illustrations were supplied by 'friends', the botanical ones by a 'Mrs P', and 'Mr Gantz of Madras' redrew some of the landscapes. The Governor, Sir Fred Adam, had allowed Smoult 'every assistance in the use of the Lithographic Department of the Chief Engineer's Office [and of] Col. Monteith of that department and his assistant'.[28] However, before the book was ready for printing Smoult was evidently transferred to Calcutta so the lithographic work (maps and the botanical plates) were in the end executed there by Jean-Baptiste Tassin. Smoult was evidently proud of his work and considered the landscapes to be 'the first attempt to produce coloured landscapes of Indian scenery'. He also provided detailed costs of preparing the plates. For example those for the three flower plates (*Cyanotis*, *Pedicularis* and *Anagallis*) were:

> Drawing on stone 32 Rs; Printing 500 copies 19 Rs; Col[ouring] 8 Rs per 100 copies; Paper 6 Rs. The total cost of each plate was therefore 148 Rs, and for the three 444 Rs.

The subject of the first lithographs recorded as being made by an Indian artist were also botanical. In 1836 Lachman Singh made lithographs after Griffith's minutely detailed analytical drawings of two species of *Podostemon*, printed at Tassin's Oriental Lithographic Press, for vol. 19 of *Asiatic Researches* [fig.21].

Madras

Virtually no information is available on the early history of lithography in Madras, though there was certainly a government lithographic press there in 1828[29], under the charge of the Chief Engineer; John and Justinian Gantz also had a lithographic establishment at Popham's Broadway, in Blacktown, and in 1827 published a series of studies of trades entitled *The Indian Microcosm*.[30]

As already noted Wight was not quite the first to consider the use of lithography for botanical purposes in the Madras Presidency, and those in Baikie's book were already in press while Wight was in Britain. His contribution, however, was both outstanding and prolific, though an aspect of his work that has been little commented on. After returning to India in 1834 two of Wight's earliest papers in the *Madras Journal of Literature and Science*,[31] on *Calotropis procera* and *Ischaemum pilosum*, were illustrated with lithographs. The prints are anonymous both as to artist and lithographer and differ from Wight's own slightly later lithographs, in that the shading takes the form of parallel lines (in imitation of engravings). Given that at this time Wight had no permanent base, they are likely to have been made at the Government Lithographic Press.

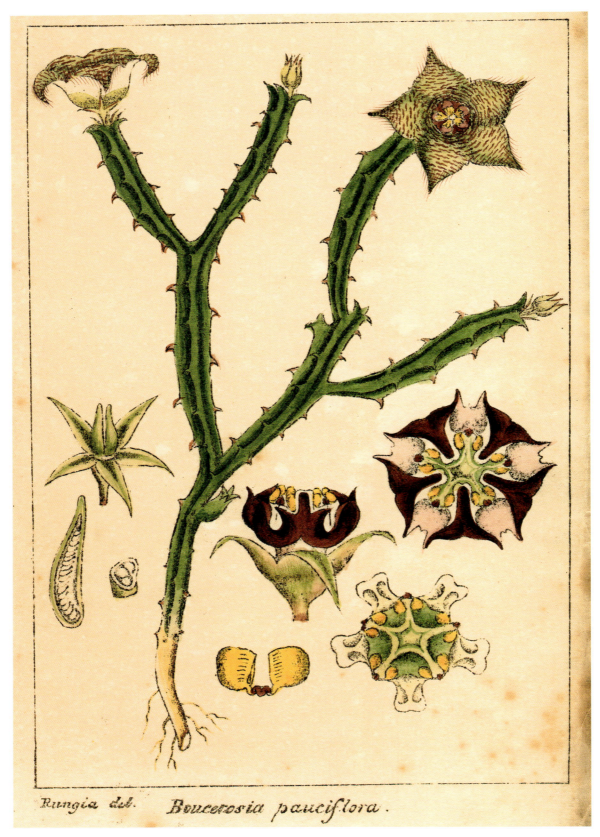

Rungia del. *Boucerosia pauciflora.*

Fig. 22. *Boucerosia* (now *Caralluma*) *pauciflora*, lithograph by Wight after a drawing by Rungiah.

When Wight was about to embark on the *Illustrations* in October 1837 Hooker had recently sent him the first parts of his own *Icones Plantarum*, illustrated by lithographs (by Allan & Ferguson of Glasgow). These were doubtless an inspiration, and Wight greatly admired:

> their execution which I think exceedingly neat and clear in the outline, now and then a little too dark in the shading but always good enough, though upon the whole inferior to the German, at least as exhibited in Nees' Genera – and also to some French Lithographers I have seen.[32]

As soon as he was able, with a settled base in Madras, Wight 'purchased a Lithographic Press, and commenced practising Lithography'.[33] This work was seen as part of Wight's official work, and Lord Elphinstone the Governor personally authorised the supply of lithographic stones from the Chief Engineer, and paper from the Superintendent of Stationery, and got the Government to subscribe to 50 copies of the *Illustrations*.[34] Wight wrote to Hooker about his own early experiments in lithography and the 'innumerable failures, from the damp and heat of the climate, clumsiness and prejudice of the natives, warpings of presses, breaking of stones, moulding of paper, drying of printing ink, and cracking of rollers'.[35] There were also problems with the process of transferring the image traced from the original drawing onto transfer paper, then onto the stone, and the behaviour of the ink in the Madras heat, such that some of the finest lines failed to print – as explained in a letter Wight wrote to Martius in response to some friendly criticism.[36] Despite these difficulties 'under which any other person would have succumbed' Wight continued with 'indomitable perseverance',[37] and in October 1837 was able to send Arnott 'specimens exhibiting my progressive improvement in the art of Lithography'.[38] The first of these to be published, this same month, was of the asclepiad *Boucerosia*

pauciflora, sent to Cole for publication in the *Madras Journal*, as a taster for the *Illustrations* [fig.22]. Wight wrote:

> nearly the whole impression … has been struck off from my own press. I may here observe that I am well aware of my present imperfections in the difficult art of lithography, but, as every successive trial exhibits some improvement on the preceding one, I am encouraged to anticipate ample success.[39]

The reviewer of the first number of the *Illustrations* in 1838 (most probably Cole himself) noted admiringly that the whole process was 'conducted on his own premises', and at this point Wight described the setup:

> The lithographic department will be executed by myself aided by my staunch retainer Rungiah who makes the drawings in transfer. Of course you are not to expect them to vie in execution with yours [Hooker's], but then they are to be coloured, which will no doubt cover many sins on the part of the lithographer, and in some measure to make up for defective execution. The cost is calculated …. [to be] about £3 per 100 4to plates.[40]

Nothing is known of Wight's press, though given the source of the Calcutta presses and Wight's connections, it seems highly likely that it might also have been made by Ruthven in Edinburgh. The largest plate Wight ever made was that of lichens, which measures 448 × 268 mm (Book 1 fig.23), so it would seem that Wight had a 'Foolscap' press, and the largest stone used was 20 × 16 inches. By this time it seems likely that Kurnool stones were being used in Madras rather than having to be imported from Germany.

When writing to elicit the Governor's support for the *Illustrations* Wight pointed out that the costs were 'nearly 50 per cent under the usual English price of such works' and that 'the colouring alone

Fig.23. *Loranthus lageniferus* (now *Tolypanthus lageniflorus*), lithograph by Dumphy, Madras, after a drawing by Rungiah, published as plate 306 of Wight's *Icones* (1840).

Fig.24. *Tolypanthus lageniflorus*, lithograph by Allan & Ferguson, Glasgow, after a drawing by Rungiah, published as plate CCXXIX/CCXXX of Hooker's *Icones Plantarum* (1839).

Fig.25. *Tolypanthus lageniflorus*, drawing by Rungiah (RBGE W132 r).

costs 3/5th of the whole sum'.[41] The early plates both of the *Illustrations* and *Icones* are largely Wight's own work – though it should be noted that the first eight plates of the *Illustrations* exist in two versions, the finer ones attributed 'R.W. Lith', the less fine bearing no lithographer's name. It was probably pressure of time that led Wight to hand over the lithography to professionals after about sixty plates of the *Icones* and about ten of the *Illustrations*. In the Prospectus for the *Icones*, dated July 1838, Wight described 'Mr Winchester the Company's Lithographer' as 'certainly the best in Madras', but as he was already undertaking the work on the *Illustrations* he was too busy to take on the *Icones*. Wight therefore had to juggle the lithography of the first volume of the latter between himself (94 plates), Winchester (21), 'Romeo' (8) and J. Dumphy, who did the majority and took over completely as lithographer for volumes 2–6 of the *Icones*, and from the second half to the end of volume 2 of the *Illustrations*.

Both Dumphy and Winchester worked at the Government Lithographic Press, which in Wight's time was situated in the Fort, at Hanover Square, its hours being 10–5.[42] Unfortunately nothing is known of either these individuals except that Dumphy's (the name suggests he was Irish) forename began with a 'J', and he lived at 'John Pereira's', in what was then called Blacktown (now Georgetown) suggesting the lowly status of a government 'Draftsman and Writer'. Dumphy was still active in 1862 (by which time the Government Lithographic Press had moved to Chepauk), when he lithographed the frontispiece and a map for Talboys Wheeler's cotton *Handbook*.[43] Winchester's name was apparently James, but a 'W. Winchester' made the prints for plates 131–4 of the *Illustrations*; perhaps a son, and it was perhaps another son, 'C. Winchester', who drew another map for Wheeler's cotton *Handbook*. Nothing is known of 'Romeo', or of the 'W. Smith' whose name appears as lithographer on some versions of plates 11 and 12[-2] of the *Illustrations*, but doubtless they also worked at the Government Lithographic Press.

After 1842 Wight was based in Coimbatore, which led to considerable logistical difficulties in dealing with the lithographers in Madras. Instructions were sent by letter and by annotations on the drawings, mainly in Telugu script. These were doubtless written by Rungiah for instructing the lithographers. A note on a sheet of floral dissections of *Bulbophyllum fuscopurpureum* on the type sheet at Kew gives some insight into the process used:

> If this plate is not struck off give these dissections in place of those attached to the drawing. If it is transferred to the stone but not printed still give these dissections make a new transfer for we are sure these are correct. I am not sure of the others which were made from dry specimens these are from fresh ones. If the plate is printed off then it can't be helped return this paper & I perhaps can find some other opportunity.

To which the lithographer has added 'Returned, as the other dissections referred to has already been printed & the Plate of the same accompanies'.

Wight evidently had a 'writer' (i.e., clerk) called Etterazooloo, based in the office of the Medical Board in Fort St George.[44] He seems to have worked on the *Icones*,[45] and it seems likely that he played a role in liaising with the lithographers in the nearby Lithographic Office.

Other lithography in Madras

In 1844 three printing presses were listed in Marsden's *Madras Almanac*, in addition to the Government Lithographic Press. Wight had connections with two of these: the 'American Mission (P.R. Hunt Supt.) Popham House' and the 'Athenaeum (J.B. Pharoah's), Mount Road'.[46] With the third, 'Gantz's Lithographic, 12 Popham's Broadway', Wight seems to have had no connection. There were also other lithographic presses in Madras around this time issuing works in Indian languages, and several of the lithographers were Muslims: for example Syed Mahomed Rahmeemtolah employed by the College of Fort St George in 1841, and the Auzamool Ukabar Press, which in 1840 issued a newspaper called 'Hindoostanee Selections'.[47] The fact of Wight's printing Telugu and Tamil plant names on his lithographs has already been noted, though by this date these could have been typeset in the letterpress if he had so wished. It is not known when Telugu typesetting first became available in South India, but in Tamil it had been available at Tranquebar as early as 1713, and in Madras, at 'what is today the Diocesan Press', since 1761.[48]

E.A. Rodrigues has been mentioned already as the colourist of four plates in the *Illustrations*, but he was also a lithographer and produced two extraordinary illustrated works on religious/mythological subjects in Madras during the 1840s. These in some ways might be seen as a curious parallel to Wight's work, demonstrating what could be called a taxonomic approach to the study of South-Indian Hindu iconography. Rodrigues was clearly a devout and extremely scholarly Christian, and the purpose of the works was to explore Hindu beliefs, and show where these overlapped with Classical philosophy and Christianity. While profoundly critical (not to say patronising) of Hinduism (for example, there were aspects that Rodrigues could not bring himself even to name), he went to enormous efforts to investigate the subject in two detailed and scholarly texts. The first was *The Hindoo Pantheon* (not to be confused with Edward Moor's more famous work of the same name) produced in 1841–5, illustrated with 140 hand-coloured lithographs. The letterpress was printed 'for the author' by R.W. Thorpe and Reuben Twigg at the SPCK's press at 'Church Street, Vepery' (the Introduction by G. Calder at the 'Asylum Press, Mount Road'). No artist's name is given, but the originals are presumably the work of a Tanjore or Trichy artist of the sort reproduced by Archer,[49] and Dallapiccola.[50] The plates were doubtless lithographed by Rodrigues himself, and are labelled 'published by E.A. Rodrigues, Oriental Lithographic Press, Madras', presumably his own private press like Wight's one of 1837. Might Wight and Rodrigues have known each other and compared notes on their similarly encyclopaedic illustrated projects? Rodrigues's second work *The Religion of Vishnoo*, three parts with twelve plates, published in 1849, is also linked indirectly with Wight as the printer of the letter press was P.R. Hunt of the 'American Mission Press', who printed the later parts of the *Illustrations*.

Hunt was also the printer of a lithographically illustrated ornithological work by Wight's friend T.C. Jerdon. While some of the hand-coloured prints in Jerdon's *Illustrations of Indian Ornithology* were produced in Britain, others were lithographed by C.V. Kistnarajoo; clearly another member of the Raju clan. The first part of this, consisting of 121 plates (price Rs 6, i.e. 12 shillings) was reviewed in Calcutta in January 1844, as surpassing 'any thing of the kind that has yet been attempted in the way of Zoological publications in India', and must have been issued in late 1843.[51]

Wight gave an explanation of the process of the sort of transfer lithography he used in the Prospectus to his *Icones* dated July 1838. As this is not bound in with all copies of the work it seems worthwhile reprinting it here:

> Lithography is essentially founded on chemical principles, or the attraction existing between the stone used (a soft close grained lime stone) and greasy substances on the one side, and the well known repulsion between oil and water on the other. A greasy line drawn on such a stone strongly adheres; the stone being then wetted, the line throws off the water retaining its attraction for any fresh portion of grease that may be brought in contact with it. A roller charged with ink, having an oily substance for its base being now passed over the stone, a portion of the ink attached itself to the line, while the water prevents its equally adhering to and soiling the rest of the stone. The line thus charged being subjected to heavy pressure, parts with the ink, which adheres to the paper to which the impression is to be communicated.
>
> Such then are the very simple principles of Lithography. The drawing may be communicated to the stone either directly by means of Lithographic chalk, a substance containing a quantity of tallow, &c. in its composition, or through the medium of a transfer drawing executed, on paper prepared for the purpose, with 'transfer' ink, also a greasy composition, which on being firmly pressed upon a dry stone, adheres and imparts the lines which are afterwards to be charged with printing ink. So far all is easy, and the principles so self-evident, that it seems wonderful the first quarter of the 19th century had nearly passed away before they were practically applied to the diffusion of knowledge.
>
> The practice however of the art of printing from stone, is as difficult as the principles are simple, and subject to so many sources of failure that it seems not less wonderful, such astonishing advances towards perfection should have been already made. The method pursued in the accompanying figures is that by transfer, or the communication of the drawing from paper, and being that with which I am best acquainted, I shall confine my remarks to it.
>
> From a bad transfer it is almost, if not actually impossible to take a good print. Much care is therefore requisite in this first operation. The transfer being completed and communicated to the stone, the whole may be destroyed in the first inking, before a single impression is taken off. This accident may happen in two ways, either the ink may be too firm and adhesive and take the lines off the stone altogether, or it may be too soft and run the adjoining fine lines into one large blotted one, technically called "smutt". Both of these accidents can, if confined to a small portion of the drawing be in some degree remedied, but never altogether corrected. In the course of printing, they are so liable to happen that it is rare for even the best printers to take off fifty consecutive impressions, without the occurrence of one or other of them in a greater or less degree. Hence the value of a well-proportioned printing ink, and still more, of one not liable to change its consistence from exposure to the air in the course of printing. This last is still a desideratum in Lithography; and until supplied we can never expect to have any considerable number of uniform impressions. Some will always be found darker and others paler, in proportion to the comparative softness or hardness of the ink, and the skill with which it has been applied. The importance of a good roller with which to ink the drawing may be imagined from the following simile of a Lithographer. "You may as soon expect to write well with a bad pen as to print delicately (in Lithography) with a bad roller". Unfortunately for the Lithographer no part of his apparatus is so difficult to make; add to these causes of failure, and many more not mentioned, the difficulty of making a fine dark and accurately proportioned ink in the first instance, its liability to change afterwards through the reaction of its component parts on each other, but especially during printing, and lastly, the great skill required in its application, only attainable by much practice.

It should be noted that this sort of lithography is essentially a fairly crude process, taking no advantage of the finer possibilities of a medium that allows an artist to draw directly on the stone, and to reproduce subtle gradations of tone – the sort practised by Gauci. Wight's method is essentially reproductive rather than artistic, and is the same method he used for reproducing the manuscript of his herbarium *Catalogue*. While perfectly adapted to the purpose he had in mind, the use of the transfer stage meant that what were reproduced were really no more than rather rough tracings of Rungiah's and Govindoo's original drawings. Despite this the drawings and their reproduction in the *Icones* were praised by that most fastidious of judges, J.D. Hooker (in his dedication of *Rhododendron wightii*), as:

> a remarkable instance of the perfection to which botanical illustrations can be brought by indomitable perseverance under the most discouraging circumstances. The first plates ... are equal to any produced at the era of their publication in India; the latter will compete with the best outline lithographs of Europe.[52]

The Drawings

The plates in this section all come from the RBGE collection, but, given the size of this, it has been possible to reproduce no more than a representative selection. In order to demonstrate the rich diversity of the South Indian flora, and following the example of Wight's own *Illustrations*, the selection has been made to cover the maximum number of plant families. The Edinburgh collection has particular strengths, probably through accidents of survival as much as being a true reflection of Wight's original collection; this bias has been maintained in the choice – for example the strong representation of the families Rubiaceae, Leguminosae, Acanthaceae and Orchidaceae. Needless to say, there has also been a presumption in favour of the most attractive drawings and those in the best condition.

The arrangement of the plants by family, or 'Natural Order', follows the natural classification of A.P. de Candolle, as given in the influential article on Botany that Wight's collaborator George Walker-Arnott wrote for the seventh edition of the *Encyclopaedia Britannica*, published in Edinburgh in 1831.

LAYOUT OF ENTRIES

Name *Followed by botanical authority*

FAMILY
Tamil and Telugu name (taken largely from Gurudeva, 2001, and from Wight's drawings and herbarium specimens)
Medium, dimensions (width × height), artist, date
Watermark

Botanical notes on the species (where possible these have been taken from Wight's own publications, but encyclopaedic works such as Mabberley (1997) and Watt (1889–93) have been heavily relied upon)
Contemporary annotations
Publication details

RBGE WIGHT COLLECTION NUMBER (SERIES)

1. Ranunculus diffusus *A.P. de Candolle*

RANUNCULACEAE

Bodycolour heightened with gum arabic, and ink, over traces of pencil, 160 × 198mm. By Rungiah, *c*.1830.

This drawing was almost certainly made from a plant from the Nilgiri Hills, which Wight & Arnott described as *Ranunculus subpinnatus*, and, along with the specimens (Wight Catalogue no. 15) in Wight's herbarium, forms the original material of this species. However, this is no longer considered distinct from *R. diffusus*, a species described earlier by Augustin Pyramus de Candolle based on Wallich specimens from Nepal. The main distribution of this subalpine buttercup is in the Sino-Himalaya, from Kashmir eastwards to N Burma and SW Yunnan at altitudes of 1300 to 3100 metres, where it grows in damp places in broad-leaved and evergreen oak forest.

Annotations by Wight: 10 (pencil, recto). Annotations by Arnott: WC. 15, Ranunculus subpinnatus (pencil, recto); Ranunculus subpinnatus, Wight ic. t. 49 (ink, recto).

Published as plate 49 of the *Icones* (1838), lithographed by Wight.

RBGE W5 R (SERIES C)

Menispermaceae

480/43

43

Cocculus Cordifolius
W. C. 44 - Wight. ic. t. 483

44

2

2. Tinospora cordifolia

(Willdenow) J.D. Hooker & Thomson

MENISPERMACEAE

Tam: chintil; Tel: thippathige; San: kundalli.

Bodycolour and ink over traces of pencil, 172 × 255mm. By Rungiah, *c.*1825.

A large climbing shrub that can reach a height of ten metres, which occurs throughout tropical parts of India, and into Burma and Sri Lanka. It has long been valued in Indian traditional medicine, in both Hindu and Muslim traditions. Elephants are said to be fond of its aerial roots. There is a very curious pencil drawing, probably by Govindoo, of this plant in the Wight collection at Edinburgh showing what appears to be some sort of rooting experiment, in which roots developing from one end of a cut section of woody stem are being trained into a water-filled glass jar.

Annotations by Wight: Menispermaceae, 43, 486/43, Turn (pencil, recto). Annotations by Arnott: 44, Cocculus cordifolius, wc. 44 – Wight ic. t. 486 (ink, recto). Other annotations: [Tamil script] Coondaniccody Tam. <u>Small.</u> (pencil, verso).

Published as plate 486 of the *Icones* (1841), lithographed by Dumphy.

RBGE W158 R (SERIES A)

3 A & B. Rorippa madagascarensis

(A.P. de Candolle) Hara

CRUCIFERAE

Bodycolour heightened with gum arabic, and ink, over traces of pencil, 234 × 305mm. By Rungiah, *c.*1834.

Watermark: [RUSE & T]URNERS [182]4.

An herbaceous weed of damp places occurring in tropical Africa and Madagascar, and scattered through India and Bangladesh. Its precise distribution in the Subcontinent is uncertain due to confusion with *R. indica* (L.) Hiern, but Wight's herbarium specimens were collected in the Nilgiris. The analytical details show a flower and a pod or 'siliqua' typical of the cabbage family, Cruciferae. The family name refers to the cross-shaped arrangement of the four petals and four sepals; the two locules of the pod are separated by a 'septum', and in this case the seeds are inserted in two rows in each 'locule'.

Published as plate 13 of the *Illustrations* (1838), lithographed by Winchester or Wight.

RBGE W346 R + V (SERIES D)

4. Maerua apetala *(Roth) Jacobs*

CAPPARACEAE

Tam: parellah marum [Wight], iruvalli; Tel: pilli adugu

Bodycolour heightened with gum arabic, and ink, over traces of pencil, 162 × 201mm. By Rungiah, *c.*1830.

A small tree that can reach four metres in height, endemic to dry forests at altitudes below 300 metres in Andhra Pradesh and Tamil Nadu. It was first described (in the genus *Capparis*) by the German botanist A.W. Roth, based on specimens collected by Benjamin Heyne, a predecessor of Wight in the post of Madras Naturalist. The plant is used medicinally: for example, a paste made from the root bark is used against leucoderma in Andhra Pradesh. The floral detail (right) shows the stamens and the long-stalked ovary attached to a common stalk called an 'androgynophore'. The plant belongs to the same family as the caper, whose flower buds are familiar as a pizza topping. The relationship is seen in the long-stalked fruits shown below the flowers at the top of this drawing, which are similar to those of the edible fruits of the caper.

Annotations by Wight: Capparideae, 174/78, Niebuhria sp. nov. (78) (pencil, recto); Niebuhria linearis, [wc.] 100.B (ink, recto). Annotations by Arnott: Wight ic. t. 174 (ink, recto). Other annotations: 3, 4, 5, 6, 7, 8, 9, 10, 11 (pencil, verso, beside pencil dissections).

Published as plate 174 of the *Icones* (1839), lithographed by Dumphy.

RBGE WI5 R (SERIES C)

5. Polygala wightiana *Wallich ex Wight & Arnott*

POLYGALACEAE

Tam: pareyahnunga chady (Wight)

Bodycolour heightened with gum arabic, and ink, over traces of pencil, 160 × 196mm. By Rungiah, *c.*1830.

An annual species of dry (including waste and cultivated) places of South India, where it occurs up to an altitude of 100 metres in the four southern states. Somewhat curiously it has also been reported from the Indonesian island of Flores. There are specimens at Edinburgh collected by Wight from Cunewady (near Dindigul), which is perhaps where he made the first collection. These early specimens were sent to the EIC herbarium in London with the dispersal of the Madras Naturalist's collection in 1828. Wallich gave these specimens a manuscript name commemorating Wight, but it fell to Wight & Arnott to describe it in their *Prodromus*, and this drawing (along with Wight's specimens) forms part of the original material of *P. wightii*. Although small, the floral details at bottom right, show the structure of the flower, familiar from the British milkworts. These are strongly bilaterally symmetric; the lower petal ('keel') has a fringed apex, which collects pollen falling from the anthers, and acts as a brush that applies the pollen to the abdomen of visiting insects.

Telugu annotations [sariyanange; kambnavada kudda].

Annotations by Arnott: [wc] 134, Polyg. Wightiana, Wight ic. t. 67 (ink, verso).

Published (with additional dissections not from this drawing) as plate 67 of the *Icones* (1838), lithographed by Dumphy.

RBGE W6 R (SERIES C)

6. Hybanthus enneaspermus

(Linnaeus) F. Mueller

VIOLACEAE

Tam: orilaithaamarai; Tel: rathnapurusha.

Bodycolour heightened with gum arabic, and ink, over traces of pencil, 175 × 242mm. By Rungiah, *c.*1825.

Watermark: [RUSE & TUR]NERS [182]4.

A prostrate herb (that may become woody at the base) widespread in dry places at low altitudes from Africa, throughout lowland India, to Australia. Linnaeus first described the plant in 1753 placing it in the genus *Viola*, which it resembles in its strongly bilaterally symmetric flowers, the lower petal forming a large lip, with a spurred, nectar containing base. Wight collected the plant in several places, firstly in the Northern Circars, then later at Trichinopoly, Pathucottah and Palamcottah. The plant has medicinal properties, and has been used as an anti-dandruff shampoo.

Annotations by Wight: Violarieae, 116 (pencil, recto). Annotations by Arnott: 309, [WC.] 115, Ionid. suffruticosum, Wight ic. t. 308 (ink, recto). Other annotations: [Tamil script] ooralattamaray (pencil, verso).

Published as plate 308 of the *Icones* (1840), lithographed by Dumphy.

RBGE W20 R (SERIES A)

7. A & B. Bergia aestivosa *(Wight & Arnott) Steudel*

ELATINACEAE

Tam: puney tangy cody [Wight]

Bodycolour heightened with gum arabic, and ink, over traces of pencil, 226 × 314mm. By Rungiah, *c*.1834.

A perennial herb with a woody stem base, occurring in the plains of S and NW India and Pakistan, where it grows along river banks. Wight & Arnott described their *Elatine aestivosa* based on specimens collected by J.G. König, and later ones collected by Wight at Pathucottah, and it is possible that this drawing represents part of the original material on which their description was based. Steudel realised that the species was better placed in the genus *Bergia*, described by Linnaeus, and named to commemorate his pupil Peter Jonas Bergius (1730–90), a Swedish botanist and physician. This is not the original drawing reproduced as plate 222 of the *Icones*.

Annotations by Arnott: Elatine (Bergia) aestivosa, Wight ic. t. 222 (ink, verso).

RBGE W376 R + V (SERIES D)

8. Abutilon crispum *(Linnaeus) Medikus*

MALVACEAE

Tam: cody taty (Wight), siruthutthi; Tel: nelabenda.

Bodycolour heightened with gum arabic, and ink, over traces of pencil, 148 × 197mm. By Rungiah, *c*.1830.

Watermark: C WILMOT 1819.

An herbaceous plant to 1.5 metres tall, native of America, but now a common pantropical weed. It is not known when it reached India, but there are specimens in the Edinburgh herbarium collected by Roxburgh prior to 1793. It is widespread in drier parts of southern India, where it ascends to 800 metres. Wight collected the plant at Gingee, while he was stationed at Negapatam, and this might well be the source of the specimen drawn by Rungiah. The floral details show the typical fused stamens of the family Malvaceae, but the fruit of this species is unusual in that the segments ('mericarps') are papery and inflated.

Annotations by Wight: 43/204 (pencil, recto). Annotations by Arnott: Abutilon crispum (pencil, verso); WC. 185, Abutilon crispum, Wight ic. t. 58 [sic, recte 68] (ink, recto). Other annotations: Malvaceae, Abutilon crispum (G. Don) (pencil, verso).

Published as plate 68 of the *Icones* (1838), lithographed by Wight, though this plate includes additional dissections not taken from this drawing.

RBGE W7 R (SERIES C)

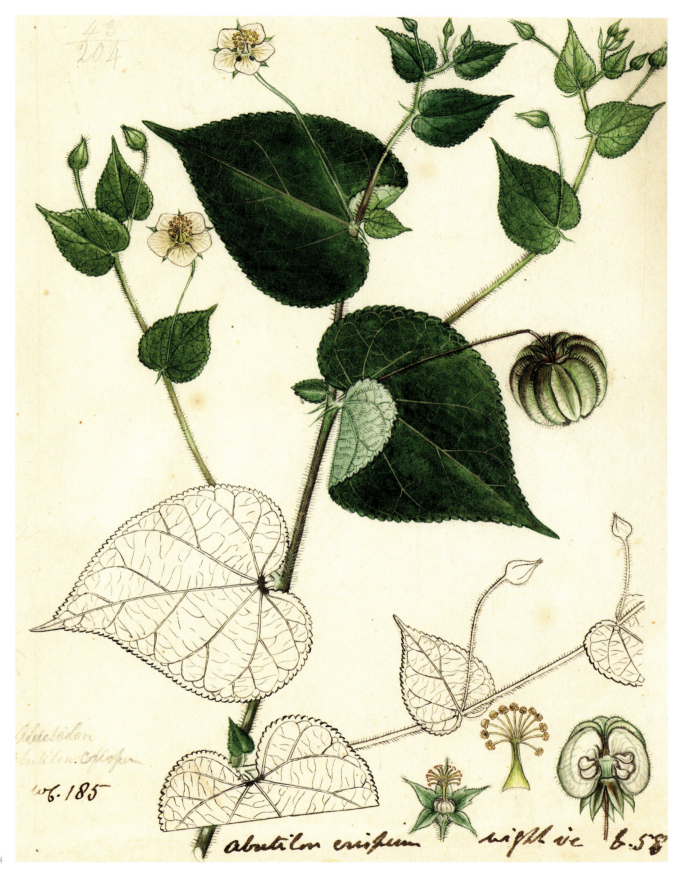

abutilon crispum   wight ic   b. 58

9. Hibiscus ficulneus *Linnaeus*

MALVACEAE

Tam: kaattu vendai; Tel: nelabenda.

Bodycolour heightened with gum arabic, and ink, over traces of pencil, 160 × 197mm. By Rungiah, *c.*1830.

Watermark: C WILMOT 1819

A small shrub to 1.5 metres tall, widespread from East Africa eastwards to Australia, and occurring throughout the hotter, drier parts of India, where it ascends to 1200 metres in the hills. It was first described by Linnaeus from Ceylon, and the epithet refers to the leaf shape, which is like that of the Mediterranean fig (*Ficus carica*). The plant is sometimes cultivated for fibre that is extracted from the stem and on which William Roxburgh carried out experiments.

Tamil annotations [illeg.].

Annotations by Wight: 196 (pencil, recto). Annotations by Arnott: WC. 205, *Abelmoschus ficulneus*, Wight ic. t. 154 (ink, recto).

Published as plate 154 of the *Icones* (1839), lithographed by Dumphy.

RBGE W9 R (SERIES C)

10 A & B. Hibiscus lunariifolius *Willdenow*

MALVACEAE

Tam: masuthutthi

Bodycolour heightened with gum arabic, and ink, over traces of pencil,
214 × 300mm. By Rungiah, *c*.1830.

The stunning floral analyses show a typical flower of the mallow
family. The top row shows the young, five-loculed fruit in
longitudinal and transverse section, with ovules attached to a
central axis. The ovary is superior, being attached above the sepals
and petals; the calyx consists of two whorls, the outer being called
the epicalyx. The filaments of the stamens are united into an
elongated tube, which surrounds the style that ends in a five-lobed
stigma – the complete structure is seen bottom right, and the male
and female parts separately bottom centre. The leaf detail shows a
covering of star-shaped ('stellate') hairs – these hairs are stinging
and hence the epithet 'pruriens' used by Roxburgh for this species.
The plant is a large herbaceous perennial or small shrub, occurring
in Africa, s India, Burma and Sri Lanka. The specific name refers to
a resemblance of the leaf to that of the European honesty (*Lunaria
annua*).

Annotations by Wight: 178, Hibiscus lunarifolius Willd. H. pruriens Roxb. Fl.
Ind. 3 pg. 196 (pencil, recto). Annotations by Arnott: Hibiscus lunariaefolius W.,
Wight ic. t. 6 (ink, recto).

The details and habit drawing on the reverse were combined and published as
plate 6 of the *Icones* (1838) lithographed by Wight.

RBGE WI02 R + V (SERIES D)

11. Ceiba pentandra *(Linnaeus) Gaertner*

BOMBACACEAE

Eng: kapok or white silk-cotton tree; Tam: ilavam; Tel: booruga

Bodycolour heightened with gum arabic, and ink, over traces of pencil, 175 × 255mm. By Rungiah, *c*.1825.

Native to South America and Africa, but commonly cultivated (and naturalised) in India and SE Asia for the silky hairs produced from the seed coat. This fibre is used for stuffing pillows and mattresses, and the plant also has medicinal uses. The tree, which can reach 30 metres in India, has a highly distinctive shape, like a cake stand, the branches being borne in whorls; the trunk is green and sometimes prickly, and develops buttresses with age. The strongly scented flowers open at night and are pollinated by bats. Wight first collected specimens of this tree while he was Madras Naturalist, when this painting must have been made. He knew it by Candolle's name *Eriodendron* (= wool-bearing) *anfractuosum*, the epithet referring to the twisted anthers, clearly shown in this drawing.

Telugu annotations [monandusham; vaikandi].

Annotations by Wight: Bombaceae, 400/228, 22/74, 226 (pencil, recto).
Annotations by Arnott: Eriodendron anfractuosum, Wight ic. t. 400 (ink, recto).

Other annotations: [Tamil script] Yalavamarum – Tam., No. 30. 2, 3, 4, 5, 6, 7, 8 [beside pencil dissections] (pencil, verso).

Published as plate 400 of the *Icones* (1840), lithographed by Dumphy.

RBGE W140 R (SERIES A)

Bombaceæ

400
228

Eriodendron
anfractuosa

12. Helicteres isora *Linnaeus*

STERCULIACEAE

Tam: kaiva, valampuri; Tel: aadasyamali

Bodycolour heightened with gum arabic, and ink, over traces of pencil, 216 × 290mm. By Rungiah, *c.*1834.

Watermark: [RUSE & TU]RNERS.

A shrub or small tree that can reach a height of five metres, widespread in tropical SE Asia. It occurs throughout India growing in forest margins and scrub jungle at altitudes below 1000m. The plant was first described by Linnaeus, based on various elements including a plate and description in Rheede's *Hortus Malabaricus*. The epithet is based on the Malayalam name 'isora murri' recorded by Rheede. The generic name refers to the curious spirally twisted fruits, which are borne in pairs. Fibre for cordage is extracted from the bark; the root, bark and fruit are used medicinally for stomach complaints.

Annotations by Wight: Helicteres Isora, W.C. 224 (ink, recto). Annotations by Arnott: Wight ic. t. 180 (ink, recto).

The floral details of this drawing (but not the habit) were published on plate 180 of the *Icones* (1839), lithographed by Wight.

RBGE W112 R (SERIES ?D)

13. Grewia orbiculata *Rottler*

TILIACEAE

Tam: nevsitti, uduppai, valukkunnu; Tel: jaana chettu, nulithada

Bodycolour heightened with gum arabic, and ink, over traces of pencil, 155 × 197mm. By Rungiah, *c.*1830.

A small tree that can reach twelve metres, occurring in the states of Andhra Pradesh, Tamil Nadu and Karnataka, where it grows in dry places up to an altitude of about 1000 metres. The yellow flowers are borne mainly between April and August. It was first described by J.P. Rottler (1749–1836), the last of the Tranquebar Missionaries, from specimens collected at Marmelong on a journey he made from Tranquebar to Madras in 1799. Marmelong was the site of the Nopalry garden, at the southern end of Mount Road in Madras, which Wight occupied in 1826–8. Rottler lived to an advanced age, latterly in Madras, and Wight bought important herbarium collections from him.

Telugu annotations [illeg.].

Annotations by Wight: Tilliaceae, 45/291 (pencil, recto). Annotations by Arnott: Wight cat. 268 (pencil, recto); Grewia rotundifolia Juss. Wight ic. t. 45 (ink, recto). Other annotations: Nechitty, Grewia vel … (pencil, recto).

Published (with additional dissections not on this drawing) as plate 45 of the *Icones* (1838), lithographed by Dumphy.

RBGE W3 R (SERIES C)

14. Elaeocarpus glandulosus *Wallich ex Merrill*

ELAEOCARPACEAE

Tam: naru makalem poovoo maram [Wight], bikki [Gamble].

Bodycolour heightened with gum arabic, and ink, over traces of pencil, 160 × 198mm. By Rungiah, *c.*1830.

Watermark: C WILMOT 1819.

A large tree, with whitish timber, that can reach 35 metres in height, occurring in the Western Ghats from Maharashtra southwards. This drawing was almost certainly made from material collected either at Courtallum or in the Nilgiris; Wight later also collected it in the Palni Hills. It is still common in the shola forest of the Palnis where Father Matthew recorded that it occurred mainly above 1800 metres. The white flowers are mainly produced between May and July and the fleshy pericarp of the massive green fruit is edible; the old leaves turn red before falling. Shown here in the floral details are the characteristic finely divided petals and the 5-lobed nectar-secreting disc surrounding the base of the ovary. The well-known, knobbly rudraksha beads (the lobed woody endocarp of the fruit) sacred to Shiva are produced by another member of this genus, *Elaeocarpus sphaericus*.

Annotations by Wight: 296 (pencil, recto). Annotations by Arnott: Elaeocarpus oblongus WC. 293 (pencil, recto); Elaeocarpus oblongus, Wight ic. t. 46 (ink, recto).

Published (with additional dissections not from this drawing) as plate 46 of the *Icones* (1838), lithographed by Wight.

RBGE W4 R (SERIES C)

15 A & B. Aegle marmelos *(Linnaeus) Corrêa*

RUTACEAE

Eng: the bael tree; Tam: villuvam; Tel: bilvachettu, maraedu

Bodycolour heightened with gum arabic, and ink, over traces of pencil, 254 × 346mm. By Rungiah, *c*.1834.

A thorny, deciduous tree to ten metres in height, occurring throughout India from the Sub-Himalaya southwards, but often cultivated. The tree is sacred to Shiva, and used in Shaivite ceremonies – the three leaflets symbolising his trident, and the processes of creation, destruction and preservation. The fruit has a hard rind, but the pulp is edible and used medicinally for bowel complaints. The generic name given by the Portuguese botanist José Corrêa da Serra is that of one of the three sisters who, in Greek mythology, guarded the garden of the Hesperides and the golden apple of Hera. One of the annotations on the drawing refers to Georg Forster's name for the plant, *Crataeva religiosa*, as used in Whitelaw Ainslie's *Materia Medica of Hindoostan*. Wight used this work extensively and one of the original intentions of his own *Icones* was to include in it illustrations of as many of the plants included in Ainslie's work as possible.

Annotations by Wight: 342, Crateva Religiosa Ainslie Mat. Med., Aegle marmelos 342 (pencil, recto). Annotations by Arnott: Aegle marmelos Corr. Roxb., Crataeva religiosa Ainslie Mat. Med. not Vahl (pencil, recto); Aegle marmelos Wight ic. t. 16 (ink, recto).

Published as plate 16 of the *Icones* (1838), lithographed by Wight.

RBGE W103 R + V (SERIES D)

16. Hypericum mysurense *Wight & Arnott*

GUTTIFERAE

Tam: awvern chady (Wight)

Bodycolour heightened with gum arabic, and ink, over traces of pencil, 159 × 200mm. By Rungiah, *c*.1830.

A shrub that can reach four metres in height, first described by Wight & Arnott in their *Prodromus* based on specimens collected in the Nilgiri Hills (where it still occurs at altitudes of 1600 to 2000 metres), and on earlier collections made by Benjamin Heyne at the spectacular hill-fort of Nundydroog north of Bangalore. It occurs from the latter southwards in the Western Ghats, and also in the central mountains of Sri Lanka, and may become dominant on deforested grassy slopes; the golden flowers are borne in February and March. This drawing was not published by Wight (it is not the original of plate 56 of the *Icones*), but almost certainly forms part of the original material on which *H. mysurense* was based. Arnott later placed the species in the segregate genus *Norysca*.

Telugu annotations: (aavaren shedy)

Annotations by Wight: 55/345 (pencil, recto). Annotations by Arnott: Norysca mysorensis Wight ic. t. 56, WC. 331 (ink, recto).

RBGE W96 R (SERIES C)

Hypericum mysorense, Heyne

Norysca mysorensis
Wight ic. t. 56
wf. 331

17. Meliosma simplicifolia (Roxburgh) Walpers

subsp. pungens (Wight & Arnott) Beusekom

MELIOSMACEAE

Tam: cembavu, kallavi

Bodycolour heightened with gum arabic and pencil, 249 × 429mm. By Rungiah, c.1845.

This drawing is included largely for botanical, rather than artistic, reasons, representing one of only two families described by Wight & Arnott – Millingtoniaceae. This family name was based on an illegitimate genus of Roxburgh's, but is now no longer regarded as taxonomically distinct from Meliosmaceae. The plant shown is an evergreen tree that can reach 20 metres, first collected by Wight in the Nilgiris, and described by Wight & Arnott as *Millingtonia pungens*. This is now treated as a subspecies of *Meliosma simplicifolia*, a species widespread in SE Asia. It occurs mainly over 2000 metres in the hills of S India (from the Nilgiris southwards) and Sri Lanka, with outlying populations (unless these represent mislabelled specimens) in Maharashtra and Sumatra.

Telugu annotations (recto: diguva kayilu arakudava vumpevarkam thirimpushayigaladi; verso: mundrinengirhillu andradanim vemiggulu, venne theranada).

Annotations by Wight: 34 & 35 (pencil, recto); Millingtoniaceae, 964/3/390, Millingtonia pungens (Wall.) (ink, recto). Annotations by Arnott: Wight ic. t. 964/3 (ink, recto).

Published as plate 964/3 of the *Icones* (1845), lithographed by Dumphy.

RBGE W424.1R (SERIES E)

18. Mesua ferrea Linnaeus

GUTTIFERAE

Eng: ironwood; Tam: naagappoo; Tel: naagachampakamu

Bodycolour heightened with gum arabic over traces of pencil, 260 × 428mm. By Rungiah, c.1840.

This was probably drawn from a tree Wight found at about 5000 feet below Coonoor in the Nilgiri Hills. It is a variable and widespread species that can reach 30 metres in height, occurring throughout India, Sri Lanka, the Malay Peninsula, Indo-China and Sumatra, but often cultivated for its spectacular flowers. The great orientalist Sir William Jones, founder of the Asiatick Society in Calcutta, thought it one of the most delightful trees on earth and that 'the delicious odour of its blossoms justly gives them a place in the quiver of Camadeva, the Hindoo god of love'. As the English name suggests the timber is hard and has been used in India for railway sleepers and bridges; its root, bark, seeds and leaves are used medicinally. Perhaps Rungiah's finest surviving drawing, the white petals are painted with great skill conveying a sense of three dimensionality unusual in Indian botanical drawings. The lead white on the petals had oxidised to a nasty shade of grey, recently chemically reversed to reveal the full glory of Rungiah's work.

Annotations by Wight: Calophylleae Guttiferae 9999961, Mesua speciosa (Chois.) Wight ic. t. 961 (ink, recto).

Published as plate 961 of the *Icones* (1845), lithographed by Dumphy.

RBGE W423.1R (SERIES ?E)

Mesua speciosa (Chris.)   Griff. 16.6.1868

18

19 A & B. Azadirachta indica *Adrien de Jussieu*

MELIACEAE

Eng: neem; Tam: veppamaram; Tel: vaepa

Bodycolour heightened with gum arabic, and ink, over traces of pencil, 250 × 344mm. By Rungiah, *c*.1830.

The renowned neem tree, which is probably native to Burma, but widely cultivated and naturalised in the Old World tropics, especially in India where it has mythic status, and legion uses. Being a member of the mahogany family its timber is useful; it is often planted as a shade tree; it is used in soaps and toothpaste; neem oil from the seeds has insecticidal and medicinal properties. In 1862 Edward Balfour recorded that 'like the shrew ash tree [*Fraxinus excelsior*, as recorded by Gilbert White] in England, it is often resorted to by the friends of the insane, who pass the sick person through a cleft in the tree, or through a stem which, having parted and re-united, forms a circular opening'. The generic name refers to the superficial similarity of the tree to *Melia azederach* (Plate 20), though the latter can immediately be distinguished by having twice divided leaves.

Annotations by Wight: 47 396 Azadarachta indica (pencil, recto). Annotations by Arnott: Azadarachta indica Wight ic. t. 17 (ink, recto).

RBGE W378 R + V (SERIES D)

20 A & B. Melia azedarach *Linnaeus*

MELIACEAE

Eng: Persian lilac; Tam: malaivembu, malie vapamarum; Tel: thurakavaepa, thooraka vaupaurmanoo.

Bodycolour heightened with gum arabic, and ink, over traces of pencil, 248 × 347mm. By Ruṇɡiah, *c*.1830.

Watermark: RUSE & TURNERS 182–.

The most stunning of Rungiah's floral dissections, showing a typical flower of the mahogany family, Meliaceae. The calyx is five-lobed, there are five white petals and the purple structure is a tube composed of fused staminal filaments; shown bottom left is a cross section of the fruit (a drupe), showing the nut (brown) with five locules, each containing a single seed, surrounded by a fleshy pericarp; on the right hand side are two details of the nut (woody endocarp) in side view and cross section. The Persian lilac is a tree that can reach a height of twelve metres, native of SE Asia and N Australia, but cultivated elsewhere, including the Mediterranean, especially in the form that produces its fragrant flowers before the leaves. Its timber has been used for cabinet making under the name 'bastard cedar', and for construction purposes, its fruits as beads, and the leaves and bark medicinally.

Annotations by Wight: 393 Melia azadarach (pencil, recto). Annotations by Arnott: Melia azedarach Wight ic. t. 160 (ink, recto).

Details and habit drawing on the reverse combined in plate 160 of the *Icones* (1839), lithographed by Dumphy.

RBGE WI07 R + V (SERIES D)

21. Ampelocissus tomentosa *(Roth) Planchon*

VITACEAE

Tam: sirunaralai, cautoo moondri; Tel: garigummadi, uddeve dracha

Bodycolour heightened with gum arabic, and ink, over traces of pencil, 239 × 318mm. By Rungiah, *c*.1830.

The family Vitaceae, to which the grape vine also belongs, is a large and taxonomically difficult one in India, but one to which Wight & Arnott paid considerable attention. This climbing species is widespread in s India, where it can be found up to an altitude of 1520 metres in the Western Ghats. In this drawing Rungiah has failed to convey the dense felty covering of rusty hairs that clothe the plant, and from which the species epithet is derived. Both unisexual and bisexual flowers are borne on the same plant: the two floral details at the bottom right show a bisexual flower (with red petals), and to their right is a cross section of a young fruit.

Annotations by Wight: Ampelideae 57/432, Vitis tomentosa (pencil, recto). Annotations by Arnott: Vitis tomentosa Wight ill. t. 57 (ink, recto); W[ight's] C[atalogue] 411 (pencil, recto).

Published (with some additional floral details not on this plate) as plate 57 of the *Illustrations* (1839), lithographed possibly by James Winchester.

RBGE W348 R (SERIES D)

22. Impatiens gardneriana *Wight*

BALSAMINACEAE

Bodycolour heightened with gum arabic, ink and pencil, 224 × 280mm. By Rungiah, 1845.

Wight was particularly interested in balsams, of which he encountered many species restricted ('endemic') to the Western Ghats. He described 28 new species, most of which are still recognised, and published a paper on them in the *Madras Journal of Literature and Science* in 1837. The species depicted here was discovered by himself and George Gardner, Superintendent of the Peradenyia Botanic Garden on Ceylon, on a joint expedition to the Nilgiri Hills in 1845. The flower position and structure is complex: one of the sepals is modified into a nectar-bearing spur, some of the pairs of sepals and petals are fused into single structures, and in some species others are missing. The flower position and which organs represented fused structures was a matter of disagreement and Rungiah's floral diagrams show different interpretations of the flower according to two German botanists: on the left (B) is that of J.A.C. Roeper (now thought to be correct, with the flower twisted through 180 degrees), and on the right (A) that of K.S. Kunth.

Annotations by Wight: Balsaminaceae, 1048, Coloured No 42/1, Impatiens Gardneriana (R.W.) (ink, recto). Annotations by Arnott: Wight ic. t. 1048 (ink, recto).

First published (hand-coloured) as plate 42/1 of the *Spicilegium* (1846), lithographed by Dumphy; reprinted (uncoloured) the same year as plate 1050 of the *Icones*.

RBGE W266 R (SERIES E)

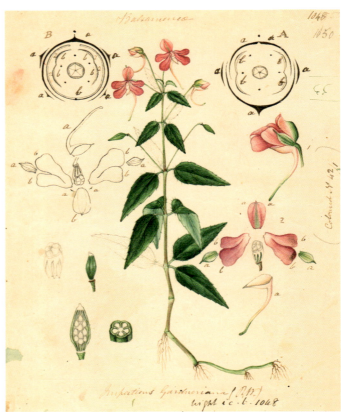

23 A&B. Impatiens munronii *Wight*

BALSAMINACEAE

Bodycolour heightened with gum arabic and pencil, 200 × 250mm (265.1);
103 × 119mm (265.2). By Rungiah, *c.*1838.

This plant was discovered in March 1838 by William Munro and the
Hon. George Stevens Gough on roadside rocks on the Koondah
Ghat near Sispara in the Nilgiri Hills. Munro and Gough were two
of the botanical correspondents who sent drawings and specimens
to Wight, at this stage based in Madras. Both were in the army:
Gough (1815–95) was the son of Viscount Gough, a famous soldier;
Munro (1818–80) later became a General, but retained his botanical
interests, especially on grasses (he was an expert on bamboos) and
part of his important grass collection is in the Edinburgh
herbarium. From the annotations 'Kunth' and 'Roeper' it can be
seen that Wight intended adding floral diagrams to this drawing as
in Plate 22.

Annotations by Wight (265.1): Balsaminaceae 1047, Impatiens Munronii (RW)
(ink, recto); Kunth, Roeper, 1049 (pencil, recto). Annotation by Arnott: ic. t.
1049 (ink, recto).

Published as plate 1049 of the *Icones* (1846), lithographed by Dumphy.

RBGE W265.1 & 2 (SERIES E)

24 A & B. Impatiens fruticosa *A.P. de Candolle*

BALSAMINACEAE

?Tam: kave gueda [Leschenault]

Bodycolour heightened with gum arabic and pencil, 197 × 260mm (204.1); 95 × 123mm (204.2). By Rungiah, *c.*1845.

A handsome shrubby species that can reach two metres in height, first discovered by the French botanist Jean Baptiste Louis Claude Theodore Leschenault de la Tour (1773–1826) in the Nilgiri Hills. Leschenault, a French botanist, was sent in 1815 to start a botanic garden at Pondicherry. The Court of Directors of the EIC in an enlightened, if uncharacteristic, moment allowed him to undertake botanical exploration of the Western Ghats, and he was the first botanist to visit the Nilgiris. Although J.S. Gamble in his *Flora of Madras* reported this species from the Palnis and Travancore hills, it is not recorded from the former by Father Matthew, and there are no specimens in the Edinburgh herbarium from anywhere other than the Nilgiris, to which it is probably restricted.

Annotations by Wight (204.1): Balsamineae, 966/450, Impatiens fruticosa (D.C.) (ink, recto). Annotations by Arnott: Wight ic. t. 966 (ink, recto).

Published (uncoloured) as plate 966 of the *Icones* (1845), lithographed by Dumphy; and later (hand-coloured) as plate 37 of the *Spicilegium*.

RBGE W204.1 & 2 R (SERIES E)

Balsamineæ

966
450

Impatiens fruticosa (D.C.)
wight ic. t. 966

25 A & B. Quassia indica *(Gaertner) Nooteboom*

SIMAROUBACEAE

Mal: karingota

Bodycolour heightened with gum arabic, and ink, over traces of pencil,
239 × 305mm. By Rungiah, 1834.

Watermark: [s & s] 1829.

The Linnaean generic name commemorates Graman Quasi, a
negro slave 'owned' by C.G. Dahlberg, who used the bark of a
related species in Surinam as a cure for fever. It belongs to a largely
tropical family, of which the only example familiar in Britain is the
introduced tree of heaven (*Ailanthus altissima*). *Quassia indica* is an
evergreen tree that can reach a height of twelve metres and is
widespread, occurring from Madagascar, throughout SE
Asia to the Philippines and the Solomon Islands. In India it
is restricted to the Malabar Coast, where Wight must have
collected the specimen depicted here. Like the Surinam
species the whole plant is bitter and the bark and roots are
used as a febrifuge.

Telugu annotation: (nutanam = new).

Annotations by Arnott: Samadera indica Wight ill. t. 68 (ink, recto).
Annotations by Wight: Feby/4 1834 14 (red crayon, verso).

Published (with the floral analyses on the reverse) as plate 68 of the
Illustrations (1839), lithographed by James Winchester.

RBGE W351 R + V (SERIES D)

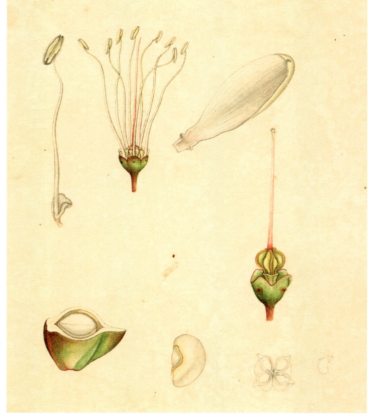

26 A & B. Balanites roxburghii *Planchon*

ZYGOPHYLLACEAE

Tam: nanjundan; Tel: gaara, ingalu mullu

Watercolour heightened with gum arabic, and ink, over traces of pencil, 250 × 351mm. By Rungiah, *c.*1834.

A small, spiny tree to six metres tall, occurring throughout drier parts of India. J.S. Gamble reported it to be characteristic of black cotton soils. Wight collected it in such a habitat in the 'Ceded Districts' when based at Bellary in 1834 and it is possible that this drawing was made there. The Indian plant was first recognised as distinct from the closely related *Balanites aegyptiaca*, the 'desert date' of Africa and the Middle East, in 1854 by the French botanist J.E. Planchon, who named it after Roxburgh. The detail of the flower on the right hand side shows a monstrous form, perhaps the result of galling by an insect. This drawing was not published by Wight (and is not the original of that published as plate 274 of the *Icones*).

Annotations by Wight: Balanites?, T[urn] O[ver]. Annotations by Arnott: wc. 2428, Balanites aegyptiaca (ink, recto).

RBGE W377 R + V (SERIES D)

27 A & B. Lophopetalum wightianum *Arnott*

CELASTRACEAE

Tam: venkottai

Bodycolour heightened with gum arabic, and ink, over traces of pencil, 240 × 307mm. By Rungiah, 1834.

Watermark: II S[MITH]

This species belongs to a family represented in Britain only by the spindle-tree (*Euonymus europaeus*). The flowers are characterised by a fleshy, nectar bearing disc, (in this case bright red), in which are embedded the ovary and five stamens. The five rounded petals are ornamented with rather brain-like ridges, from which the generic name (meaning 'crested petals') is derived. An evergreen tree that can reach a height of thirty metres, occurring in the southern part of the Western Ghats. Both genus and species were described by Arnott in 1839, based on a Wight collection from which this drawing was doubtless made. This is one of no fewer than 256 species named to commemorate Wight. As 110 of these are still in use, there is no danger of forgetting Wight when studying the Indian flora.

Telugu annotations (nutanam [= new] February).

Annotations by Wight: Lophopetalum corymbosum – ovules numerous in each cell of the ovary, T[urn] O[ver] (pencil recto); February/9 1834 19 (red crayon, verso). Annotations by Arnott: W[ight's] C[atalogue no.] 2440 Lophopetalum wightianum Arn. Wight ic. t. 162 (ink, recto).

Published as plate 162 of the *Icones* (1839), lithographed by Winchester.

RBGE WIO9 R + V (SERIES D)

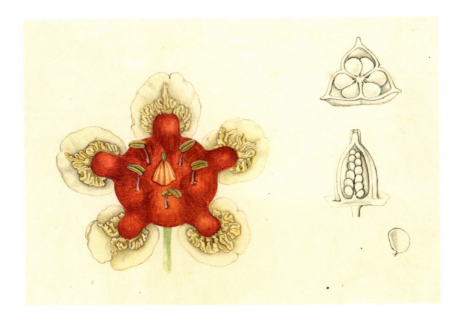

28 A & B. Turpinia nepalensis

Wight & Arnott

STAPHYLEACEAE

Badaga name (recorded in the Nilgiris by J.S. Gamble): nila

Bodycolour heightened with gum arabic and pencil, 218 × 249mm;
111 × 127mm. By Rungiah, *c*.1845.

A moderately large tree that can reach a height of 20
metres, occurring in the Sino-Himalaya, Burma, Thailand
and the Western Ghats of India. In the Palni and Nilgiri
Hills it can be dominant in shola forests between altitudes
of 1600 and 2300 metres, flowering mainly in April–May.
In the Palnis and Nilgiris the shola forests have been greatly
reduced in extent due to clearance and aggressive invasion
by acacias and eucalyptus; because of its quick growth
Father Matthew recommended *Turpinia* for use in shola
regeneration programmes. The generic name given by E.P.
Ventenat commemorates the French botanist and botanical
artist Pierre Turpin (1775–1840). This species was described
by Wight & Arnott based on specimens collected by Wallich
in Nepal in 1821, and Wight's specimens probably from the
Nilgiris.

Annotations by Wight: Staphyleaceae, Celastrineae, 972/491, Turpinia
nepalensis (Wall.) (ink, recto).

Published (uncoloured) as plate 972 of the *Icones* (1845), lithographed
by Dumphy; reprinted (hand-coloured) as plate 44 of the *Spicilegium*.

RBGE W210.1 & 2 R (SERIES E)

29 A & B. Ventilago madraspatana *Gaertner*

RHAMNACEAE

Tam: pappili, vembadaam; Tel: errasurugudu

Bodycolour heightened with gum arabic, and ink, over traces of pencil, 256 × 352mm. By Rungiah, *c.*1834.

A slender, climbing shrub, endemic to the western Deccan and eastern slopes of the Western Ghats up to altitudes of 1200 metres. Both genus and species were first described by Joseph Gaertner in his pioneering work on the seeds and fruits of plants, a copy of which was in Wight's library. This species was based partly on specimens in the herbarium of Sir Joseph Banks, sent to him from Madras probably either by Roxburgh or one of the Tranquebar missionaries. The fruit, shown in the pencil sketches later added to the drawing by Rungiah, is a winged samara. The bark of the root is the source of a red dye used for textiles.

Annotations by Wight: 514 Ventilago madraspatana, 57 (pencil, recto); Connective of the anthers distinctly projects beyond the cells tho not represented in this figure (pencil, verso). Annotations by Arnott: Ventilago maderaspatana Wight ic. t. 163 (ink, recto).

Published as plate 163 of the *Icones* (1839), lithographed by Winchester.

RBGE W110 R + V (SERIES D)

30. Spondias pinnata *(Linnaeus f.) Kurz*

ANACARDIACEAE

Eng: hog plum; Tam: akkara pattai, kaattuma, mumbulichi, marimaa, pullipullama; Tel: adavimaamidi, ambaala chettu

Bodycolour heightened with gum arabic, and ink, over traces of pencil, 176 × 256mm. By Rungiah, *c.*1830.

A deciduous tree that can reach a height of 20 metres, occurring throughout India, Sri Lanka and S E Asia. In South India it occurs up to an altitude of 600 metres. It is commonly planted for its edible fruit, which can reach the size of a goose egg; the inner part becomes sweet, but according to Sir George Watt is usually used unripe as an acid vegetable in fish or vegetable curries, or pickled. A gum flows from wounds of the bark, which Wight recorded was 'sold in the Bazaars as gum arabic'. Watt, as had Rheede in *Hortus Malabaricus*, reported that the fruit and other parts, including the bark, were used medicinally for various purposes, but Wight had never heard of such uses. Wight knew this tree as *Spondias mangifera*, an illegitimate name given by Willdenow, its epithet referring to the similarity of the fruits to those of the mango, which belongs to the same family

Annotations by Arnott: W C. 534 (pencil, recto); Spondias mangifera, Wight ill. t. 76 (ink, recto). Other annotations: [Tamil script] Poolie mangaie No. 105 (pencil, verso).

Published as plate 76 of the *Illustrations* (1839), lithographed by Winchester.

RBGE W352 R (SERIES A)

Spondias mangifera
wight ill. b. 76

31 A & B. Pterocarpus indicus *Willdenow*

LEGUMINOSAE (PAPILIONOIDEAE)

Eng: Burmese rosewood, Andaman redwood

Bodycolour heightened with gum arabic, and ink, over traces of pencil, 197 × 319mm. By Rungiah, *c.*1834.

A large tree widely distributed from the Indonesian islands northwards to Burma, but not native in S India. This drawing was almost certainly made from a specimen growing in the Nopalry, a garden set up in Madras for growing cacti as the host for the cochineal insect, where Wight was based 1826–8. Wight collected specimens in May 1826 that ended up in the EIC herbarium in London. In Wallich's catalogue of this collection he called these specimens *P. dalbergioides*, but when Wight & Arnott revised the genus for their *Prodromus*, they realised it was distinct and named it after Wallich; however, it is now regarded as synonymous with an earlier species of Willdenow. In Burma its rose-scented timber, a form of the renowned padouk wood, is highly valued.

Published as plate 78 of the *Illustrations* (1839), lithographed by James Winchester.

Annotations by Wight: 825 Pterocarpus Wallichii (pencil, recto).

RBGE W379 R + V (SERIES D)

32 A & B. Senna alata *(Linnaeus) Roxburgh*

LEGUMINOSAE (CAESALPINIOIDEAE)

Tam: seemaiyagathi; Tel: mettataamara

Bodycolour heightened with gum arabic, and ink, over traces of pencil, 239 × 303mm. By Rungiah, 1833.

Watermark: [s & s] 1829.

This handsome shrub or small tree (formerly placed in the genus *Cassia*) is a native of Central America and the Caribbean, but has been widely cultivated as an ornamental and is now commonly naturalised throughout the tropics. It is not known when the plant was first introduced to India, but Roxburgh knew it on the Coromandel Coast in the 1780s, and Wight first collected it there in 1822. Roxburgh recorded that Indian doctors used it to cure 'all poisonous bites and other venereal outbreakings, and [that it] also strengthens the body. The leaves are very often employed to cure ring-worms. They are well rubbed into the parts affected, once or twice a day, and generally with great success'. The specific epithet refers to the four broad wings of the narrow pod.

Annotations by Wight: 253, 60 890 Cassia alata (pencil, recto); 1833 (red crayon, verso).

Published as plate 253 of the *Icones* (1840), lithographed probably by Wight.

RBGE WI27 R + V (SERIES D)

33 A & B. Caesalpinia crista *Linnaeus*

LEGUMINOSAE (CAESALPINIOIDEAE)

Tel: mulluthige

Bodycolour heightened with gum arabic, and ink, over traces of pencil, 241 × 305mm. By Rungiah, *c.*1834.

Watermark: [s & s] 1829.

Leguminosae is one of the largest families of flowering plants and one of the most useful to mankind. It is especially well represented in the Indian flora and is divided into three major subfamilies. This shows a typical flower of the subfamily Caesalpinioideae, with bilateral symmetry, five sepals and five petals, one of which (called the 'vexillum' by Wight) is modified as a landing platform for an insect pollinator. The fruit is a 'legume' that characterises the family (most familiar as a pea-pod) and gives it its name; in this case it is one-seeded. *Caesalpinia crista* is a spiny, climbing shrub widespread in s, se and e Asia, reaching n Australia and the Pacific Islands.

Annotations by Wight: April/5 42 (red crayon, verso); Leguminosae 369, Caesalpinia paniculata (pencil, recto).

Published as plate 36 of the *Icones* (1838), lithographed by Wight.

RBGE WI04 R + V (SERIES D)

Cæsalpinia
869 paniculata

Cæsalpinia paniculata (Roxb.)

34 A & B. Saraca asoca *(Roxburgh) de Wilde*

LEGUMINOSAE (CAESALPINIOIDEAE)

Eng: Ashoka tree; Tam: asogam; Tel: ashokamu

Bodycolour heightened with gum arabic, and ink, over traces of pencil, 242 × 302mm. By Rungiah, 1833.

Watermark: S & S 1829.

Although belonging to the same subfamily as *Caesalpinia* (Plate 33), the floral structure is very different: the flower is subtended by two small bracteoles and the four petal-like sepals are united into a long tube; the petals are lacking. Roxburgh created a new genus for this tree, dedicated to his mentor Sir William Jones, and coined an epithet from its Indian name, literally meaning 'free of sorrows'. It perhaps also commemorates the great Mauryan emperor Ashoka, who converted to Buddhism, and had improving edicts inscribed on rocks across his empire (one of which promoted the planting of roadside trees). Jones encouraged such linking of east and west in plant names, but sadly the genus is no longer recognised as distinct from Linnaeus's earlier *Saraca*. It is a small tree found wild in the Himalaya, E Bengal, S India, Sri Lanka, Burma, Malaya and Indonesia, but is also commonly cultivated. It is used medicinally (for gynaecological conditions) and is sacred both to Hindus and Buddhists. When Sita was abducted by Ravana, she escaped his caresses by taking refuge in a grove of ashoka trees, and in Burma the Buddha is believed to have been born (and given his first sermon) beneath one.

Annotations by Wight: 1833/unfinished (red crayon, verso); Leguminosae 206/881; 881 Jonesia asoca (pencil, recto). Telugu annotation: arakudananapudinadi.

Published as plate 206 of the *Icones* (1839), lithographed by Wight.

RBGE W116 R + V (SERIES D)

Wight, Ic.Pl.Ind.Or. i. 206.

Jonesea
881 asoca

Jonesia Asoca Roxb.

35 A & B. Xylia xylocarpa *(Roxburgh) Taub*

LEGUMINOSAE (MIMOSOIDEAE)

Eng: Burma iron wood; Tam: erul; Tel: channangi

Bodycolour heightened with gum arabic, and ink, over traces of pencil, 197 × 319mm. By Rungiah, *c.*1834.

This drawing shows a typical flower of the subfamily Mimosoideae (to which acacias also belong), which are usually small and aggregated into dense heads. The flowers have radial symmetry, in this case with five fused sepals and five fused petals; as usual in this group the filaments of the stamens are long. Also shown here is the woody legume to which both the generic and specific names refer. The generic name was given by George Bentham, who knew Wight and worked on his specimens belonging to the families Labiatae and Scrophulariaceae. A tall tree occurring in India (especially the Western and Eastern Ghats), Burma and Indo-China. The timber is valuable, and the heartwood is said to be as strong as teak and so hard that nails cannot be driven into it. It has been used for purposes where great strength is required such as railway sleepers and the hubs of wooden wheels. This drawing was not published by Wight.

Annotations by Wight: April/11 48 (red crayon, verso); 831 Inga xylocarpa (pencil, verso).

RBGE W380 R + V (SERIES D)

36. Parkinsonia aculeata *Linnaeus*

LEGUMINOSAE (CAESALPINIOIDEAE)

Eng: Jerusalem thorn, prickly Parkinsonia; Tam: parangivel; Tel: seemathumma

Bodycolour heightened with gum arabic over traces of pencil, 195 × 247mm. By Rungiah, *c.*1826.

Native to tropical America, this spiny shrub is widely cultivated in the tropics, especially as a hedge plant. It is not known when it was first introduced to India, but Wight collected it in his first Indian period, doubtless in the Northern Circars. The generic name given by Linnaeus commemorates John Parkinson (1566–1650) the London apothecary, herbalist and pioneering garden writer. A fibre can be extracted from the stems. This, one of Rungiah's earliest drawings, was sent to India House in London with the dispersal of the Madras Naturalist's collection in 1828. The dramatic layout owes much to Rungiah's native artistic tradition that would become somewhat tamed, though by no means eradicated, under Wight's influence.

Annotations by Wight: 436 Parkinsonia aculeata (pencil, recto); 436 Madras R.W. (red ink, verso), 69 (black ink, verso).

RBGE W401 R (SERIES A)

37 A&B. Smithia blanda *Wight & Arnott*

LEGUMINOSAE (PAPILIONOIDEAE)

Bodycolour heightened with gum arabic and pencil, 221 × 251mm (218.1),
113 × 143mm (218.2). By Rungiah, c.1845.

The genus commemorates Sir J.E. Smith, who studied botany with
Professor John Hope at the Royal Botanic Garden Edinburgh in
1781–3, and went on to purchase Linnaeus's herbarium from his
widow and found the Linnean Society of London. It was named by
William Aiton, superintendent of the Royal Gardens at Kew. The
epithet '*sensitiva*' given to the first species of the genus was not used
in classical Latin, and in this context cannot mean 'responsive to
stimulus'; but rather 'tender, delicate' applying certainly to the
plant, but by association doubtless also intended as a (somewhat
dubious) complement to the then 30–year old Smith. This allusive
naming seems to have been continued by Wallich, who first applied
the even more unusual epithet '*blanda*' to the plant depicted here, for
specimens in the East India Company Herbarium collected in
Meghalaya by Francis d'Silva. While this adjective can mean
'pleasing or charming', it can also mean 'flattering, fawning or
caressing', and from the tone of some of Smith's letters one wonders
if Wallich (and Wight & Arnott who provided a description for the
plant) were being slightly wicked. The plant is widespread
throughout India.

Annotations by Wight: Papilionaceae Leguminosae Hedysareae 986, Smithia
blanda (ink, recto).

Published (uncoloured) as plate 986 of the Icones (1845), lithographed by
Dumphy; reprinted (hand-coloured) as plate 59 of the *Spicilegium* (1847).

RBGE W218.1 & 2 R (SERIES E)

38 A & B. Indigofera cassioides

Rottler ex A.P. de Candolle

LEGUMINOSAE (PAPILIONOIDEAE)

Bodycolour heightened with gum arabic and pencil, 225 × 281mm (372.1), 101 × 125mm (372.2). By Rungiah, *c*.1847.

Wight & Arnott worked hard on the account of the family Leguminosae for their *Prodromus*. Robert Graham, Regius Keeper of the RBGE, had originally promised to write it for them, but at the last minute went back on his word and they had to do it themselves at break-neck speed. This ornamental shrub can reach 2.5 metres in height and is widespread throughout hilly parts of India, and also in Nepal, Burma, SW China and Indo-China. This specimen was doubtless drawn from a specimen from the Nilgiri Hills, where Wight described it as a 'beautiful object .... when in full flower ... in February', the effect is the more marked as it often flowers when leafless. This plant belongs to the same genus as *Indigofera tinctoria*, the source of the blue dye indigo. This is one of the few drawings made especially for the *Spicilegium Neilgherrense*.

Annotations by Wight: Papilionaceae Leguminosae Loteae 48, Indigofera pulchella (ink, recto); 100 copies [required, i.e., the edition size] (pencil, recto).

Published (hand-coloured) as plate 55 of the *Spicilegium* (1847), lithographed by Dumphy.

RBGE W372.1 & 2 R (SERIES E)

39 A & B. Crotalaria semperflorens *Ventenat*

LEGUMINOSAE (PAPILIONOIDEAE)

Bodycolour heightened with gum arabic and pencil, 216 × 282mm (214.1),
111 × 142mm (214.2). By Rungiah, *c*.1845.

These drawings were probably made from a specimen from the
Nilgiri Hills, where Wight recorded it as abounding in 'woods and
thickets of Ootacamund … in flower at all seasons quite enlivening
the thickets among which it grows with the number and brilliancy of
its blossoms'. It is a shrub that can reach five metres in height. The
Nilgiri plant was described by Wight & Arnott as a new species,
Crotalaria wallichiana, but this is not now regarded as distinct from
the appropriately named *C. semperflorens*, a native of s India that also
occurs in Indonesia (could it perhaps have been introduced by Tamil
settlers?). *C. semperflorens* was first described by the French botanist
E.P. Ventenat (illustrated by an engraving after Redouté) from
specimens cultivated in the garden of J.M. Cels at Montrouge near
Paris, to which it had been introduced by Lahaye, collector on the
d'Entrecasteaux voyage sent in search of La Pérouse.

Published (uncoloured) as plate 982 of the *Icones* (1845), lithographed by
Dumphy; reprinted (hand-coloured) as plate 54 of the *Spicilegium* (1847).

Annotations by Wight: Papilionaceae Leguminosae Loteae 982/579, Crotalaria
Wallichiana (W & A) (ink, recto).

RBGE W214.1 & 2 R (SERIES E)

40. Rubus ellipticus *Smith*

ROSACEAE

Bodycolour heightened with gum arabic, and ink, over traces of pencil,
161 × 197mm. By Rungiah, *c*.1830.

A suberect or scrambling shrub occurring at altitudes of 1220–2220
metres in the Western Ghats (Karnataka southwards) and Sri
Lanka, and widespread from the Himalaya eastwards to Thailand,
Burma, Vietnam and the Philippines. It also occurs as an
introduction in Australia and East Africa. The yellow, raspberry-like
fruit is eaten, raw or made into a preserve in the Himalaya. Wight
knew this under a Roxburgh name based on its vernacular name in
the West Himalaya 'gauri phul', but it had been earlier described by
J.E. Smith based on collections made by Francis Buchanan in Nepal
in 1802. This was published in one of his articles for Abraham Rees's
Cyclopaedia, a 39 volume work owned by Wight, that was the only
book for which he had to pay customs duty when he returned to
Britain on furlough in 1831 (unlike his other books he did not intend
to take it back with him to India). This drawing was probably made
from a specimen collected in the Nilgiri Hills.

Annotations by ?Arnott (partly erased): 230, Rubus Gowrephul Roxb., WC. 1002,
Wt. icon t. 230 Mysore (pencil, recto).

The floral details on the verso (but not this habit drawing) were published as plate
230 of the *Icones* (1839), lithographed by Romeo.

RBGE W78 R (SERIES C)

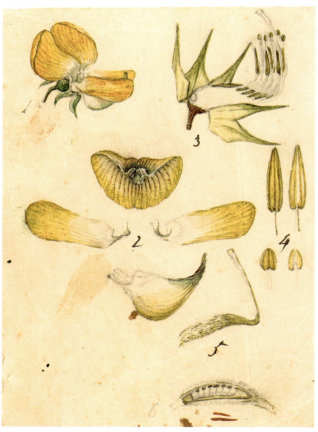

41 A & B. Lagerstroemia speciosa

(Linnaeus) Persoon

LYTHRACEAE

Eng: pride of India; Tam: kadalai, poomaruthu; Tel: vaaragogu

Bodycolour heightened with gum arabic, and ink, over traces of pencil, 319 × 394mm. By Rungiah, 1834.

Watermark: C WILMOT 1819.

A tree that in the wild may reach a height of 18 metres. It is native in hilly parts of W and NE India, Sri Lanka, Burma, China and the Malay Peninsula, but is often grown as an ornamental in Indian gardens (and elsewhere in the tropics). E.G. Balfour, with whom Wight corresponded over the plant products to be sent from Madras to the Great Exhibition of 1851, described how 'in full blossom, in the morning, the tree looks as if mantled with roses, but the flowers change through the day to a beautiful purple, making it appear at evening … like a bower of English lilacs'. This painting would therefore appear to have been made towards evening. The soft, red timber was used in Wight's time for building purposes and, because of its durability under water, for making boats and water casks. This is one of the few drawings by Rungiah that is dated. The main drawing was not reproduced by Wight, though some of the floral details on the reverse were.

Annotations by Wight: 953 Lagerstroemia reginae (pencil, recto); March/I 23/ 1834 (red crayon, verso).

RBGE W413 R + V (SERIES ?D)

Carallia?
93 Regina

42 A & B. Potentilla indica *(Andrews) F.T. Wolf*

ROSACEAE

Bodycolour heightened with gum arabic and pencil, 272 × 219mm (221.1); 93 × 121mm (221.2). By Rungiah, *c*.1845.

Widespread in montane regions of Asia, and common in the Himalaya from Afghanistan to China, northwards to Korea and Japan, and south to Malaysia. This drawing was almost certainly made from specimens collected in the Nilgiri Hills, where it occurs in damp woods. Wight noted that the bright red fruit though 'very tempting to the eye' was 'watery, mawkish and disagreeable to the taste'. This drawing is unique in that the leaves left uncoloured by Rungiah have subsequently been marked with green 'dashes', as a short-hand instruction for the painters colouring the plates for the *Spicilegium*.

Annotations by Wight: Dryadeae Rosaceae 989/924, Fragaria indica (Andr) (ink, recto).

Published (uncoloured) as plate 989 of the *Icones* (1845), lithographed by Dumphy; reprinted (hand-coloured) as plate 62 of the *Spicilegium* (1847).

RBGE W221.1 & 2 R (SERIES E)

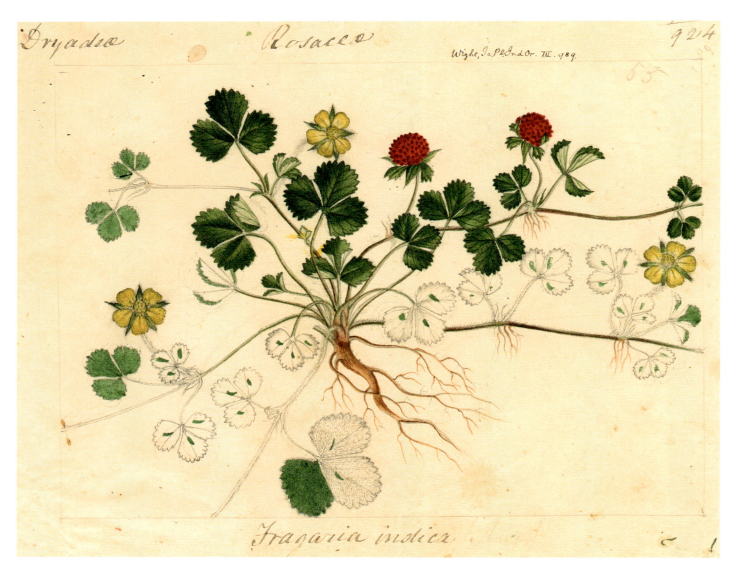

43 A & B. Kandelia candel *(Linnaeus) Druce*

RHIZOPHORACEAE

Tam: kandal; Tel: kandigala, thuvarkandam

Bodycolour and ink over traces of pencil, 243 × 308mm. By Rungiah, *c.*1830.

Watermark: s & s 1829.

A shrub or small tree (to 7 metres tall) widespread on muddy shores and tidal creeks from the west coast of India, around the Bay of Bengal and Indonesia, to China and southern Japan. Both generic and specific names are taken from the Malayalam name applied generally to mangroves and this species was first described and illustrated in 1686 under the name 'tsjerou-kandel' by Rheede in the *Hortus Malabaricus*. Linnaeus based his *Rhizophora candel* on Rheede's plate, and Wight & Arnott (when transferring it to a new genus) gave it a new, superfluous specific name commemorating Rheede. The use of its bark, crushed with ginger and long pepper to treat diabetes is given in *Hortus Malabaricus* and Sir George Watt recorded that in Cochin its bark was used for tanning. In many mangroves the single seed starts to develop while the fruit is still attached to the tree, with a lengthening of the part between the seed leaves and the root (the 'hypocotyl'). The lower drawing shows two stages in this process: in the young fruit still attached to the branch at the centre the narrow pointed green hypocotyl has just pierced through the apex of the greenish-brown pericarp; the detail at the bottom shows the stage at which the whole fruit (with reflexed, persistent petals) falls from the tree, with the hypocotyl greatly developed into a hooked, cigar-shaped structure.

Annotations by Wight: 89/960, Kandelia Rheedei, 960, 65 (pencil, recto). Other annotations: Rhizophoreae, Kandelia Rheedei (W. & A.) (pencil, recto); Jany 6 (red chalk, verso).

Published as plate 89 of the *Illustrations* (1840), lithographed by ?Wight.

RBGE W354 R + V (SERIES D)

44 A & B. Carallia brachiata *(Loureiro) Merrill*

RHIZOPHORACEAE

Tel: kaaralli

Bodycolour heightened with gum arabic, and ink, over traces of pencil, 255 × 352mm. By Rungiah, 1833.

Although another member of the mangrove family, this is not one of the coastal species, though it resembles them in that it can develop aerial roots around the base of the trunk under wet conditions. It is a tree that can reach 50 metres in height and is not uncommon in the evergreen forests of the Western Ghats, where it ascends to 1220 metres, and is widely distributed from Madagascar, throughout SE Asia, reaching N Australia. The hard timber is red with a silvery grain and has been used for cabinet making, musical instruments and building purposes; the plant also has medicinal uses. The floral analyses show Rungiah's exceptional ability to convey, by means of shading, a sense of depth to the rococo laceration of the petals. Also shown is the semi-inferior ovary, with a brown, nectar producing disc at the point of attachment of the seven-lobed calyx, and 14 stamens inserted opposite and between the petals.

Telugu annotations: (vennaipedirna vellu rashiti rindi).

Annotations by Wight: 1833 (red crayon, verso); Carallia corymbosa RW T[urn] O[ver] (pencil, recto). Annotations by Arnott W[ight's] C[atalogue no.] 2447 Carallia ceylanica β (ink, recto).

Published as plate 90 of the *Illustrations* (1840), lithographed probably by Winchester.

RBGE W355 R + V (SERIES D)

45 A & B. Combretum latifolium *Blume*

COMBRETACEAE

Watercolour and ink over traces of pencil, 272 × 225mm. By Rungiah, *c.*1830.

This species is a member of a family of tropical trees and climbers to which the myrobalan (*Terminalia chebula*) also belongs. It is a large, woody climber, and was probably gathered by Wight (or his collectors) in Malabar. Specimens in the EIC herbarium were named 'Combretum Wightianum' by Wallich, but it was Wight &

Arnott who provided a description of it. However, *Combretum wightianum* is no longer recognised as distinct from *C. latifolium*, a widespread species occurring from s India and Sri Lanka through Burma, Indo-China and Malaysia to Indonesia, first described from Java by the Dutch botanist C.L. Blume.

Annotations by Wight: §Combreteae Combretaceae 981, Combretum Wightianum (pencil, recto).

Published as plate 227 of the *Icones* (1839), lithographed by Dumphy.

RBGE WI23 R + V (SERIES D)

46 A & B. Sonerila speciosa *Zenker*

MELASTOMATACEAE

Bodycolour heightened with gum arabic and pencil, 222 × 248mm (228.1); 108 × 125mm (228.2). By Rungiah, *c.*1845.

Many members of the family Melastomataceae have sumptuously coloured flowers, and attractive leaf venation, and the family seems to have been of special interest to Wight. This one is a succulent herb and was found by Wight at the Kaitie Falls, a favourite picnic spot in the Nilgiri Hills, close to which his patron Lord Elphinstone (Governor of Madras) had a bungalow and garden. Wight also found it growing above the Avalanche Bungalow, flowering in February. The plant is restricted to the southern part of the Western Ghats, and was described by the German botanist J.C. Zenker, Professor of Botany at Jena, from specimens sent to him by his cousin the Rev Bernhard Schmid, a missionary friend of Wight based in Ootacamund.

Annotations by Wight: Melastomeae Melastomaceae 1000 or 995/2, Sonerila speciosa (Zenker) (ink, recto); 67/2 or 70 (pencil, recto).

Published (uncoloured) as plate 995/2 of the *Icones* (1845), lithographed by Dumphy and reprinted (hand-coloured) as plate 67/2 of the *Spicilegium* (1847).

RBGE W228.1 & 2 R (SERIES E)

Melastomeæ   Melastomaceæ   1000 or 995½

1001

67½ or 79

Sonerila Speciosa (Zenker)

47. A & B. Osbeckia aspera *(Linnaeus) Blume* var. **wightiana** *(Bentham ex Wight & Arnott) Trimen*

MELASTOMATACEAE

Bodycolour heightened with gum arabic and pencil, 217 × 250mm (231.1); 112 × 124mm (231.2). By Rungiah, *c.*1845.

This drawing shows another characteristic feature of Melastomataceae: the anthers, which shed pollen through an apical pore. This species is a shrub that can reach two metres in height, first collected by Wight in the Nilgiri Hills prior to 1828, and sent home with the Madras Naturalist's collections and incorporated into the EIC herbarium. This vast collection was curated between 1828 and 1832 by Nathaniel Wallich, with the help of various specialists. Among these helpers was George Bentham, who worked on the specimens of Melastomataceae, and who named this collection after Wight. Bentham provided no description in the catalogue of the herbarium, and it fell to Wight & Arnott to provide one in 1834, giving rise to the erroneous impression that Wight (with Arnott) might have named the plant after himself. Restricted to the southern part of the Western Ghats, it is now treated as a variety of *O. aspera*, which also occurs in Sri Lanka.

Annotations by Wight: Melastomeae Melastomaceae 997, Osbeck.a Wightiana (Benth) (ink, recto).

Published (uncoloured) as plate 998 of the *Icones* (1845), lithographed by Dumphy, and reprinted (hand-coloured) as plate 70 of the *Spicilegium* (1847).

RBGE W231.1 & 2 R (SERIES E)

Melastomeæ   *Melastomaceæ*

Osbeckia Wightiana (Benth)

Wight, Ic.Pl. Ind. Or.
1. 194.

Alangium 10-petalum

Wight Cat
1062

48. Alangium salviifolium

(Linnaeus f.) Wangerin

ALANGIACEAE

Tam: alangi; Tel: uduga

Bodycolour heightened with gum arabic, and ink, over traces of pencil, 60 × 197mm. By Rungiah, *c.*1830.

A deciduous tree to 20 metres tall, widespread in SE Asia. In S India it occurs in the plains and foothills up to an altitude of 600 metres, often growing by roadsides. The hard wood is scented and has been used for ornamental work. The tree also has medicinal uses and has been used as a substitute for ipecacuanha. Wight knew this species by Lamarck's name *A. decapetalum*, a species based on a plate in Rheede's *Hortus Malabaricus*, but this is no longer regarded as distinct from *A. salviifolium* a species described by the younger Linnaeus from material collected in Ceylon by J.G. König. The specific epithet refers to the resemblance of the leaves (particularly the undersides, with a network of raised veins) to those of the sage (presumably *Salvia officinalis*).

Telugu annotations: (aashiralimbe, thandakam nanidi).

Annotations by Wight: 1005, 96, Alangium 10–petalum (pencil, recto). Annotations by Arnott: Wight Cat. 1062 (pencil, recto. Other annotations: Auseyr-Aulingey (pencil, recto); 194/1005, Alangieae, Alangium decapetalum (Lam.) (pencil, verso).

Published as plate 194 of the *Icones* (1839), lithographed by Winchester.

RBGE WI7 R (SERIES C)

49. Syzygium aqueum *(N.L. Burman) Alston*

MYRTACEAE

Bodycolour heightened with gum arabic, and ink, over traces of pencil, 254 × 347mm. By Rungiah, *c.*1830.

The family Myrtaceae was a special interest of Wight's, and the one on which he arguably did his best taxonomic work. This is a tree that can reach a height of twenty metres, perhaps native in Indonesia and Sri Lanka, but cultivated for its edible fruit, especially in Bengal and Burma. Wight did not record where he collected this plant, and his specimens and this drawing are likely to have been made from a cultivated specimen, perhaps in Madras. The fruit is whitish and has a curious shape – like a child's top, with a flattened apex.

Annotations by Arnott: Jambosa aqueum W & A, W[ight's] C[atalogue no.] 1080.

Published as plate 216 of the *Icones* (1839), lithographed by Wight.

RBGE WI2I R (SERIES D)

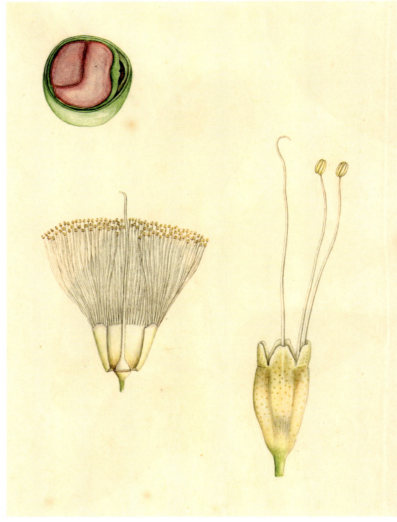

50 A & B. Syzygium zeylanicum

(Linnaeus) A.P. de Candolle

MYRTACEAE

Tam: marungi

Bodycolour heightened with gum arabic, and ink, over traces of pencil,
198 × 318mm. By Rungiah, *c.*1834.

Watermark: C WILMOT 1819.

A shrub or small, evergreen tree to ten metres in height, occurring
in wet evergreen forest in the Western Ghats, and also in NE India,
Sri Lanka, Burma and w Malaysia. Wight collected it on the
Malabar Coast before 1831, and this drawing was probably made
from these collections . The species was first described (in the genus
Myrtus) by Linnaeus, from specimens collected in Ceylon by Paul
Hermann. This drawing was not published by Wight (it is not the
original of plate 73 of the *Icones*). Generic concepts in this family
have changed since Wight's time and this is one of the many species
that he treated under the genus *Eugenia*. The oil glands that are
characteristic of this family (which also includes the genus
Eucalyptus) are particularly conspicuous on the calyx tube.

Annotations by Wight: 72 (pencil, recto). Other annotations: April/13 50 (red
chalk, verso).

RBGE W383 R + V (SERIES D)

51 A&B. Syzygium densiflorum

Wight & Arnott

MYRTACEAE

Tam: naval; Tel: neredu

Bodycolour heightened with gum arabic and pencil, 218 × 273mm; 99 × 121mm.
By Rungiah, *c*.1845.

A large evergreen tree to 60 metres in height, restricted to the
Nilgiri and Palni Hills. Father Matthew recorded it as one of the
most representative shola trees of the Upper Palnis; the peak
flowering occurs from March to May, the dark purple fruits ripen in
July–August, and the new foliage, which is red, appears from
February to April. The plant described as *S. arnottianum* by Walpers
is no longer regarded as distinct from *S. densiflorum* which was
described by Wight & Arnott based on Wight specimens from the
Nilgiris. A specimen at Edinburgh collected by Wight's friend
H.F.C. Cleghorn is annotated 'one of the principal timbers of the
Nilgiris'.

Annotations by Wight: 999 [deleted], 997, Arnottiana (pencil, recto); 997,
Myrteae, Myrtaceae, Eugenia (A) montana (RW (ink, recto).

Published (uncoloured) as plate 999 of the *Icones* (1845), lithographed by
Dumphy; reprinted (hand-coloured) as plate 72 of the *Spicilegium*.

RBGE W232.1 & 2 R (SERIES E)

52. Careya arborea *Roxburgh*

LECYTHIDACEAE

Tam: aymaa, kumbi; Tel: budda dharmi, kumbhi

Bodycolour and ink over traces of pencil, 256 × 349mm. By Rungiah, *c*.1830.

A deciduous tree to 20 metres tall, occurring throughout India and
Sri Lanka, and eastwards into Burma, Thailand and N Malaysia. It
was first described by Roxburgh, who named the genus for his
friend the Baptist missionary the Rev William Carey. Carey was a
polymath who went to India in 1794 and in 1801 became professor
of Sanskrit at the College of Fort William, Calcutta. In 1820 he
founded the Agricultural and Horticultural Society of India to
which Wight sent specimens and reports on economic botany for
publication in their journal. The fibrous bark of this species has
been used for cordage and for medicinal purposes. Roxburgh noted
that its wood was used in the Northern Circars to make large
mortars in which 'to bruise various kinds of oil-seeds'.

Telugu annotations: (aavimavu maram).

Annotations by Wight: 99–100, Myrtaceae subord. Barringtonieae, Careya
arborea Roxb. (pencil, recto). Annotations by Arnott: Careya arborea R. WC.
1084 – But the painter has not represented the two rows of stamens (the inmost
and outermost) which want anthers (pencil, recto). Other annotations: 99/1039,
Suborder Barringtoniae, Careya arborea (Roxb.) (pencil, verso).

Published as plate 99 of the *Illustrations* (1841), lithographed by Winchester.

RBGE W359 R (SERIES D)

53. Ludwigia perennis *Linnaeus*

ONAGRACEAE

Tam: nattypoondoo, musalkathilai; Tel: lavanga kaaya

Bodycolour heightened with gum arabic over traces of pencil, 176 × 253mm. By
Rungiah, *c*.1825.

A herb of damp places, such as rice fields and beside streams,
widespread from E Africa to India and Malesia. Wight knew this
plant as *L. parviflora* Roxburgh, but this is not regarded as distinct
from the earlier *L. perennis*, described by Linnaeus based on
material from Ceylon and a plate in Rheede's *Hortus Malabaricus*.
When identifying his specimens Wight & Arnott always referred to
the early Indian literature, and annotated them accordingly – one
such specimen at Edinburgh is annotated with the Rheede
reference, and another with a reference to a plate in Leonard
Plukenet's *Phytographia*. In the latter a specimen is depicted that was
evidently sent from Madras to London in the late seventeenth
century, and to which Plukenet gave the phrase name 'Lysimachia
non papposa, humilis, Maderaspatana, Clinopodii lutei foliis non
crenatus, fructu Caryophylloide, parvo'. From this can be seen the
boon conferred to botany by Linnaeus's binomial nomenclature.
This drawing was not published by Wight (it is not the original of
plate 101 of the *Illustrations*).

Telugu annotations: (antidi).

Annotations by Wight: 107 (pencil, recto). Annotations by Arnott: Ludwigia
parviflora WC 1088 (pencil, recto). Other annotations: [Tamil script]
Nattypoondoo Tam., No. 5 (pencil, verso).

RBGE W396 R (SERIES A)

53

54 A & B. Cucurbita moschata *(Lamarck) Poiret*

CUCURBITACEAE

Eng: pumpkin, winter squash; Tel: potti gummadi

Bodycolour heightened with gum arabic, and ink, over traces of pencil, 353 × 255mm. By Rungiah, *c.*1830.

The family Cucurbitaceae was of particular interest to Wight and he published a paper on the peculiar structure of its fruits – familiar as melons, pumpkins and loofahs, and technically known as 'pepoes'. Charles Darwin, at a time when he was interested in families with no apparently close relations, commented on Wight's paper. The taxonomically complex squashes originated in Central and South America where they have been cultivated since antiquity. Depicted here is a 'keeping-squash' referrable to the species that might, perhaps, be the original from which many others were derived. This drawing was probably made at Negapatam, and the fine image of the fruit (which weighed 15 lbs – 6 kg) was only discovered when it was removed from the backing sheet to which it had been glued for filing in the Cuttings Collection.

Annotations by Wight: Cucurbiteae, §9 but should be §8 – 507/1056 (pencil, recto). Annotations by Arnott: W[ight's] C[atalogue no.] 1140, Cucurbita maxima Duch[esne] (ink, recto); Rheed Mal. 8 t. 2 certe, referred to Cucurbita pepo (pencil, recto); lb 15 – Wt (pencil, verso).

Published as plate 507 of the *Icones* (1841), lithographed by Dumphy.

RBGE W419 R + V (SERIES ?D)

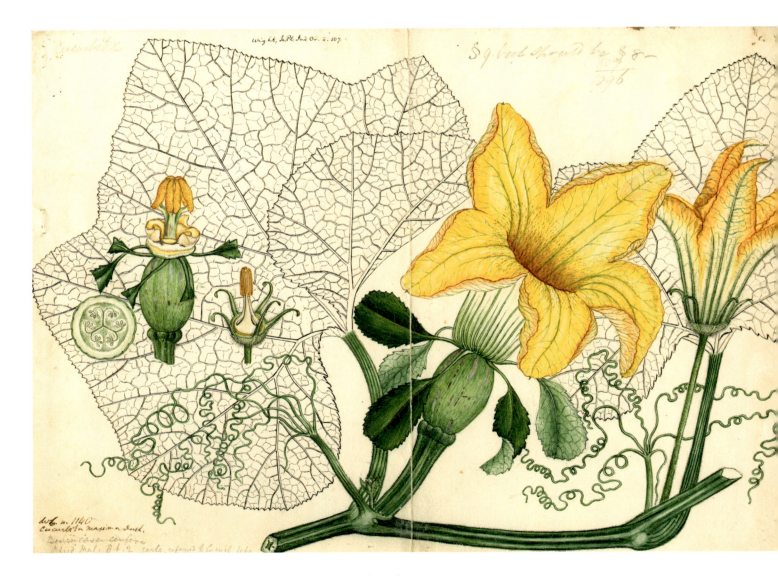

55. Diplocyclos palmatus *(Linnaeus) Jeffrey*

CUCURBITACEAE

Tam: iyvirali; Tel: lingadonda

Bodycolour heightened with gum arabic, and ink, over traces of pencil, 176 × 254mm. By Rungiah, *c.*1825.

A climber that can reach six metres, widespread in tropical E and Central Africa, and S and SE Asia and Australia. It is sometimes cultivated as an annual in Europe for its attractive, bright red, silver-mottled, cherry-like fruits. Arnott's annotation refers to a plate of the species in Rheede's *Hortus Malabaricus* of 1688, where one of its recorded medicinal uses, taken with honey and sugar, was as a remedy for 'fever, cough, abscess and internal gas'. This drawing shows Rungiah's sense of design at its best, and was almost certainly painted at Negapatam. He later added floral details in pencil on the reverse for its publication in the *Icones*.

Annotations by Wight: 500/1072, B. laciniosa, ienalarie, §7 (pencil, recto); No. 8 (pencil, verso). Annotations by Arnott: Rheed. Mal. 8 t. 19 certe (pencil, recto).

Published as plate 500 of the *Icones* (1841), lithographed Dumphy.

RBGE WI60 R (SERIES A)

56. Momordica dioica *Willdenow*

CUCURBITACEAE

Tam: palupaagakaiungu, tholoopaavai; Tel: angaakara, karkotaki

Bodycolour heightened with gum arabic, and ink, over traces of pencil, 159 × 196mm. By Rungiah, *c.*1830.

A dioecious climber widespread in India, Sri Lanka and Malaysia. The tuberous root is used medicinally, especially that of the female plant, which is larger than that of the male. Sir George Watt, in 1891, recorded that on the Konkan (the coast south of Bombay) juice from the root was used to counteract the inflammation caused by contact with urine of the house lizard! The fruit, when green and tender, can be eaten in curries. This drawing was probably made while Wight was at Negapatam, and shows the male plant.

Telugu annotations: (left) sheeranoor, dullupave.

Annotations by Wight: 1087, §7 (pencil, recto). Annotations by Arnott: Momordica dioica Rottl[er], Rheed. Mal. 8 t. 12 certe (pencil, recto); W[ight's] C[atalogue no.] 1127, Momordica dioica α (ink, recto).

Published as plate 505 of the *Icones* (1841), lithographed by Dumphy.

RBGE W43 R (SERIES C)

57. Solena amplexicaulis (Lamarck) Gandhi

CUCURBITACEAE

Tam: pulivanji, ramacovacodee; Tel: tiddanda

Bodycolour heightened with gum arabic, and ink, over traces of pencil, 160 × 199mm. By Rungiah, c.1830.

A dioecious climber, widespread in tropical Asia. This drawing shows the habit of the female plant, with supplementary details of the male flower and a section of the fruit. The leaves, roots and fruits of the plant are all edible, and its roots and seeds are the source of medicinal purgatives and stimulants. This species was first described in the genus *Bryonia* by Lamarck, its specific epithet referring to the clasping leaf bases; but Arnott later transferred it to his (no longer recognised) genus *Karivia*. The species is now placed in the genus *Solena*, described in 1790 by the Portuguese botanist João de Loureiro in his *Flora Cochinchinensis*, the name coming from the Greek word for a tube, in reference to the stamens. Wight collected the plant at Negapatam, which is probably where Rungiah made this drawing.

Telugu annotations: (ramakuvamkodi).

Annotations by Wight: §5 Karivia (pencil, recto); 502/1078, Bryonia amplexicaulis Karivia Arnott (pencil, verso). Annotations by Arnott: W[ight's] C[atalogue no.] 1121, B[ryonia] amplexicaulis Lam. (ink, recto).

Published as plate 502 of the *Icones* (1841), lithographed by Dumphy.

RBGE W41 R (SERIES C)

58. Trichosanthes tricuspidata Loureiro

CUCURBITACEAE

Tam: ankoratthai, shavaripalam; Tel: avvagooda

Bodycolour heightened with gum arabic over traces of pencil, 175 × 254mm. By Rungiah, c.1830.

A large woody climber to 12 metres, occurring in upland parts of India, eastwards to China, Japan, Malaysia and tropical Australia. In the Western Ghats it occurs between 1000 and 1600 metres; the white flowers (unfinished in this drawing) are produced between November and February. Wight noted that the fruits of this species (which he knew as *T. palmata* Roxburgh) were 'considered poisonous by the natives'. This is another genus named by Loureiro from Indo-China, the name referring to the hair-like divisions of the petals; the epithet refers to three-lobed leaves, but as in many members of this family leaf shape is very variable, and in the specimen depicted here the leaves are seven-lobed.

Annotations by Wight: 104–5 (pencil, recto). Annotations by Arnott: Trichosanthes palmata Roxb., laciniosa Klein (pencil, recto); WC 1137. Trichosanthes palmata β.

Plate 105 of the *Illustrations* (1841), lithographed by Winchester is similar, but was probably based on a related drawing.

RBGE W361 R (SERIES A)

59. Adenia wightiana *(Wallich ex Wight & Arnott)* *Engler* subsp. **wightiana**

PASSIFLORACEAE

Bodycolour heightened with gum arabic, and ink, over traces of pencil, 159 × 201mm. By Rungiah, *c.*1830.

An herbaceous or slightly woody climber that can reach eight metres, first collected by Wight at Gingee in 1826, and later at Narthamala. This drawing represents original material of *Modecca wightiana*, a name given to the plant by Wallich, but validated with a description by Wight & Arnott in the *Prodromus*. Two subspecies are now recognised – the one shown in this drawing from s India and Sri Lanka, where it occurs on dry hills up to 800 metres, and another subspecies in E Africa. The genus is related to the passion flowers (*Passiflora*), and was known to Wight & Arnott as *Modecca*, a genus based by Lamarck on a plate in *Hortus Malabaricus*, but later realised not to be distinct from Forsskål's earlier genus *Adenia* (a name derived from the Arabic 'aden' applying to plants with swollen stems such as Forsskål's *Adenia venenata*).

Telugu annotations: (shirukuraku).

Annotations by Arnott: Modecca wightiana Wall., WC 1155 (ink, recto).

Published as plate 179 of the *Icones* (1839), lithographed by Winchester.

RBGE W16 R (SERIES C)

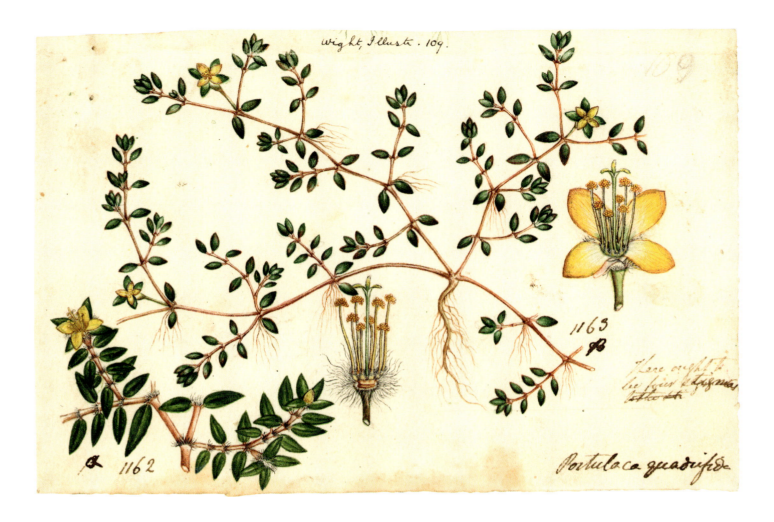

Wight, Illustr. 109.

1163

Portulaca quadrifida

1162

60 A & B. Portulaca quadrifida *Linnaeus*

PORTULACACEAE

Tam: passalaikkeerai, cunnoopasalee; Tel: sannapayalaaku, nalabutchalee.

a. Bodycolour heightened with gum arabic, and ink, over traces of pencil, 174 × 120mm. By Rungiah, *c.*1830.

b. Pencil and watercolour, 115 × 130mm. By Rungiah, *c.*1840.

A small, creeping annual, widespread in tropical Africa and Asia, and in South India occurring on coastal plains up to an altitude of about 600 metres. The species was first described from Egypt by Linnaeus, and the species name refers to the four petals. The habit drawing was probably made while Wight was at Negapatam, and shows two varieties, the lower one with larger leaves and longer hairs on the nodes of the stem. When Wight later wanted James Winchester to make a lithograph of the drawing for the *Illustrations*, he must have asked Rungiah to draw the floral details on a supplementary sheet. This latter has been chewed by an insect larva, one of the hazards to which paper is exposed in tropical climes.

Annotations by Wight: 109 (pencil, recto). Annotations by Arnott: There ought to be four stigmas, Portulaca quadrifida, [Wight's Catalogue nos.] 1163β, 1162 α.

Published as plate 109 of the *Illustrations* (1841), lithographed by Winchester.

RBGE W363 1 & 2 (SERIES E)

Opuntia Dillenii Haw.

61. Opuntia stricta *(Haworth) Haworth* var. **dillenii** *(Ker Gawler) L.D. Benson*

CACTACEAE

Tam: sappaatthukkalli; Tel: naagadaali, naagajemmudu

Bodycolour over traces of pencil, 255 × 352mm. By Rungiah, *c.*1830.

This prickly pear is native to coastal sites in the West Indies, around the Gulf of Mexico, southwards to northern South America. It has been widely introduced in the tropics, grown as an impenetrable hedging material. The setting up of the garden in Madras called the 'Nopalry', by Dr James Anderson, was in order to grow opuntias on which to raise the cochineal insect. Wight made no comment on such a use of this species when he reproduced this drawing in the *Illustrations*, but it could have been one of those introduced by Anderson, though the correct host for the insect is the related species *O. cochinillifer*. When Maria Graham (sister-in-law of Robert Graham) visited Madras in 1810 she noted that 'I saw also the Nopaul, a kind of prickly pear, on a species of which the cochineal insect lives, and which is now cultivated in Madras as an esculent vegetable. It was brought here merely as a curious exotic, but was discovered by Dr Anderson to be a valuable antiscorbutic, and has since been used in all men of war on the Indian stations, which are now almost free from that dreadful malady scurvy. The nopaul keeps fresh, and even continues to vegetate long after it is gathered; it makes an excellent pickle, which is now issued to the ships of war'.

Annotations by Wight: 114 (pencil, recto). Annotations by Arnott: Opuntia Dillenii Haw.,– DC. Prod. 3 p. 472 (ink, recto). Other annotations: [Tamil script] Supal Kullie Tam– (pencil, recto); No. 128, 113 (pencil, verso); Cacteae 86 (ink, verso).

Published as plate 114 of the *Illustrations* (1841), lithographed by Winchester.

RBGE W364 R (SERIES D)

62 A & B. Trachyspermum roxburghianum *(A.P. de Candolle) Craib*

UMBELLIFERAE

Sans: ajamoda; Tam: ashamtagam

Bodycolour heightened with gum arabic, and ink, over traces of pencil, 246 × 330mm. By Rungiah, *c.*1834.

Wight collected this species at Courtallum, but it is widely cultivated in gardens throughout India. The seeds are used for flavouring curries, and the leaves were formerly used by Europeans in India as a substitute for parsley. The plant, like many members of its family, has medicinal properties, and Sir George Watt in 1889 recorded that it was 'useful in hiccup, vomiting and pain in the bladder'. The floral analyses show a typical flower of the family Umbelliferae. The inferior ovary is composed of two carpels which split apart when ripe; at the ovary apex is a nectar secreting disc and swollen style bases ('stylopodia'). The five petals (unusually well developed in this species) and five stamens are borne on the apex of the ovary. The immature fruit bottom left is atypical in having three (rather than the usual two) styles. The section of the immature fruit shows a covering of glandular hairs. This drawing was not published by Wight.

Telugu annotation: (samusham).

Annotations by Wight: 116 117, Pimpinella involucrata (pencil, recto).

RBGE W385 R + V (SERIES D)

63 A & B. Sanicula elata

Buchanan-Hamilton ex D. Don

UMBELLIFERAE

Bodycolour heightened with gum arabic and pencil, 217 × 270mm (236.1); 96 × 119mm (236.2). By Rungiah, *c*.1845.

Very widespread, occurring in montane areas of Africa and throughout the Himalaya to China and Malaysia. It was first named by Francis Buchanan, a pupil of John Hope in Edinburgh, applied to a collection he made on what was the first botanical visit to Nepal in 1802–3. The name was provided with a description ('validated') by David Don, son of RBGE Curator George Don, in a Flora of Nepal that he published in 1825. This drawing was almost certainly made in the Nilgiri Hills, where Wight recorded the plant as 'common in almost every wood about Ootacamund, flowering during the rainy season. It often attains a large size, three or four feet in height'. In this species the mericarps (details 2, 6, 8, 9) are covered in hooked hairs – an adaptation to animal dispersal.

Annotations by Wight: Saniculeae Umbelliferae 1004/1134, Sanicula elata (Ham) (ink, recto).

Published (uncoloured) as plate 1004 of the *Icones* (1845), lithographed by Dumphy; reprinted (hand-coloured) as plate 79 of the *Spicilegium* (1847).

RBGE W236.1 & 2 R (SERIES E)

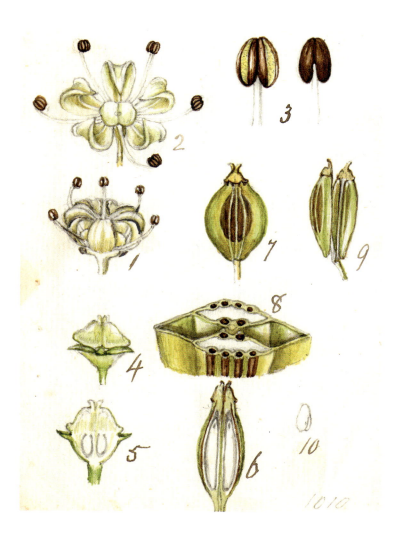

64 A & B. Heracleum hookerianum

Wight & Arnott

UMBELLIFERAE

Bodycolour heightened with gum arabic and pencil, 213 × 268mm (241.1); 96 × 120mm (241.2). By Rungiah, *c*.1845.

Wight described 16 new species of Umbelliferae including this endemic of the Nilgiri Hills, where it grows in pastures and on slopes that homesick Britons called 'downs'. It was first collected by Wight or his collectors prior to 1831 and named jointly with Arnott, in their *Prodromus*, after their friend William Hooker, then Professor of Botany at Glasgow. Generic limits in this family are notoriously difficult and Wight later thought it should be placed in the parsnip genus (*Pastinaca*), though the original treatment is now followed, as might be guessed from its resemblance to the common British hogweed (*Heracleum sphondylium*). In this family the structure of the fruit is of great taxonomic importance, as seen in Rungiah's wonderfully clear analysis. The inferior ovary develops into a fruit that splits into two mericarps (detail 9); of particular diagnostic importance are the oil glands ('vittae') shown here in brown, in surface view (7) and cross section (8).

Annotations by Wight: Peucedaneae Umbelliferae 1010/1152, Pastinaca Hookeriana (RW) Heracl: Hookerianum (W & A) (ink, recto).

Published as plate 1010 of the *Icones* (1845), lithographed by Dumphy.

RBGE W241.1 & 2 R (SERIES E)

65 A & B. Schefflera racemosa *(Wight) Harms*

ARALIACEAE

Mal: serencha; Tam: aalandai, ettilemaram, kannaa, malardai

Bodycolour heightened with gum arabic and pencil, 220 × 249mm (242.1); 113 × 142mm (242.2). By Rungiah, *c*.1845.

The family Araliaceae is closely related to Umbelliferae, but its members are usually woody, forming shrubs, trees or, as in the case of the European ivy (*Hedera helix*), climbers. The species shown here is a tree that can reach a height of 25 metres, occurring in the southern Western Ghats and Sri Lanka. In the Palni Hills it is common in shola forest between 1200 and 2200 metres, often growing beside streams; the greenish flowers are borne mainly between October and March. It was first described (in the genus *Hedera*) by Wight from plants growing, literally, on his doorstep, 'woods behind Kelso land', in Ooty where this drawing (which represents original material of the species) was doubtless made. The flowers in this family (like those of Umbelliferae) are usually arranged in umbels, but in this species the partial inflorescences are racemes (to which the epithet refers), arranged in a panicle.

Telugu annotations: (venna thirinudi).

Annotations by Wight: H. racimosa (pencil, recto); 1013, Araliaceae, Hedera racimosa (R.W.) (ink, recto).

Published (uncoloured) as plate 1015 of the *Icones* (1845), lithographed by Dumphy; reprinted (hand-coloured) as plate 85 of the *Spicilegium* (1847).

RBGE W242.1 & 2 R (SERIES E)

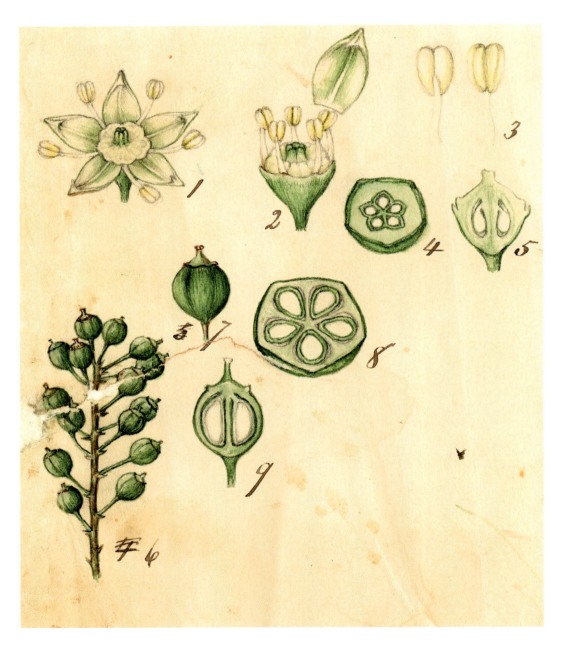

Wight, Ic.Pl.Ind.Or. iii. 1015.   *Araliaceæ*   1015

Hedera racimosa (R.W.)

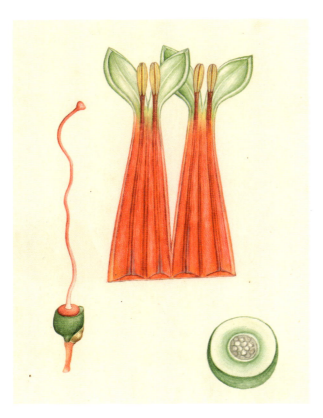

66 A & B. Helixanthera obtusata

(Schultes) Danser

LORANTHACEAE

Bodycolour heightened with gum arabic, and ink, over traces of pencil, 195 × 316mm. By Rungiah, *c.*1834.

Watermark: C WILMOT 1819

Mistletoes are parasitic or semi-parasitic plants belonging to either of two largely tropical families: Loranthaceae and Viscaceae. The shrubby species shown here is semi-parasitic, having green leaves and therefore capable of making some of its own sugars by photosynthesis, though also obtaining nutrients from its host plant. This species can parasitize a wide variety of hosts, including *Rhododendron*, *Daphniphyllum*, *Symplocos*, and even introduced species of *Acacia*. It occurs in the Nilgiri and Palni Hills especially between altitudes of 1500 and 1900 metres. In the floral analyses are shown the green, inferior ovary, the colourful corolla attached to its apex, which consists of four petals; the lower, red parts are closely appressed to form a tube; the filaments of the four stamens are fused to the petals and in this species the calyx is merely a rim around the ovary apex.

Annotations by Wight: April/3 40 (red crayon, verso); 119/1178, Loranthus obtusatus 1178 (pencil, recto).

Published as plate 119 of the *Illustrations* (1841), lithographed by Winchester.

RBGE W366 R + V (SERIES D)

67. Dendrophthoe falcata

(Linnaeus f.) Ettingshausen

LORANTHACEAE

Tam: plavithil, pulluruvi, sangattanmarattubulluruvi; Tel: badanika

Bodycolour heightened with gum arabic, and ink, over traces of pencil, 221 × 308mm. By Rungiah, *c.*1830.

This drawing shows the plant described by Augustin Pyramus de Candolle (from the Nilgiris) as *Loranthus amplexifolius*, but which is now treated as a form of *Dendrophthoe falcata*, a widespread and very variable parasitic shrub that occurs from India through SE Asia to Australia. In S India this species occurs in the plains and foothills up to 1800 metres, and parasitises trees from a wide range of families, including neem, mango, *Terminalia*, but especially legumes including various *Bauhinia* and *Acacia* species and also the flame of the forest, *Butea monosperma*. Wight collected this species at 'Dindigul', perhaps referring to the Palni Hills where Father Matthew recorded it between 1600 and 1800 metres.

Annotations by Wight: /1187 (pencil, recto). Annotations by Arnott: W.C. 1245, Loranthus amplexifolius DC. Other annotations: [Tamil script] Sengatanmanarathoopilloorwee (pencil, recto); No. 16 of Icon (pencil, verso).

Published as plate 301 of the *Icones* (1840), lithographed by Winchester.

RBGE W128 R (SERIES ?D)

Wight, Ic.Pl. Ind.Or. i. .301.

W.C. 1245
Loranthus amplexifolius DC.

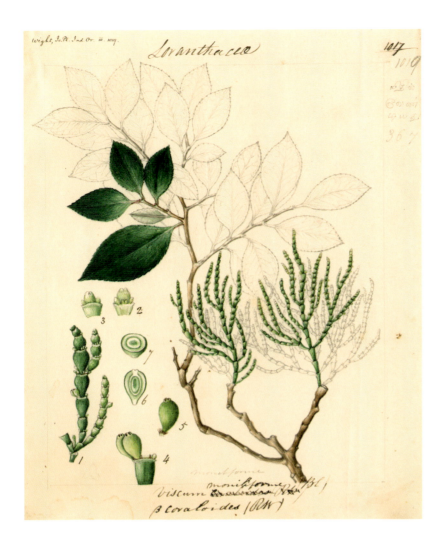

68. Korthalsella japonica

(Thunberg) Engler

VISCACEAE

Bodycolour and pencil, 219 × 277mm. By Rungiah, *c.*1845.

The plant shown here belongs to the same family as *Viscum album*, a British species associated with druids and Christmas osculation. It is a parasitic shrub with characteristically jointed stems, widespread from Africa to SE Asia and Japan. In South India it occurs in the Western Ghats at altitudes above 1520 metres, where it parasitises a wide range of tree species in shola forest, especially *Rhododendron*, *Vaccinium*, *Eurya* and *Ilex*. When Wight published this drawing, based on a plant from the banks of the Pycarah River in the Nilgiris, he stated the host to be an *Agapetes* (though it looks more like a *Vaccinium*). This drawing is part of the original material of Wight's var. *coraloides*, of *Viscum moniliforme*, but this is no longer regarded as worth recognising, being merely a form with shorter stem joints, and hence resembling coral. Although the species is usually monoecious, with male and female flowers borne separately on the same plant, Wight noted this to be dioecious, and he knew only female plants, as shown in the floral details 2–7. The pencil annotation at top right is an instruction to the printer, referring to the edition size (367 plates) of the *Icones*.

Annotations by Wight: 1019, moniliforme (pencil, recto); 1017, Loranthaceae, Viscum moniliforme (Bl.) β coraloides (RW) (ink, recto). Other annotations: [Telugu script] 367.

Published as plate 1019 of the *Icones* (1845), lithographed by Dumphy.

RBGE W246 R (SERIES E)

69. Dendrophthoe falcata

(Linnaeus f.) Ettingshausen

LORANTHACEAE

Tam: plavithil, pulluruvi, sangattanmarattubulluruvi; Tel: badanika

Bodycolour heightened with gum arabic, and ink, over traces of pencil, 176 × 256mm. By Rungiah, *c.*1825.

Watermark: RUSE & T[URNERS] 182–.

This drawing represents another form of the variable *Dendrophthoe falcata*, differing from that shown in Plate 67 in leaf shape and flower colour. In the Palni Hills this form apparently occurs at lower altitudes than the one with amplexicaul leaves.

Annotations by Wight: 302/1186 (pencil, recto). Annotations by Arnott: Loranthus longiflorus Desr. WC. 1242 (ink, recto). Other annotations: No. 79, [Tamil script] Mamarattoo Pillooroong.

Published as plate 302 of the *Icones* (1840), lithographed by Winchester.

RBGE W129 R (SERIES A)

302
1186

Loranthus longiflorus Desr.
WC. 1242

69

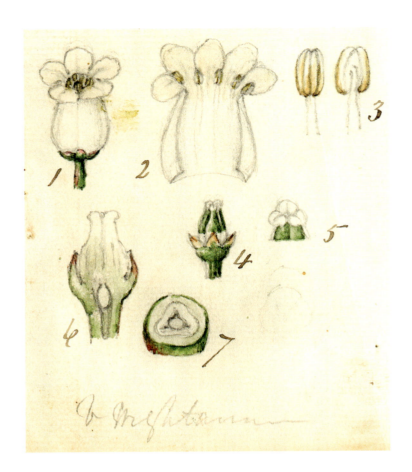

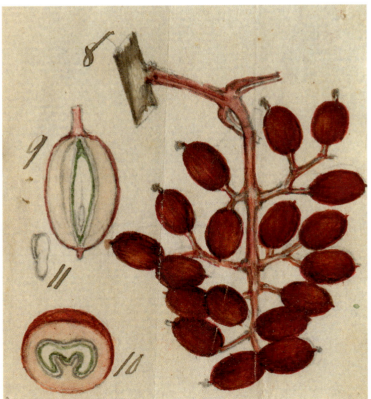

70 A, B & C. Viburnum erubescens

Wallich ex A.P. de Candolle

CAPRIFOLIACEAE

Bodycolour heightened with gum arabic, and pencil; 210 × 269mm (251.1); 83 × 92mm (251.2); 61 × 86mm (251.3). By Rungiah, *c.*1845.

One of the most unpleasant smelling cabinets in the herbarium is that containing the genus *Viburnum*, and this is one of the culprits. The plant shown here was described by Wallich as *Viburnum wightianum*, based on Wight specimens from the Nilgiris. This, however, is no longer recognised as distinct from the widespread *V. erubescens* a species first described from Nepal and Kumaon, with an epithet that refers to the pink blush of the flowers. This is a large, deciduous shrub to four metres tall, widespread in the Sino-Himalaya from Kumaon to sw China, and also in the mountains of the southern Western Ghats. In the Nilgiri and Palni Hills it occurs above 1850 metres at the edge of shola forest.

Annotations by Wight: 90 (pencil, recto); 1022/1203, Viburnum Wightianum (Wall.) (ink, recto).

Published (uncoloured) as plate 1024 of the *Icones* (1845), lithographed by Dumphy; reprinted (hand-coloured) as plate 90 of the *Spicilegium* (1847).

RBGE W251.1, 2, & 3 (SERIES E)

Wight, Ic.Pl.Ind.Or. iii. 1024.

1022
1203

Viburnum Wightianum (Wall)

Hedyotea   Rubiacea

312
1266
wight, Ic. Pl. Ind. Or. i. 312.

Nᵒ 1306
Hedyotis racemosa Lam.

Hedyotis
racemosa
Lam

71. Oldenlandia paniculata *Linnaeus*

RUBIACEAE

Bodycolour heightened with gum arabic, and ink, over traces of pencil,
178 × 256mm. By Rungiah, *c*.1825.

Watermark: RUSE & T[URNERS] 182–.

A succulent herb to 50 cm tall, occurring in moist places in the
plains of India and Sri Lanka. This is one of very few drawings
annotated with a locality in English, which records that Wight saw
the plant at Negapatam in 1828, though the drawing appears to
be earlier. The taxonomy and generic placement of this and
related species are confused, and this plant (known to Wight as
Hedyotis racemosa) has commonly been known as *O. biflora* L. The
root of a related species, *O. umbellata* L., the 'chayroot', is the
source of a red dye, and some of the cotton experiments in the
Tinnevelly District came up against a problem when locals who
had rights to dig up this valuable commodity demanded
compensation when they were denied access to land taken over
for cotton.

Annotations by Wight: Hedyoteae, Rubiaceae, 1266, Hedyotis racemosa
Turn (pencil, recto); Very common in this neighbourhood + [see below] in
moist soil particularly about the edges of tanks – Oct. 1828 + Negapatam
(pencil, verso). Annotations by Arnott: WC. 1306 Hedyotis racemosa Lam.
(ink, recto); Filaments inserted … the mouth (pencil, recto).

Published as plate 312 of the *Icones* (1840), lithographed by Dumphy.

RBGE W23 R (SERIES A)

72 A & B. Gardenia latifolia *Aiton*

RUBIACEAE

Tam: kumbay; Tel: peddabikki

Bodycolour heightened with gum arabic, and ink, over traces of pencil,
160 × 197mm. By Rungiah, *c*.1830.

A small, deciduous tree occurring in dry hills in west, central and
SW India, and also in the NW Himalaya. Its fine-grained wood
has been used for making combs. In *Flora Indica* Roxburgh, who
knew the plant in the Northern Circars, recommended its
cultivation as an ornamental for its glossy leaves and large,
fragrant flowers. It was introduced to Kew by R.A. Salisbury in
1787, and was first described from this cultivated material by
William Aiton in *Hortus Kewensis*. The generic name
commemorates the Aberdeenshire born Alexander Garden, who
practised medicine at Charleston, South Carolina, and
corresponded with Linnaeus.

Telugu annotations: (kambepuram).

Annotations by Wight: 759, Gardenia latifolia … (pencil, recto);
Gardeniaceae Rubiaceae 1218, Gardenia latifolia (Ait) See the other side for
dissections (ink, recto); 2, 3, 4 (ink, verso). Annotations by Arnott: Gardenia
latifolia Ait vix Roxb. WC. 1279 [deleted] (ink, recto). Other annotations:
Kumbay Marom (pencil, recto).

Published as plate 759 of the *Icones* (1844), lithographed by Dumphy.

RBGE W45 R + V (SERIES C)

73. Hydrophylax maritima *Linnaeus f.*

RUBIACEAE

Bodycolour heightened with gum arabic, and ink, over traces of pencil, 202 × 162mm. By Rungiah, *c.*1830.

A creeping, succulent herb occurring on sand dunes on both east and west coasts of Peninsular India, and in Sri Lanka. Both genus and species were described by the younger Linnaeus from specimens collected by the Tranquebar missionary J.G. König at Gudulur (now Cuddalore) on the Coromandel Coast – both generic name and epithet refer to the habitat of the plant, and the binomial can be translated as 'seaside water sentinel'. It is one of the plants recommended by Hugh Cleghorn as useful for binding sand in a paper published in 1857, the result of a request by the Madras Military Board who were concerned about how to 'consolidate the drifting sand thrown up near Colonel Cotton's groynes' on Madras beach.

Annotations by Wight: 760, Hydrophyllax maritima (pencil, recto); Spermacoceae, Rubiaceae, 1357, Hydrophyllax maritima, 1, 2, 3, 22 (ink, recto). Annotations by Arnott: 1369 [deleted] (ink, recto).

Published as plate 760 of the *Icones* (1844), lithographed by Dumphy.

RBGE W46 R (SERIES C)

74 A & B. Pleiocraterium verticillaris

(Wight & Arnott) Bremekamp

RUBIACEAE

Bodycolour heightened with gum arabic and pencil, 253 × 225mm (255.1);
93 × 122mm (255.2). By Rungiah, *c.*1845.

A strange, rosette-forming herb endemic to the Nilgiris at altitudes
between 1830 and 2130 metres, where it is still locally dominant in
grassland between Avalanche and Sispara. It was first described (in
the genus *Hedyotis*) by Wight & Arnott based on a specimen sent by
Wight to the EIC herbarium in London. In 1939 the Dutch botanist
C.E.B. Bremekamp made it the type of a new genus with a curious
distribution – of the other members one is from Sri Lanka (*P.
plantaginifolium*, originally described by Arnott based on plants
collected by Colonel & Mrs Walker, but which had also been
collected by Wight on his 1836 visit), and the other two from the
mountains of northern Sumatra. The generic name refers to the
cup-shaped leaf bases. The Indian species is heterostylous (like the
British primrose), having two types of flower with either a long or a
short style (an adaptation to out-crossing) and Rungiah has shown
here the long-styled form, with the stigma exserted from the
corolla. The three other species are homostylous, in which all
flowers have long styles.

Telugu annotations: (101 prasada).

Annotations by Wight: Hedyotideae, Rubiaceae, 1029/1253, Hedyotis
verticillaris (Wall.) (ink, recto).

Published as plate 1029 of the *Icones* (1845), lithographed by Dumphy; reprinted
(hand-coloured) as plate 94 of the *Spicilegium* (1847).

RBGE W255.1 & 2 R (SERIES E)

75 A & B. Mitragyna parvifolia

(Roxburgh) Korthals

RUBIACEAE

Tam: chinnakadambu, nichulam; Tel: battagenupu

Bodycolour heightened with gum arabic, and ink, over traces of pencil, 245 × 331mm. By Rungiah, *c*.1834.

A large, deciduous tree to 30 metres tall, occurring in dry deciduous forests throughout India and Sri Lanka, and also in Bangladesh and Burma, ascending to 1220 metres in the Himalaya. The timber has been used for various domestic purposes, such as for making agricultural implements, furniture and household utensils; it is easily worked and takes a polish, but rots easily if exposed to wet. The tree was first described (in the genus *Nauclea*) by Roxburgh, who knew it in the mountains of the Northern Circars. This is the true kadamba tree, under which Krishna frolicked with the milkmaids (gopis). The generic name refers to the stigma, shaped like a bishop's mitre, shown clearly in the floral details.

Annotations by Wight: 1207, Cinchonaceae, Rubiaceae (pencil, recto). Other annotations: Cinchonaceae, Rubiaceae, 1207, Nauclea parvifolia (Roxb.) (pencil, verso).

Published as plate 123 of the *Illustrations* (1841), lithographed by Winchester.

RBGE W415.1 R + V (SERIES D)

76. Launaea sarmentosa *(Willdenow) Kurtze*

COMPOSITAE

San: gojhiva

Bodycolour heightened with gum arabic, and ink, over traces of pencil, 156 × 202mm. By Rungiah, *c*.1830.

A perennial herb of sandy soils, which creeps by means of stolons. It occurs from E Africa through India (both coasts) and Sri Lanka, to Mauritius and Malaysia. This is one of the plants discussed by Cleghorn in 1857 with a view to stabilising the mobile sand of Madras beach, but he considered that 'no species of the Compositae possesses sufficient strength to effect the object in view'. There has been much confusion over the generic placement of this plant. It was first described and illustrated in Willdenow's *Phytographia*, based on specimens collected by J.G. Klein. The RBGE has Rottler's own copy of this rare book, which must have been acquired in Madras by Cleghorn. When Wight published this relatively early drawing of Rungiah's, he appears to have asked him to make some additional floral analyses on a supplementary sheet. The combined result was published in the Compositae section of the *Illustrations* the plates of which were coloured by E.A. Rodrigues. Rodrigues was an intriguing man who used lithography to produce an extraordinary, almost taxonomic, study of South Indian Hinduism, printed by the American Mission Press that produced Wight's later works.

Telugu annotations: (illeg).

Annotations by Wight: Lactuceae, Compositae – Cichoraceae, (Microrhynchus sarmentosus D.C. prod.), Lactuca sarmentosa R.W. cont., Prenanthes sarmentosa (pencil, recto). Annotations by Arnott: Lactuca sarmentosa Wight – DC WC. 1504 (ink, recto).

Published as plate 133 of the *Illustrations* (1848–50), lithographed by Winchester.

RBGE W371.1 R (SERIES C)

77 A & B. Grangea maderaspatana

(Linnaeus) Poiret

COMPOSITAE

Tam: maashipathri; Tel: manchipathri

Bodycolour heightened with gum arabic, and ink, over traces of pencil, 199 × 159mm (275.1); pencil, 107 × 124mm (275.2). By Rungiah, c.1830 and c.1845.

Watermark: C WILMOT 1819.

A prostrate herb occurring in moist sandy and waste places from tropical Africa eastwards through India to Malaysia and China. The plant was first described and illustrated by Leonard Plukenet in two forms, one of which came from Madras (hence the epithet). Linnaeus treated these forms as synonymous under the name *Artemisia maderaspatana*, which Poiret transferred to *Grangea*, a genus described by Michel Adanson (possibly named after the French mathematician Joseph Louis La Grange). This is another case where Rungiah later supplemented an early drawing with some exquisite floral analyses in pencil, in this case for publication in the *Icones*. In this species the small individual flowers ('florets') that make up the head ('capitulum') are all identical, with no elongation of one of the corolla lobes as is found in the outer row of florets in *Senecio* (Plate 80) or all the florets in *Launaea* or *Chaetoseris* (Plates 76, 78).

Telugu annotations: (illegible)

Annotations by Wight: Asteroideae, [DC Prodr.] 5.372 (pencil, recto); Asteroideae, Compositae, 1097, Grangea Madraspatana (Poir.) (ink, recto). Annotations by Arnott: Grangea maderaspatana, WC. n. 1449 [deleted] 1419 (ink, recto).

Published as plate 1097 of the *Icones* (1846), lithographed by Dumphy.

RBGE W275.1 & 2 R (SERIES C/E)

78 A, B & C. Chaetoseris hastata

(A.P. de Candolle) Shih

COMPOSITAE

Bodycolour heightened with gum arabic and pencil, 217 × 271mm (283.1), 97 × 121mm (283.2). By Rungiah, *c.*1845.

Watermark (283.2): [HARRIS &] TREMLETT [1837].

Wight sent his pre-1831 herbarium specimens of the family Compositae to the great Candolle in Geneva, who based many new species on them both in Wight's *Contributions to Indian Botany* and in the Compositae volumes of his own great *Prodromus*. The latter work, which pioneered a system of natural classification of which Wight & Arnott were keen promoters, was the last attempt to treat the Flora of the whole world at species level. In 1846 Wight published a conspectus of Candolle's classification of the Compositae and, in various books and papers, described a small number of new species, including this handsome sowthistle (as *Mulgedium neilgherrense*) from the Nilgiri Hills. In fact it was not new, having been described earlier by Candolle, based on specimens collected in Nepal by Wallich. Several species (notably *Rhododendron arboreum*) exhibit a similar distribution pattern – mainly Sino-Himalayan, but with outlying populations in the Nilgiri Hills.

Annotations by Wight (14.1): Cichoraceae Compositae 1144, Mulgedium Neilgherryense (W) see other side (ink, recto). Annotation by Arnott: 7. 247 (pencil, recto; a reference to Candolle's *Prodromus*).

Published (uncoloured) as plate 1144 of the Icones (1846), lithographed by Dumphy; reprinted (hand-coloured) as plate 119 of the *Spicilegium* (1848).

RBGE W283.1 R + V, 283.2 R (SERIES E)

79 A. Acmella calva *(A.P. de Candolle) R.K. Jansen*
79 B. Acmella oleracea *(Linnaeus) R.K. Jansen*

COMPOSITAE

Tam: palvali poondu

Bodycolour heightened with gum arabic, and ink, over traces of pencil,
159 × 198mm (278.1); bodycolour heightened with gum arabic and pencil,
111 × 126mm (278.2). By Rungiah, *c.*1830 and *c.*1845.

Acmella calva is a perennial herb to 75 cm tall, occurring in damp
places up to altitudes of 2500 metres in India, Nepal and Sri Lanka,
and eastwards to Burma, Thailand and s China, also occurring in
Java and the Philippines. It was first described (in the genus
Spilanthes) by Augustin Pyramus de Candolle, based on Wight's
specimens from Cunnawady and Mysore. This drawing was
probably made from one of these specimens, in which case it
represents original material of the species. In Nepal and Sri Lanka

the plant is chewed for relief from toothache, and according to J.S.
Gamble, in his *Flora of Madras*, the flower heads have a hot, burning
taste.

The supplementary sheet shows floral details of a related species,
Acmella oleracea, made from plants growing in a coconut plantation at
Coimbatore. This annual, known only in cultivation and as an
escape, is probably derived from a Peruvian species. It is grown for
ornamental and medicinal purposes (it is also effective against
toothache) and has insecticidal properties. These supplementary
details were mistakenly added to the plate of *A. calva* when
lithographed for the *Illustrations*, and the correct ones (on the reverse
of the sheet of *A. calva*) were omitted.

Annotations by Wight: Senecionideae, 100, [DC Prodr.] 5. 620 (pencil, recto);
Senecionideae, Compositae, 1109, Spilanthes calva (D.C.), B S. oleracea (Jacq)
Turn over (ink, recto); 1, 2, 3, 4, 5, 6 (ink, verso).

Published as plate 1109 of the *Icones* (1846), lithographed by ?Dumphy.

RBGE W278.1 & 2 R (SERIES C/E)

Senecionideæ   Compositæ   1109

Wight, Icbl. Ind. Or.
iii. 1109.

5. 620.

Spilanthes calva (D.C.)
B *S. oleracea. (Jacq)*

Turnovii

80 A & B. Senecio intermedius *Wight*

COMPOSITAE

Bodycolour heightened with gum arabic and pencil, 218 × 250mm (282.1); 108 × 124mm (282.2). By Rungiah, *c.*1845.

This member of one of the largest of all genera (with about 1250 species worldwide) is relatively unusual in being a climber. It was discovered by Wight climbing on trees and bushes near the Avalanche Bungalow in the Nilgiri Hills, where it flowers in February and March. It occurs between altitudes of 1200 and 1800 metres in the southern part of the Western Ghats, and is still recognised as a distinct species, though closely related to the more widespread *Senecio scandens*. Rungiah's beautiful pencil details show a capitulum (1 – a condensed inflorescence), details of stamens (5) and the achene (9–10), the receptacle and calyx-like involucral bracts (2), a detail of a barbed pappus hair (6), two views each of a rayless, bisexual disc floret (3, 4), and one of the outer 'ray florets', which are female and in which one of the corolla lobes is greatly and asymmetrically developed (7, 8).

Annotations by Wight: Senecionideae Compositae 1135, Senecio intermedius (RW) (ink, recto).

Published as plate 1135 of the *Icones* (1846), lithographed by Dumphy.

RBGE W282.1 & 2 R (SERIES E)

81 A&B. Diospyros malabarica

(Desrousseaux) Kosteletzky

EBENACEAE

Eng: false mangosteen; Tam: thumbika; Tel: thumiki chettu

Bodycolour heightened with gum arabic, and ink, over traces of pencil, 237 × 335mm. By Rungiah, *c.*1835.

Many of the plants represented in the drawings are of herbaceous plants, of a sort more or less familiar from temperate floras; however, it is trees that are the most characteristic element of tropical floras. Trees were not neglected by Wight and his artists, for example, this member of the ebony family is a medium-sized, evergreen, dioecious tree, and this drawing shows the female plant. It is widespread throughout moist parts of India, Sri Lanka, Burma and the Malay Peninsula – this drawing was made from a Malabar specimen, and Wight also knew it as a cultivated tree in Madras. The sticky pulp of the fruit (Roxburgh called the plant *Embryopteris glutenifera*) has been used for caulking the seams of wooden boats and in book-binding. The astringent fruit has been used for tanning and yields a brown dye; it also has medicinal properties, on which account it was, in 1868, included in the *Pharmacopoeia of India*, of which Wight was one of the editors. Unlike some other members of the family its timber is not of high quality and is used only for general building purposes.

Annotations by Wight: Ebenaceae, Embryopteris glutenifera ♀ (Roxb.) Turn over (pencil, recto).

Published as plate 844 of the *Icones* (1844/5), lithographed by Dumphy.

RBGE WI68 R + V (SERIES D)

82. Caralluma umbellata *Haworth*

APOCYNACEAE

Tam: kalmulaiyaan, sirunkalli; Tel: kundelu kommulu

Bodycolour and ink over traces of pencil, 159 × 197mm. By Rungiah, *c.*1830.

The milkweed family, Asclepiadaceae, was one of Wight's greatest botanical interests and, with Arnott's help, published no fewer than 18 new genera and 118 new species in the family, which is now no longer recognised as distinct from Apocynaceae. Some of their new genera are no longer recognised, such as *Boucerosia* (a name referring to the ox-like horns of the corona shown here in one of the floral details) in which Wight & Arnott placed this species. The family exhibits highly specialised adaptations to insect pollination, and this succulent species, from dry habitats in s India and Sri Lanka, has foul-smelling flowers pollinated by carrion insects. This drawing was probably made from specimens collected at Dindigul while Wight was stationed at Negapatam.

Annotations by Wight: Stapelieae Asclepiadeae 495 (pencil, recto). Annotations by Arnott: Boucerosia umbellata w & a [Wight's Catalogue no.] 1519 (ink, recto).

Published (with additional details supplied by Rungiah) as plate 495 of the *Icones* (1841), lithographed by Dumphy.

RBGE WI59.1 R (SERIES C)

83 A & B. Hoya ovalifolia *Wight & Arnott*

APOCYNACEAE

Watercolour and ink over traces of pencil, 243 × 303mm. By Rungiah, *c.*1834.

Watermark: [s] & s 1829.

An epiphytic, trailing perennial, occurring in the Western Ghats from Karnataka southwards, and in Sri Lanka, but apparently rare. First described from specimens from the Nilgiris, this drawing was made from a Malabar specimen. The beautiful magnified details of the waxy flowers show the structure clearly – the upper left figure shows a flower with the corolla and calyx removed, showing the pink scales developed from the stamens that form a corona protecting the anthers. In the top right figure the scales have been removed to show the anthers, attached to and alternating with the stigma lobes. When an insect, such as a butterfly, visits the flower and puts its tongue into the slits between the coronal scales, the sticky translators that join the pollen masses (pollinia) from two adjacent anthers become attached to the insect. The double unit (pollinarium) shown at the extreme right becomes detached when the insect removes its tongue and may be transferred to the next flower visited.

Telugu annotations: (illegible).

Annotations by Wight: Pergularieae, Asclepiadeae, 847, 5, Hoya ovalifolia (W & A), 114 (pencil, recto); 1, 2, 3, 4, 6 (pencil, verso). Other annotations: Jany 4 (red chalk, verso).

Published as plate 847 of the *Icones* (1844–5), lithographed by Dumphy.

RBGE WI69 V + R (SERIES D)

83B

Porgularieæ   Asclepiadeæ   847

Hoya ovalifolia

84 A & B. Toxocarpus kleinii *Wight & Arnott*

APOCYNACEAE

Bodycolour heightened with gum arabic, and ink, over traces of pencil, 175 × 255mm. By Rungiah & R.K. Greville, *c.*1825 & *c.*1830.

A slender climber that may reach eight metres, native of the plains and foothills of s India and Sri Lanka. It was based by Wight & Arnott on various collections including ones made by Wight at Vellangany near Negapatam, where it was found climbing in hedges near the sea; this drawing represents part of the original material. The original material also included specimens from the Tranquebar Missionaries, and the species was named to honour one of them,

J.G. Klein. This is an early drawing of Rungiah's and the small coloured floral details below the habit drawing proved inadequate. When the drawing was sent to Hooker (who added the name '*Metaplexis dichotoma*'), he must have asked R.K. Greville to examine the flowers of the accompanying specimens microscopically, and it was he who added the pencil details on the verso.

Annotations by Wight: Secamoneae, Metaplexis dichotoma, Asclepiadeae, 5, 3 Toxocarpus Kleinii (w & A, Turn (pencil, recto); 2, 4, 5, 6 (pencil, verso). Annotations by Arnott: Toxocarpus Kleinii w & A w[ight] c[atalogue] 1560 (ink, recto). Annotations by W.J. Hooker: Metaplexis dichotoma (ink, recto).

Published as plate 886 of the *Icones* (1844–5), lithographed by Dumphy.

RBGE WI75 R + V (SERIES A/B)

Secamoneœ   Asclepiadeœ   886

5

Toxocarpus Kleinii
Wb. 1560   Toxocarpus Kleinii (W&A)   Turner

Metaplexis
dichotoma.

85. Ceropegia candelabrum *Linnaeus*

APOCYNACEAE

Tel: bachhalimanda, langatai, pullamanda
Bodycolour heightened with gum arabic, and ink, over traces of pencil, 256 × 350mm. By Rungiah, *c.*1830.

A perennial twiner, arising from a tuberous root, widespread in s and e India up to 900 metres, and also occurring in Sri Lanka. The roots are edible and have been used medicinally. Roxburgh's *C. tuberosa* is no longer regarded as distinct from *C. candelabrum*, a species based by Linnaeus on an illustration and description in Rheede's *Hortus Malabaricus*. In the genus *Ceropegia* the relatively small sexual parts are in a swollen chamber at the base of a tubular corolla that acts as an insect trap; in this species the insects are attracted by the hairy apical lobes of the corolla, which are mobile. Seen here are the characteristic paired fruits ('follicles') of the family, which split to release the seeds that are wind dispersed by means of an apical corona of hairs.

Annotations by Arnott: Ceropegia tuberosa wc. 1516 (ink, recto); wc. 1516 (ink, verso).

Published as plate 353 of the *Icones* (1840), lithographed by ?Dumphy.

RBGE W417.1 R (SERIES ?D)

Ceropegia tuberosum
W. 1816

86 A & B. Wrightia tinctoria *(Roxburgh) R. Brown*

APOCYNACEAE

Eng: dyer's oleander, ivory wood; Tam: irumpaalai, vetapaalai; Tel: ankudu, paalavareni

Bodycolour heightened with gum arabic, and ink, over traces of pencil, 153 × 196mm. By Rungiah, *c.*1830.

Watermark: C WILMOT 1819.

A small, deciduous tree to 15 metres tall, widespread in dry deciduous forest in Peninsular India, up to altitudes of 1300 metres. The epithet refers to the dyeing properties of the leaves, which yield an indigo blue with which William Roxburgh experimented at Samulcottah around 1790. Wight sent seed of the plant to the Agricultural and Horticultural Society in Calcutta for their museum in May 1845. The fine-grained, whitish wood is used for turning and carving. The genus commemorates William Wright, a medical pupil of John Hope in Edinburgh, who made an important contribution to knowledge of the flora and ethnobotany of Jamaica, and was named by Robert Brown. This drawing was not published by Wight (it is not the original of plate 444 of the *Icones*).

Telugu annotations: (marathanam, velpale).

Annotations by Wight: Wrightia (pencil, recto). Other annotations: Veppalay Marom (pencil, recto).

RBGE W79 R + V (SERIES C)

87. Vallaris solanacea *(Roth) Kuntze*

APOCYNACEAE

Tel: china maalathi, naagamalle, paalamallethivva

Bodycolour heightened with gum arabic, and ink, over traces of pencil, 201 × 154mm. By Rungiah, *c.*1830.

A large twining shrub to ten metres high, occurring throughout India and Sri Lanka, eastwards into Burma, Indo-China and s China. It occurs in dry forest and hedges up to an altitude of 1520 metres, but is also commonly cultivated in gardens for its attractive flowers. First described (in the genus *Peltanthera*) by the German botanist A.W. Roth, based on specimens collected by Benjamin Heyne, one of Wight's predecessors as Madras Naturalist. The epithet refers to a resemblance in flower shape to those of a member of the genus *Solanum*; and the generic name, coined by N.L. Burman in his *Flora Indica* (1768), is an allusion to the plant's cultivated habitat – *vallus* being Latin for a stake in a fence or palisade.

Annotations by Wight: Vallaris Heynii Spr. (pencil, recto).

RBGE W83 R (SERIES C)

88. Strychnos cinnamomifolia

Thwaites var. **wightii** *A.W. Hill*

LOGANIACEAE

Bodycolour heightened with gum arabic, and ink, over traces of
pencil, 159 × 198mm. By Rungiah, *c*.1830.

Watermark: C WILMOT 1819.

A very large shrub that climbs by means of unbranched
tendrils (not shown in this drawing), occurring in
evergreen forests of the Western Ghats from Karnataka
southwards, at altitudes of up to 900 metres. The genus is
known for its poisonous alkaloids, and the queried
identification on the drawing refers to the related *Strychnos
nux-vomica*, a tree that is the source of strychnine.
According to J.S. Gamble in his *Flora of Madras* the seeds of
the variety depicted here contain the alkaloid brucine. This
variety was described and named for Wight by Sir Arthur
Hill, who met an untimely end in 1941 when thrown from
his horse while riding in the Mid Surrey Golf Course,
which adjoins Kew Gardens of which he had been its
notable Director since 1922.

Annotations by Wight: Strychnos n vomica? (pencil, recto).
Annotations by Arnott: S. potatorum, see Wight ic. Vol 2d part 2d t.
434 (pencil, verso). Other annotations: Yetty-Marom (pencil, recto).

RBGE W71 R (SERIES C)

89. Exacum pedunculatum *Linnaeus*

GENTIANACEAE

Tam: kana poondu

Bodycolour heightened with gum arabic, and ink, over traces of
pencil, 158 × 198mm. By Rungiah, *c*.1830.

An annual herb usually under 30 cm, occurring in
grassland and moist places in the lowlands throughout
India and Sri Lanka up to an altitude of 900 metres. It was
described by Linnaeus based on an illustration and
description in Plukenet's *Phytographia* that seems to have
come from Malabar. Like many members of the gentian
family it contains bitter elements and according to Sir
George Watt can be used as a substitute for chiretta. It is
related to the Persian violet (*Exacum affine*), widely grown
as a pot plant, introduced from the island of Socotra by
Isaac Bayley Balfour who later became Regius Keeper of
RBGE. The figure at bottom right shows the bent style
characteristic of the genus.

Telugu annotations: (sletheriyad [= cannot say], kadederisavidi).

Annotations by Wight: Chironeae, Gentianeae, 336, Exacum
pedunculare, Sabaea carinata (pencil, recto). Annotations by Arnott:
Exacum pedunculare L. (ink, recto). Other annotations: The name of
this plant is not known (pencil, recto).

Published as plate 336 of the *Icones* (1840), lithographed by Dumphy.

RBGE W29 R (SERIES C)

90. Crescentia cujete *Linnaeus*

BIGNONIACEAE

Tam: thiruvottukkaai; Eng: calabash tree

Bodycolour heightened with gum arabic, and ink, over traces of pencil, 159 × 200mm. By Rungiah, *c.*1830.

An evergreen tree that can reach a height of ten metres, native to dryish parts of Mexico and c America, but commonly cultivated for its curious appearance and fruits. The flowers, which open at night, are bat pollinated, and borne directly on the trunk ('cauliflorous'). From these develop the large, round fruits (to 50cm diameter), which have a hard skin and are used as utensils and as bailers for canoes; the pulp has medicinal uses. The generic name given by Linnaeus commemorates the thirteenth century Italian writer on rural matters, Pietro Crescenzi, and the epithet is taken from the plant's vernacular name recorded by the French missionary Charles Plumier in the West Indies. It was introduced to the Calcutta Botanic Garden in 1795, but it is not known when it reached Madras though an old specimen still grows in the garden of the Agri-Horticultural Society there.

Annotation by ?Arnott: Crescentia (pencil, recto).

RBGE W75 R (SERIES C)

91. Ipomoea cairica *(Linnaeus) Sweet*

CONVOLVULACEAE

Tam: kodie cundengathery

Bodycolour heightened with gum arabic, and ink, over traces of pencil, 159 × 198mm. By Rungiah, *c.*1830.

A perennial twiner, widely cultivated for its attractive flowers and now naturalised in disturbed habitats throughout the Old and New World tropics. Its original home may have been in the Americas, but it was first described from Egypt by the sixteenth century Swiss botanist Caspar Bauhin. Linnaeus coined its specific name, meaning 'belonging to Cairo', in 1759. This drawing was probably made while Wight was stationed at Negapatam, but none of the specimens in his herbarium is localised.

Annotations by Arnott: Ipomoea pulchella Ch[oisy], W[ight's] C[atalogue] 2292 (ink, recto).

Published as plate 156 of the *Icones* (1839), lithographed by Wight.

RBGE WII R (SERIES C)

[143]

92. Merremia hederacea

(N.L. Burman) H.G. Hallier

CONVOLVULACEAE

Tam: yelikkaadhu thazhai

Bodycolour heightened with gum arabic, and ink, over traces of pencil,
161 × 202mm. By Rungiah, *c.*1830.

A perennial twiner, widespread in the Old World tropics, from
Africa eastwards to China, Australia and the Pacific Islands. The
specific name refers to the ivy-shaped leaves, and the generic name
commemorates Blasius Merrem (1761–1824), Professor of Natural
Sciences at Marburg in Germany. Rungiah, like many Indian
artists, seems to have taken a particular delight in climbing plants,
and the opportunity to arrange these decoratively around the page.
This is seen both here and in drawings of the family Cucurbitaceae
(Plates 54–58). This drawing was probably made while Wight was
stationed at Negapatam, but he had first collected the species at
Rajahmundry as early as 1822.

Annotations by Arnott: C[onvolvulus] dentatus R[oxburgh], C. rostratus
Koen[ig] (pencil, recto); Ipomoea chryseides Ch[oisy], W[ight's] C[atalogue]
2288 (ink, recto).

Published as plate 157 of the *Icones* (1839), lithographed by Wight.

EW12 R (SERIES C)

93 A & B. Argyreia nervosa *(N.L. Burman) Bojer*

CONVOLVULACEAE

Eng: Elephant creeper; Tam: samudrappachai; Tel: samudrappaala

Bodycolour heightened with gum arabic, and ink, over traces of pencil,
282 × 243mm. By Rungiah, *c.*1835.

An extensively spreading and ornamental creeper. While
Rungiah conveys the habit and the pink flowers well, he fails
with the striking silvery hairs that densely clothe the
undersides of the leaves. The plant is widespread in India and
very commonly cultivated both there and more generally in SE
Asia. Wight first collected it at Rajahmundry in 1822. It was
probably this plant of which Wight wrote in 1851: 'a very large

and handsome plant has got the name of snake-creeper, under the impression that snakes will not approach it! A foolish fancy, as I have seen snakes taking shelter under the abundant cover it affords for their concealment to such an extent that I was obliged to destroy a handsome arbour of it to get rid of them'. This shows both the biological hazards of gardening in India and differing cultural perceptions!

Annotations by Wight: Convolvuleae Convolvulaceae, Argyreia speciosa (Sweet) Turn (ink, recto); 851 [Wight's Catalogue] 2250 (pencil, recto).

Published as plate 851 of the *Icones* (1844/5), lithographed by Dumphy.

RBGE WI7I R + V (SERIES ?D)

94. Hewittia malabarica *(Linnaeus) Suresh*

CONVOLVULACEAE

Bodycolour heightened with gum arabic, and ink, over traces of pencil, 160 × 197mm. By Rungiah, *c.*1830.

A twining perennial herb, widespread in tropical s and s e Asia and Africa, and introduced to the West Indies. It often occurs in disturbed habitats such as thickets, forest margins and roadsides, up to an altitude of 900 metres, and Wight recorded it as 'common enough near the Coast'. The Swiss botanist J.D. Choisy, an expert on Convolvulaceae, based his genus *Shutereia* on this species, named after James Shuter, but Wight & Arnott had at almost exactly the same time commemorated Shuter in a genus in Leguminosae, and it is the latter name that has been 'conserved'. Shuter was Wight's predecessor as Madras Naturalist and generously gave him his botanical books when he left India in 1826. Wight & Arnott coined the replacement name *Hewittia* for Choisy's *Shutereia*, but made no comment as to whom this name commemorates: it is most likely (though it would have been a mis-spelling) to have been after the botanical phrenologist Hewett Cottrell Watson.

Annotations by Wight: Convolvuleae, Convolvulaceae, 835, 12, 13 [deleted], Hewetia bicolor (w & a, Shuteria bicolor (Ch) (pencil, recto). Annotations by Arnott: Shuteria bicolor Chois., w c. n. 2299 (ink, recto).

Published as plate 835 of the *Icones* (1844–5), lithographed by Dumphy.

RBGE W53 R (SERIES C)

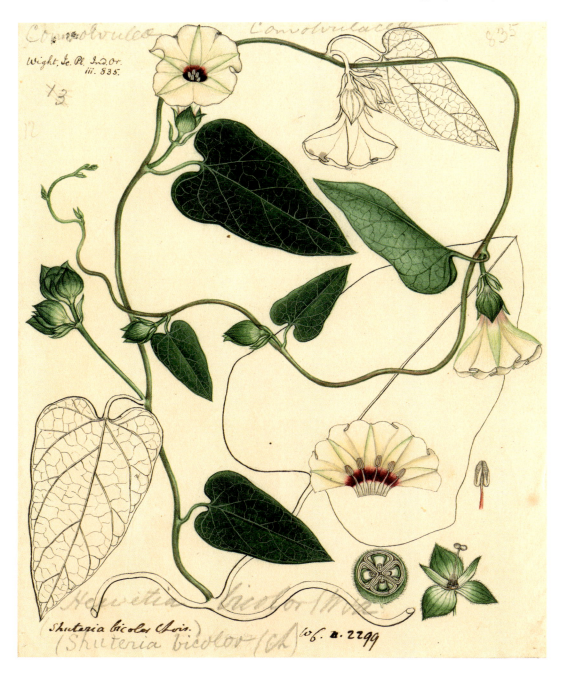

95. Ipomoea dichroa *Choisy*

CONVOLVULACEAE

Tam: paal nirathai

Bodycolour heightened with gum arabic, and ink, over traces of pencil, 160 × 196mm. By Rungiah, *c*.1830.

An annual climber widespread in tropical Africa. In India its distribution is rather unusual, apparently occurring only in the north (where it ascends to 1070 metres in the NW Himalaya and Nepal) and in the extreme south. In the *Icones* Wight described it as occurring 'twining over bushes in jungles near the bottom of the hills', and there are specimens at Edinburgh collected at Cunewady,

possibly where this drawing was made. Wight described the leaves as 'white powdery beneath, the flowers a beautiful rose pink colour and the whole plant covered with long soft hairs'.

Telugu annotations: (illegible).

Annotations by Wight: Convolvulaceae, Convolvuleae, 14, 10 [deleted], 837, Ipomoea pilosa (Ch.) (pencil, recto). Annotations by Arnott: Ipomoea pilosa Ch., WC. n. 2289 (ink, recto).

Published as plate 837 of the *Icones* (1844–5), lithographed by Dumphy.

RBGE W54 R (SERIES C)

96. Trichodesma indicum

(Linnaeus) Lehmann

BORAGINACEAE

Tam: kavil thumbai; Tel: guvvagutthi

Bodycolour heightened with gum arabic, and ink, over traces of pencil, 160 × 200mm. By Rungiah, *c.*1830.

An erect herb to 40 cm tall, occurring from Afghanistan southwards throughout India, and also in Mauritius. It grows in disturbed places such as fields and roadsides and Wight recorded it as 'very common … on dry sandy soil'. This drawing is accompanied by a long manuscript description of the plant by Wight (in English), and is probably one of those sent to Hooker between 1828 and 1831, but which Hooker decided not to publish in the *Botanical Miscellany*. It was not published by Wight, and is not the drawing reproduced as plate 172 of the *Illustrations*. The floral detail bottom right shows the characteristic appendages to the anthers, which are extended and twisted into a cone. Wight stated that members of this genus were 'sufficiently common on the plains of India to have found their way into the Native materia medica', but did not say for what purpose.

Telugu annotations: (virapuram, kalida thumve).

Annotations by Wight: Trichodesma indicum; draw again [beside cross-section of ovary] (pencil, recto). Other annotations: Kaladay-Toombay.

RBGE W406 R (SERIES B)

97. Solanum torvum *Swartz*

SOLANACEAE

Tam: malaichundai, sundaikaai; Tel: kondavuste

Bodycolour heightened with gum arabic, and ink, over traces of pencil, 174 × 253mm. By Rungiah, *c.*1830.

A shrub that can reach three metres in height, first described by the Swedish botanist Olof Swartz from Jamaica. It is now a widespread weed occurring throughout the tropics, and appears to have been introduced to India in the late eighteenth century (the oldest specimen in the Edinburgh herbarium is from the garden of the Tranquebar Missionaries, collected in 1798). Sir George Watt, in 1893, recorded that its berries were sometimes eaten at times of famine. This drawing was probably made at Negapatam, where Wight collected specimens now in the Edinburgh herbarium. Wight commented that this drawing was 'imperfect in not representing the tomentum [hairy leaf covering]'. As will be seen in other drawings Rungiah, in common with other Indian artists, had difficulty in representing hairy surfaces in paint.

Annotations by Wight: Solaneae, Solanaceae, 345, malay choondee, Solanum torvum (pencil, recto); No. 121 [Tamil script] (pencil, verso). Annotations by Arnott: Solanum torvum Sw., W[ight's] C[atalogue] 1577 (ink, recto).

Published as plate 345 of the *Icones* (1840), lithographed by Dumphy.

RBGE W33 R (SERIES A)

Solanea   Solanaceo   Wight, Jc. Pl. Int. Or. ii. 345.

345

malay Choondey

Solanum torvum Sw.
S. torvum (with fruit?)
Solanum torvum   Aug 6. 15 77

98 A&B. Aeginetia indica *Linnaeus*

OROBANCHACEAE

Watercolour and pencil, 186 × 229mm, watermark: C & E H (181.1);
110 × 150mm (181.2). By Rungiah, *c.*1845.

A parasitic herb occurring throughout India and eastwards to
Burma, Thailand, China, Japan and also in Borneo, the Philippines
and New Guinea. In s India it occurs in evergreen and deciduous
forest in the hills up to an altitude of 910 metres (to 1820 metres in
the Himalaya), and parasitises a variety of host plants. Wight
recorded it as very abundant among decaying vegetation in jungles
near Paulghaut, which is doubtless where this specimen was drawn.
The species was based by Linnaeus on an illustration and
description in Rheede's *Hortus Malabaricus*, and Wight stated that
his illustration exactly matched that of Rheede. The top right
analysis shows a cross section of the fruit, with two highly
convoluted placentas on which are borne large numbers of minute
seeds.

Annotations by Wight: Orobancheae, 895, 13, Aeginetia indica (Roxb.) (pencil,
recto)

Published as plate 895 of the *Icones* (1844–5), lithographed by Dumphy.

RBGE WI81.1 & 2 R (SERIES E)

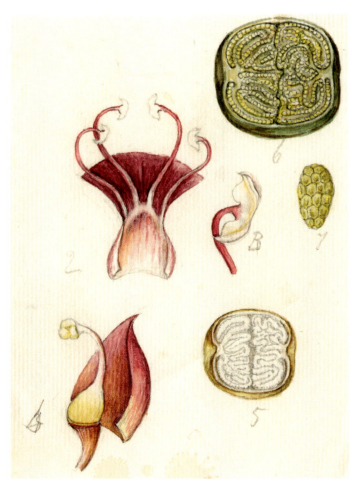

99 A & B. Dopatrium lobelioides

(Retzius) Bentham

SCROPHULARIACEAE

Bodycolour heightened with gum arabic, and ink, over traces of pencil, 160 × 198mm. By Rungiah, *c.*1830.

An annual, emergent aquatic herb that grows in flooded rice fields in South India and Sri Lanka. It was first described (in the genus *Gratiola*) by the Swedish botanist Anders Retzius, from material collected by J.G. König at Tranquebar – the epithet doubtless referring to the similarity (both in habit and flower) to the northern submerged aquatic *Lobelia dortmanna*. It was transferred to the genus *Dopatrium* by George Bentham who used Wight's specimens for his important work on Indian Scrophulariaceae. This drawing is included for the stunning half-flower, but in the text of the *Icones* Wight was rightly critical of the cross-section of the fruit, the structure of which was clearly not properly understood by Rungiah.

Annotations by Wight: Gratioleae, Scrophularineae, 859, 18, Turn, 127, Dopatrium lobelioides (Benth.) (pencil, recto); 1, 2, 3, 4, 5 (pencil, verso)

Published as plate 859 of the *Icones* (1844–5), lithographed by Dumphy.

RBGE W60 V + R (SERIES C)

100. Limnophila aquatica *(Roxburgh) Alston*

SCROPHULARIACEAE

Bodycolour heightened with gum arabic, and ink, over traces of pencil, 160 × 198mm. By Rungiah, *c*.1830.

Emergent, aquatic annual, which can reach a height of 60 cm, occurring in the plains of India from Bengal southwards, and in Sri Lanka. The leaves on the upper part of the stem, borne above the water, are undivided, but the submerged leaves, shown here in two uncoloured whorls, are very finely divided – such heterophylly is a feature of many water plants. This species grades into *L. indica*, a glabrous plant with smaller, white flowers. Saldhana & Nicolson for the Hassan district of Karnataka treated the two as conspecific but noted that the form shown here tended to grow in more or less permanent pools, though Wight recorded it from rice fields. Wight also noted that the purple flowers are fragrant. The plant was first described (in the genus *Cyrilla*) by Roxburgh in his *Plants of the Coast of Coromandel*.

Telugu annotations: (tharunagiri malai yiri).

Annotations by Wight: Gratioleae, Scrofularineae, Limnophilla racimosa (Benth) (pencil, recto). Annotations by Arnott: 861, Limnophila [gratissima (deleted)] racemosa Benth W.C. n. 2181 (ink, recto). Other annotations: Neernetty Pausey.

Published as plate 861 of the *Icones* (1844–5), lithographed by Dumphy.

RBGE W61 R (SERIES C)

101. Leucas vestita *Bentham*

LABIATAE

Tam: thumbai

Bodycolour heightened with gum arabic, and ink, over traces of pencil, 157 × 197mm. By Rungiah, *c*.1830.

Watermark: C WILMOT 1819.

A stout herb to 1.5 metres tall, occurring in the southern Western Ghats. Father Matthew recorded it as common in the Palni Hills between 1500 and 2400 metres, occurring at the edges of shola forests. It was first described by Bentham in his monograph of the genera and species of the Labiatae of the EIC herbarium that he undertook for Wallich, published in *Plantae Asiaticae Rariores*. The epithet refers to the brownish hairs that cover the vegetative parts of the plant and the upper lip of the corolla. The original material included specimens from Silhet (no longer regarded as belonging to this species) and specimens collected by Wight probably in the Palni Hills. Bentham was one of Wallich's greatest helpers in his vast undertaking of curating, naming, and cataloguing the EIC herbarium. After Wallich had to return to India in 1832 Bentham continued work on the lithographed catalogue, and again helped with the distribution of the final specimens and last parts of the catalogue after Wallich retired to England in 1846.

Telugu annotations: (male peru thumbai).

Annotations by Wight: 338 (pencil, recto). Annotations by Arnott: Leucas vestita Spr., WC. n. (ink, recto).

Published as plate 338 of the *Icones* (1840), lithographed by Dumphy.

RBGE W31 R (SERIES C)

102. Leucas biflora *(Vahl) R. Brown*

LABIATAE

Bodycolour heightened with gum arabic, and ink, over traces of pencil,
156 × 197mm. By Rungiah, *c.*1830.

An annual or short-lived perennial herb growing in dry forest in the
foothills of s India and Sri Lanka up to an altitude of 1300 metres
(though there is confusion between this and the N Indian species *L.
procumbens*). It was first described by Paul Hermann and Johannes
Burman in their pre-Linnean works on Ceylon and given a binomial
(in the genus *Phlomis*) by Linnaeus's pupil Martin Vahl; it was
transferred to the genus *Leucas* by Robert Brown in 1810 in his
Prodromus Florae Novae Hollandiae, a work that largely established
the use of the Jussieuan system of natural classification in Britain.
Wight noted that the plant was variable in habit and this form was
chosen to suit the size of the plate! However, it can often grow to
more than a metre 'lying along the ground, but sometimes climbing
… among bushes'.

Telugu annotations: (venjanam munjai).

Annotations by Wight: 25, 866, Leucas biflora (pencil, recto); Stachydeae,
Labiatae, Leucas biflora (R. Br.), 1, 2, 3, 4 (ink, recto). Annotations by Arnott:
Leucas biflora W.C. n. 2155 (ink, recto). Other annotations: Vellay-Toomlay
(pencil, recto).

Published as plate 866 of the *Icones* (1844–5), lithographed by Dumphy.

103. Clerodendrum serratum *(Linnaeus) Moon*

VERBENACEAE

Tam: angarvalli; Tel: bhaarangi, gantubaarangi

Bodycolour heightened with gum arabic, and ink, over traces of pencil, 238 × 305mm. By Rungiah, *c.*1830.

A shrub that can reach three metres in height, occurring throughout India and Sri Lanka, eastwards into Indo-China and China, and Indonesia. Wight collected it at Courtallum and in the Nilgiri and Palni Hills, where it occurs up to an altitude of 1800 metres. The roots and leaves have medicinal properties and the root was recorded by Sir George Watt in 1889 as being used to cause fermentation in the manufacture of rice beer. As can be seen from this drawing the flower is adapted for insect pollination, with the dark blue lip acting as a landing platform, and the stamens so positioned as to deposit pollen on the back of the visiting insect.

RBGE W389 R (SERIES D)

104. Clerodendrum inerme (*Linnaeus*)

Gaertner

VERBENACEAE

Tam: pinaarichanganguppi, pinchil, sangam; Tel: pisingi

Bodycolour heightened with gum arabic, and ink, over traces of pencil, 177 × 258mm. By Rungiah, *c.*1825.

A straggling shrub, widespread on saline soils from India through S E Asia to S China, Australia and the Pacific. However, it has been widely introduced, both as a garden plant and to stabilise coastal soils, for example in the West Indies, Zaire and Brazil. This drawing was not published by Wight, but was sent to Hooker (the name is in his hand), along with a sheet of notes, bearing a description, and information on habitat and uses. This records that 'the expressed juice of the leaves is mixed with butter milk & drank to cause vomiting wh. the natives say it does as effectively as Ipecacuana'. Wight also noted that the plant was 'much employed as an edging to garden walks for which its shining dark green foliage peculiarly adapts it'.

Annotations by W.J. Hooker: Clerodendron inerme Spr. (ink, recto). Other annotations: No. 80 (pencil, verso).

RBGE W435 R (SERIES B)

105. Acanthus ilicifolius *Linnaeus*

ACANTHACEAE

Tam: attumulli, kaludaimulli, nier mulli; Tel: alchi

Bodycolour heightened with gum arabic, and ink, over traces of pencil, 174 × 252mm. By Rungiah, *c.*1830.

A shrub that can reach a height of 2.5 metres. It is widespread in S and S E Asia, from India to China and Australia, where it grows in brackish habitats such as mangrove swamps. In Indonesia the plant has been used as a desiccant, placed in rice sacks to keep them dry, and in Malaysia it is used medicinally. The drawing was probably made at Negapatam, where Wight collected the plant in saltmarshes. Wight placed this species in the genus *Dilivaria*, a name based by Jussieu on a vernacular name recorded in the Philippines by J.G. Kamel, but this is no longer recognised as distinct from the genus *Acanthus*. The specific epithet given by Linnaeus refers to the resemblance of the leaves to those of the European holly (*Ilex aquifolium*).

Telugu annotations: (uppukari [= salt water] neerum [= chili powder]).

Annotations by Wight: Acantheae, Acanthaceae, 459, Nier moollie Tam (pencil, recto); No. 41 (pencil, verso). Annotations by W.J. Hooker: Acanthus ilicifolius (pencil, recto). Annotations by Arnott: Dilivaria ilicifolia W[ight's] C[atalogue] 1976 (pencil, recto).

Published as plate 459 of the *Icones* (1841), lithographed by Dumphy.

RBGE W150.1 R (SERIES A)

Acanthus ilicifolius Acanthaceae
Acanthea

459

Dilivaria ilicifolia
wb. 1976
Nier moolli Jam

105

106 & 107. Crossandra infundibuliformis *(Linnaeus) Nees*

ACANTHACEAE

Tam: kanagaambaram, pavalakkurinji, sembayiravuppundu, munjabayeravappundu; Tel: kanakaambramu.

Bodycolour heightened with gum arabic, and ink, over traces of pencil; 148 × 201mm (151.1), 149 × 202mm (152.1). By Rungiah, *c*.1830.

Watermark (151.1): J[ones] & M[ather] 1823.

This small shrub, which can reach a height of about one metre, is native to Africa, India and Sri Lanka, and in South India is also commonly cultivated in gardens and near temples. The flowers are often used in garlands for women's hair and the plant is allegedly an aphrodisiac. While on leave in Britain, Wight sent his specimens of the family Acanthaceae to Christian Nees von Esenbeck in Breslau. In 1832 Nees described *Crossandra axillaris*,

based on Wight specimens, very possibly the ones from which this drawing was made. However, *C. axillaris* is no longer regarded as being distinct from *C. infundibuliformis* (unless as a variety). It was Nees who transferred this Linnaean species to the genus *Crossandra*, described by Richard Salisbury and named for its fringed anthers. The drawings were probably made while Wight was stationed at Negapatam, and while Rungiah's floral details do not show the anthers, they do show the characteristic seeds, covered with fringed scales, which become sticky when wet.

Telugu annotations: (151.1: shembhairavapudi; 152.1: manjibhairavapondu).

Annotations by Wight (151.1): C. infundibuliformis (pencil, recto). Annotations by Arnott: Crossandra axillaris W[ight's] C[atalogue] 1978 (pencil, recto).

Annotations by Arnott (152.1): Cross. infundibuliformis β N[ees ab] E[senbeck] W[ight's] C[atalogue] 1977b (pencil, recto).

Published as plates 460 and 461 of the *Icones* (1841), lithographed by Dumphy.

RBGE W151.1 R & 152.1 R (SERIES C)

Crossandra afillani
wG. 1978

108. Lepidagathis pungens *Nees*

ACANTHACEAE

Bodycolour heightened with gum arabic, and ink, over traces of pencil, 158 × 195mm. By Rungiah, *c.*1830.

A rigid, branched, low-growing shrub, endemic to the plains of the extreme SE of India. It had first been collected by the Tranquebar missionaries, and Wight collected it at Cunewady, Palamcottah, Madurai and Cape Comorin. It was one of many genera in the family described by the German botanist C.G. Nees von Esenbeck, the Greek name (literally 'scaly ball of thread') referring to the shape of the inflorescence buds. In addition to Acanthaceae Nees also undertook extensive work on Wallich's and Wight's plants of the families Lauraceae, Solanaceae, Cyperaceae and Gramineae.

Telugu annotations: (kangi nandi sherandu; parelarinde).

Annotations by Arnott: Lepidagathis pungens WC. 1973 (pencil, recto).

Published as plate 456 of the *Icones* (1841), lithographed by Dumphy.

RBGE WI48.1 R (SERIES C)

109. Andrographis echioides *(Linnaeus) Nees*

ACANTHACEAE

Bodycolour heightened with gum arabic, and ink, over traces of pencil, 159 × 247mm. By Rungiah, *c.*1830.

An erect, annual herb that can grow to a height of 45 cm. It is widely distributed in the drier parts of India from the Punjab southwards, and also in Sri Lanka and Burma. It was first described (in the genus *Justicia*) by Linnaeus, based on various earlier descriptions and illustrations from Ceylon and Malabar; the epithet refers to a superficial resemblance of the inflorescence to that of the common European viper's bugloss (*Echium vulgare*). Nees in his monograph of Acanthaceae in Wallich's *Plantae Asiaticae Rariores* referred the plant to his new genus *Andrographis*; the name suggests a resemblance of the anthers to writing or letters, which Wallich interpreted as referring to the bearded anther bases shown here in the half-flower at bottom right.

Annotations by Wight: Andrographideae, Acanthaceae, 467, Andrographis echioides (Nees) (pencil, recto). Annotations by Arnott: Andrographis echioides WC 2026 (pencil, recto). Other annotations: [Tamil script] Chovaramthanghy Tam. (pencil, verso).

Published as plate 467 of the *Icones* (1841), lithographed by Dumphy.

RBGE WI57.1 R (SERIES A)

110. Lysimachia leschenaultii *Duby*

PRIMULACEAE

Tam: thoo do poo chady (Wight)

Bodycolour heightened with gum arabic, and ink, over traces of pencil, 257 × 351mm. By Rungiah, *c.*1830.

An erect, perennial herb restricted to the Nilgiri and Palni Hills, where it may be locally abundant in marshy meadows mainly between 2000 and 2300 metres. The species was described, based on specimens collected in the Nilgiris by Leschenault de la Tour, by Jean Duby, a pastor in Geneva who wrote the account of Primulaceae for Candolle's *Prodromus*. In the *Illustrations* Wight noted that it had been 'extensively introduced into gardens on the Neilgherries'. The Greek generic name was taken by Linnaeus from Dioscorides, and probably refers to the medicinal property by which the yellow-flowered European members of the genus are still known: literally 'loose-strife'; however, a more fanciful derivation from Lysimachus would be appropriate in this case as, before becoming a King of Thrace and northern Asia Minor in 306 BC, he had been a distinguished member of Alexander the Great's bodyguard on his Persian and Indian expedition. This drawing was not published by Wight (it is not the original of plate 1204 of the *Icones*).

Telugu annotations: (thavutu shedi).

RBGE W386 R (SERIES D)

111. Digera muricata *(Linnaeus) Martius*

AMARANTHACEAE

Tam: thoyyakeerai; Tel: chanchalikoora.

Bodycolour heightened with gum arabic, and ink, over traces of pencil, 159 × 197mm. By Rungiah, *c.*1830.

An annual herb to 50 cm tall, widespread from tropical Africa and Madagascar eastwards through Arabia and India to Malaysia and Indonesia. In s India it occurs in dry cultivated and waste places in the lowlands and foothills, flowering mainly from November to January. Wight recorded that 'the leaves and tender tops are used by the Natives in their curries'. The flowers are borne in threes, a fertile central one subtended by two sterile ones each consisting of a bracteole and a curious serrated scale. These are correctly shown in the bottom row of analyses, but in the upper one Rungiah incorrectly shows the two sterile flowers as fused (doubtless due to the poor microscope or lens he had at this stage). The genus was described by Linnaeus's pupil Pehr Forsskål from Yemen, the name being derived from an Arabic name for the plant – 'Didjar'. Forsskål took part in the Danish expedition to Egypt and Arabia (1761–3), and Carsten Niebuhr edited his important *Flora Aegptiaco-Arabica* after his premature death on the expedition at the age of 31.

Telugu annotations: (thirumonampali [= marriage] jebbukaswaram; sunnambu [= lime] kire [= green vegetable] thuil).

RBGE W86 R (SERIES C)

112. Aerva javanica *(N.L. Burman) Schultes*

AMARANTHACEAE

Tam: perumbulai; Tel: peddapindikonda, magabeera

Bodycolour and ink over traces of pencil, 159 × 197mm. By Rungiah, *c.*1830.

A perennial herb, often woody at the base, widespread in drier parts of the tropics and subtropics of the Old World, and introduced to Australia and elsewhere. This species is dioecious and, curiously, only the female form, as shown here, occurs in Tamil Nadu. Wight recorded it as 'an exceedingly common and troublesome weed'. It was first described and illustrated by N.L. Burman in *Flora Indica* in 1768, based on a plate and description in Plukenet, and on plants raised (presumably in the Amsterdam Botanic Garden) from seeds from Java. The inadequacy of illustrations in the works of Burman and Plukenet was one of the factors that inspired Wight's efforts to produce his own great illustrated works reproducing the drawings of Rungiah and Govindoo.

Telugu annotations: (velleakanupula).

RBGE W87 R (SERIES C)

113. Suaeda monoica *Forsskål ex J.F. Gmelin*

CHENOPODIACEAE

Tam: karuvumari, umarinandi; Tel: koyyalamoora, oligura dubbu

Bodycolour heightened with gum arabic, and ink, over traces of pencil, 149 × 202mm. By Rungiah, *c*.1830.

Like many members of the family Chenopodiaceae this plant grows on saline soils, such as salt marshes and at the edges of tidal lagoons. It is a large woody shrub that can reach a height of three metres and is widespread from Africa eastwards to India and Sri Lanka. Wight first collected it in the Northern Circars, and later at Tuticoreen. The leaves are edible, and like other members of the family yield soda when burnt (though of lower quality than the ash of *Salsola*). It was first described from specimens collected by Pehr Forsskål in Yemen, in Gmelin's edition (the 13th) of Linnaeus's *Systema Naturae*. This drawing was not published by Wight, and is one of the series probably prepared for Hooker, accompanied by a sheet with notes by Wight including a long description of the plant and details of its habitat.

Tamil annotation: (pevu mini).

Annotation by Wight: Chenopodium sp nov? (pencil, recto).

RBGE W408 R (SERIES B)

114. Persicaria glabra *(Willdenow) M. Gomez*

POLYGONACEAE

Tam: atalari; Tel: burada gogu

Bodycolour heightened with gum arabic, and ink, over traces of pencil, 159 × 198mm. By Rungiah, *c*.1830.

A herb that can reach two metres in height, widespread in the Old World tropics. In s India it occurs in moist places, such as stream and river banks, up to an altitude of 1500 metres. It was first described by C.L. Willdenow, director of the Berlin botanic garden, in the fourth edition of Linnaeus's *Species Plantarum*, the edition used by Roxburgh and Wight. In this important work Willdenow based many new species on specimens collected by the Tranquebar missionaries, including this one which was first collected by J.G. Klein in 1795, who recorded that the plant's Tamil name was 'mudalei pundu'. The leaves and young shoots are edible. This drawing was not published by Wight, and is one of those probably prepared for Hooker; associated with it is a sheet of notes in Wight's hand with a long plant description and the habitat is given as 'moist soil near the banks of rivers & water channels', where it flowers 'the greater part of the year'.

Telugu annotation: (chegalyeri [= small canal]; modalarihadu).

Annotation by Wight: Polygonum glabrum? Other annotation: Aulary-Poondoo (pencil, recto).

RBGE W410 R (SERIES B)

115. Begonia malabarica *Lamarck*

BEGONIACEAE

Bodycolour heightened with gum arabic, and ink, over traces of pencil,
251 × 349mm. By Rungiah, *c.*1830.

A large succulent herb that can reach a height of three metres, and
which flowers from January to May in damp forests in the southern
part of the Western Ghats. In the Palni Hills it ascends to an altitude
of 2100 metres. The genus is monoecious, bearing separate male
and female flowers on the same plant: the male flower is shown in
the central of the three floral details bottom right, the female to its
left, and a cross section of the fruit to its right – showing the ovules
attached to three placentas. Although many begonias are grown for
their ornamental foliage and flowers, the ungainly habit of this
species would tend to preclude such a use.

RBGE W384 R (SERIES D)

116. Phoebe wightii *Meisner*

LAURACEAE

Aecidium periphericum *Nees*

UREDINALES (RUST FUNGI)

Bodycolour heightened with gum arabic, and ink, over traces of pencil, 160 × 197mm. By Rungiah, *c.*1830.

This drawing is of exceptional scientific, if not aesthetic, interest. Wight's pre-1831 collections of the laurel family were among those he sent for study by Nees von Esenbeck in Breslau. Nees was the expert on the family and wrote an account of it for Wallich's *Plantae Asiaticae Rariores* in 1832, and a monograph in 1836, which both included new species based on Wight's collections. This drawing is mentioned in the monograph, and represents type material not only of the flowering plant host, which Nees described as *Phoebe paniculata* var. *minor*, but also of the parasitic fungus visible on the underside of its leaves. The fungus is in its cup ('aecial') stage, one of five phases of the life cycle of a rust, which Nees described, based on this drawing, as *Aecidium periphericum*. This name has been overlooked by mycologists. No locality is given on the related herbarium specimen, but it is likely to have been collected in either the Nilgiri or Palni Hills.

Annotations by Arnott: Return (pencil, recto: probably addressed to Nees); Folia subtus fungum gerunt, Ocotea W[ight's] C[atalogue] 2236 = 2/5 (ink, recto).

RBGE W72 R (SERIES C)

117. Casearia tomentosa *Roxburgh*

FLACOURTIACEAE

Tam: kadichai; Tel: chilaka duddi

Bodycolour heightened with gum arabic, and ink, over traces of pencil, 160 × 197mm. By Rungiah, *c.*1830.

In drier, open areas, this species, which is widespread in India and Sri Lanka, forms a small tree or bush, but in wet forest it can grow into a tree eight metres high. Although the habit drawing does not show the characteristic pubescence of this species, this is of the sort that Rungiah found impossible to depict in paint, and confirmation of the identification is found in the tiny hairs shown on the microscopic floral details (pedicel apex and tepal margins). Wight (who knew the plant as *Casearia elliptica*) recorded it as 'not uncommon in Southern India in jungles near the coast' and 'frequent among the bushes usually found about old "Bowries" near pagodas', presumably meaning what are now called Sacred Groves. According to the forester Dietrich Brandis (quoted by Sir George Watt) the pounded fruit may be used to poison fish.

Telugu annotations: (selavatam; peralingi).

Annotations by ?H.F.C. Cleghorn: not figured anywhere ?, Saymydaceae, Casearia glomerata Roxb. (pencil, recto). Other annotation: Pare-Anlingey (pencil, recto).

RBGE W70 R (SERIES C)

118. Aristolochia indica *Linnaeus*

ARISTOLOCHIACEAE

Tam: adagam, isuraver, karudakkodi, peraumarundu; Tel: nella eeshvari

Bodycolour heightened with gum arabic, and ink, over traces of pencil, 175 × 256mm. By Rungiah, *c*.1825.

An herbaceous twiner that may reach six metres, widespread from Nepal and Bengal south through India to Sri Lanka, occurring 'in almost every kind of soil & situation' in the plains and foothills, up to 650 metres. The curious shape of the flower (which acts as a trap for insect pollinators) has given rise to the use of the plant as an antidote to snake bite, on the principle of the 'doctrine of signatures'. For this purpose Wight recorded that the root was 'powdered, mixed with a little water & made into a bolus [large pill] with a few grains of black pepper and as soon as possible swallowed, another portion without pepper being at the same time applied to the wound'. Wight also noted a more credible use of its tonic qualities 'in cases of indigestion'. The fresh leaves have been used in treating rheumatism and the bitter root and stems, which have stimulant and tonic properties, for fever and diarrhoea. This drawing was not published by Wight, and is one of those sent to Hooker from Negapatam, accompanied by two sheets bearing descriptions of the plant, and notes on its habitat and uses.

Annotations by ?Wight: Parroomaroondoo (pencil, recto). Annotations by others: Aristolchia indica (pencil, recto)

RBGE W437 R (SERIES A/B)

119. Euphorbia corrigioloides *Boissier*

EUPHORBIACEAE

Tel: erra paala alumu

Bodycolour heightened with gum arabic over traces of pencil, 178 × 254mm.
By Rungiah, *c.*1830.

This drawing was not published by Wight, and is one of those sent to
Hooker from Negapatam, accompanied by a description and notes
on habitat ('usually on the banks which are raised in the fields to
retain the water with which they are irrigated'). Wight also referred
to the difficulty of identifying this plant from the only works he had,
by Sprengel and Persoon, and left it to Hooker to decide if it was a
new species. In fact it would have been, had Hooker only realised, as
it was not described until 1860 by the Swiss botanist Edmond
Boissier based on a collection made by Benjamin Heyne. The
epithet refers to a resemblance to the European strapwort *Corrigiola
litoralis* (Caryophyllaceae). The plant is a procumbent perennial
herb growing from a tap root, and occurs in the plains of s India up
to 500 metres, from the Northern Circars and Bellary southwards.
In the genus *Euphorbia* what appears to be a single flower is in fact an
inflorescence ('cyathium') of monoecious flowers, the reduced male
ones, each consisting of a single stamen, arranged on a cup around a
single central female one. Around the edge of the cup is a series of
glands (in this case four in number), and the petal like-structures are
appendages to the glands.

Annotations: [Tamil script] Vail ammampatcharici Tam, No. 91.

RBGE W439 R (SERIES A/B)

Euphorbia

130

120. Euphorbia rosea *Retzius*

EUPHORBIACEAE

Bodycolour heightened with gum arabic over traces of pencil, 174 × 256mm.
By Rungiah, *c.*1830.

A perennial herb growing from a woody taproot, occurring from
Afghanistan southwards through the Indian Peninsula to Sri
Lanka. In s India it occurs on poor soils including ccastal sands,
and in scrub jungles. It was described by the Swedish botanist
Anders Retzius from specimens collected by J.G. König,
doubtless found near Tranquebar. This species differs from *E.
corrigioloides* (Plate 119) in having the appendages of two of the
glands greatly enlarged. This is one of the series of drawings sent
to Hooker with accompanying descriptions, but this was
published neither by Hooker nor Wight.

RBGE W438 R (SERIES A/B)

121. Sauropus bacciformis *(Linnaeus) Airy Shaw*

EUPHORBIACEAE

Tam: cottagachy, cattachy poondoo (Wight)

Bodycolour heightened with gum arabic over traces of pencil, 177 × 255mm.
By Rungiah, *c.*1830.

An annual or biennial herb growing from a taproot, widespread
from India and Sri Lanka eastwards to Malaya, China, the
Philippines and Indonesia. In s India it occurs on the plains up
to an altitude of 500 metres, growing on fallow land, bunds of
paddy fields and in sandy, saline areas near the sea. This was one
of the species sent back to his old teacher Linnaeus by J.G. König
from Tranquebar, and described in Linnaeus's *Mantissa
Plantarum* of 1767. The flowers are unisexual and both male and
female are clearly seen here – both attached to the plant and in
the floral details, bottom right. The ovary develops into a
somewhat berry-like capsule to which the epithet refers. This
drawing was not published by Wight, and is one of those sent to
Hooker from Negapatam, with a plant description and notes on
habitat ('common … in almost all soils & in flower at all
seasons').

Annotations by Arnott: Agyneia phyllanthoides, receptacles separate, capsule
open, seed (pencil, recto). Other annotations: [Tamil script] Colagachy Tam,
No. 113,

RBGE W440 R (SERIES A/B)

122. Pellionia heyneanum *Weddell*

URTICACEAE

Tam: cul ottoo (Wight)

Bodycolour heightened with gum arabic, and ink, over traces of pencil, 252 × 349mm. By Rungiah, *c.*1830.

Watermark: [RUSE & T]URNERS [182]4.

A perennial herb, with creeping woody stems and asymmetric leaves, occurring in very wet places in evergreen forest in the southern Western Ghats and Sri Lanka at altitudes of 450 to 1830 metres. This, one of the few drawings of Rungiah annotated with a locality in Telugu, was made from a Courtallum specimen. It is not surprising that Arnott could not identify this plant since, although it was named in the EIC herbarium as *Procris heyneana*, it was not

formally described until 1856, when Hugh Algernon Weddell placed it in the genus *Pellionia*, in his monograph of Urticaceae. *Pellionia*, described by Gaudichaud-Beaupré, commemorates the naval officer Alphonse Pellion who accompanied Freycinet on his second circumnavigation of 1817–20. Weddell was from 1850–7 'aide-naturalist' at the Muséum d'Histoire Naturelle in Paris and, while preparing the monograph, in September 1854 visited Wight at Grazeley to look at his specimens of Urticaceae, including this species and possibly even this drawing. The plant is monoecious, the male flowers are borne in branched cymes (as seen upper centre), the female in the smaller, more contracted ones below.

Telugu annotations: (Kuttalam; shugale yuroshum; shailan gari kodi [= creeper]).

Annotations by Arnott: Procris? Urticeae.

RBGE W393 R (SERIES ?D)

123. Aponogeton natans

(Linnaeus) Engler & K. Krause

APONOGETONACEAE

Tam: kotti kizhangu; Tel: namma dumpa

Bodycolour heightened with gum arabic over traces of pencil, 176 × 256mm. By Rungiah, *c.*1830.

A submerged aquatic, growing from a perennial tuber (embedded in the substrate), with leaves floating on the water surface and an emergent spike of flowers. It occurs throughout the plains of India from Uttar Pradesh southwards. Wight noted that the leaves were used as 'greens & made into curry'. This drawing was not published by Wight, but is one of those sent to Hooker from Negapatam. With it are no fewer than three manuscript sheets with plant descriptions and notes on habitat and uses, showing the care Wight took before submitting such work to the great Hooker. Wight noted that the tubers were eaten by the natives though 'not much relished at least in the Tanjore country', but a reminiscence of Wight's boyhood is to be found in the statement that 'to my pallet it was disagreeable tho' it put me somewhat in mind of the taste of the common earth nut (*Bunium*) [now = *Conopodium majus*] which I [along with every other Scottish schoolboy of the time] formerly thought very good eating'. Arnott thought this plant belonged to subfamily Saureae of the dicot pepper family (Piperaceae) but observed that it had 'floated for some time between the Dicotyledones and Monocotyledones'. It is now known to be a monocot.

Annotations: No. 104 [+ Tamil script] (pencil, verso).

RBGE W442 R (SERIES A/B)

124 A & B. Eria braccata *(Lindley) Lindley*

ORCHIDACEAE

Bodycolour and pencil, 226 × 283mm (294.1); 100 × 125mm (294.2). By Govindoo, *c.*1850.

This small tree-dwelling ('epiphytic') orchid was first described (in the genus *Dendrobium*) by John Lindley, based on a drawing and immature specimens collected by James Macrae while Superintendent of the Ceylon botanic gardens. The unusual epithet (meaning 'wearing trousers') probably refers to the bract sheathing the base of the singly-borne flower, which probably appeared more prominent on the specimens in bud that Lindley had to hand. The plant is also found in the Western Ghats as far north as Maharashtra and is said to be common in the Nilgiris between altitudes of 1900 and 2100 metres. It was from Pycarrah in the Nilgiris that Wight described *Eria reticosa*, of which this drawing forms part of the original material, but which is not now regarded as distinct from *E. braccata*. Wight's epithet refers to the net-like covering around the pseudobulb, formed from a decayed leaf sheath – a feature, rather surprisingly, not noted by Lindley.

Annotations by Wight: 1637, Eria, E. reticosa R.W. Pycarah June on rocks & branches of trees 42 (pencil, recto); Malaxideae Orchideae 1637, Eria reticosa (RW) (ink, recto).

Published as plate 1637 of the *Icones* (1851), lithographed by Dumphy.

RBGE W294.1 & 2 R (SERIES E)

125 A & B. Vanda testacea *(Lindley) H.G. Reichenbach*

ORCHIDACEAE

Bodycolour over traces of pencil, 224 × 249mm (307.1); 108 × 124mm (307.2). By Govindoo, *c.*1850.

An epiphytic species first described by Lindley from Ceylon, and occurring in hilly parts of India, Burma, China and Thailand, ascending to 2000 metres in the Himalaya. The epithet refers to the flower colour, Lindley defining '*testaceus*' as yellowish-brown, 'like that of unglazed earthenware'. Wight's epithet '*parviflora*' that is noted on the drawing was not validly published, as although it appears on the published plate in the *Icones*, it was corrected in the simultaneously issued text.

Annotations by Wight: 120, Vanda parviflora (pencil, recto); Vandeae, Orchideae, 1669, Vanda parviflora (RW) (ink, recto).

Published as plate 1669 of the *Icones* (1851), lithographed by Dumphy.

126. Seidenfadeniella rosea *(Wight) Sathish Kumar*

ORCHIDACEAE

Bodycolour heightened with gum arabic over traces of pencil, 203 × 320mm. By Govindoo, *c*.1850.

Watermark: [crowned rampant lion in cartouche].

When he described this species from the Nilgiri Hills in 1851 Wight was not happy with the generic placement, and only in 1994 was it accommodated in a new genus named to commemorate the Danish orchidologist Gunnar Seidenfaden. The plant is a pendulous epiphyte restricted to the Nilgiri Hills and the adjacent Palghat and Wynad districts, possibly extending northwards into Coorg. It occurs between 1500 and 2300 metres, and flowers from February to July.

On the drawing is a note written by Wight instructing the lithographer how to compose the plate. The original version of the section with the inflorescences and floral analyses evidently did not satisfy Wight, and Govindoo had to redraw it on a separate piece of paper. This he attached to the sheet, signing his name in Telugu script across the join, presumably to authenticate the change. The signature is upside down with respect to the plant and Govindoo must have taken the stem to be negatively geotropic.

Telugu annotations: (Govindoo).

Annotations by Wight: Vandeae Orchideae 1685 Sarcanthus roseus (RW) (ink, recto); Shorten this part of the stem by leaving out all between the 2 lines but put a little gap with a × between the ends & cut off part of the other root (pencil, recto).

Published as plate 1685 of the *Icones* (1851), lithographed by Dumphy.

RBGE W321 R (SERIES E)

127. Spiranthes sinensis *(Persoon) Ames*

ORCHIDACEAE

Bodycolour heightened with gum arabic and pencil, 202 × 259mm. By Govindoo, *c*.1845.

Watermark: C WILMOT 1840.

One of the commonest ground-dwelling ('terrestrial') orchids of the hilly parts of S E Asia. As suggested by the specific name it was first described from China, by the Dutch South African botanist Christiaan Persoon. The generic name refers to the characteristically spirally twisted spike seen also in the British 'ladies tresses'. Wight recorded this plant as abundant in pastures in the Nilgiri Hills, where it flowers from June to October.

This sheet is a fascinating collage, made up by Wight of drawings and floral details originally made by Govindoo on separate sheets, but amalgamated when Wight realised that they all belonged to a single variable species. That on the left was the form described by the London-based orchidologist John Lindley as *Spiranthes wightiana*, the other two were regarded as two further distinct species by the French botanist Achille Richard.

Annotations by Wight: Neotteae Orchideae 1724, Spiranthes australis (Lind[ley] (ink, recto).

Published as plate 1724 of the *Icones* (1851), lithographed by Dumphy.

RBGE W334 R (SERIES E)

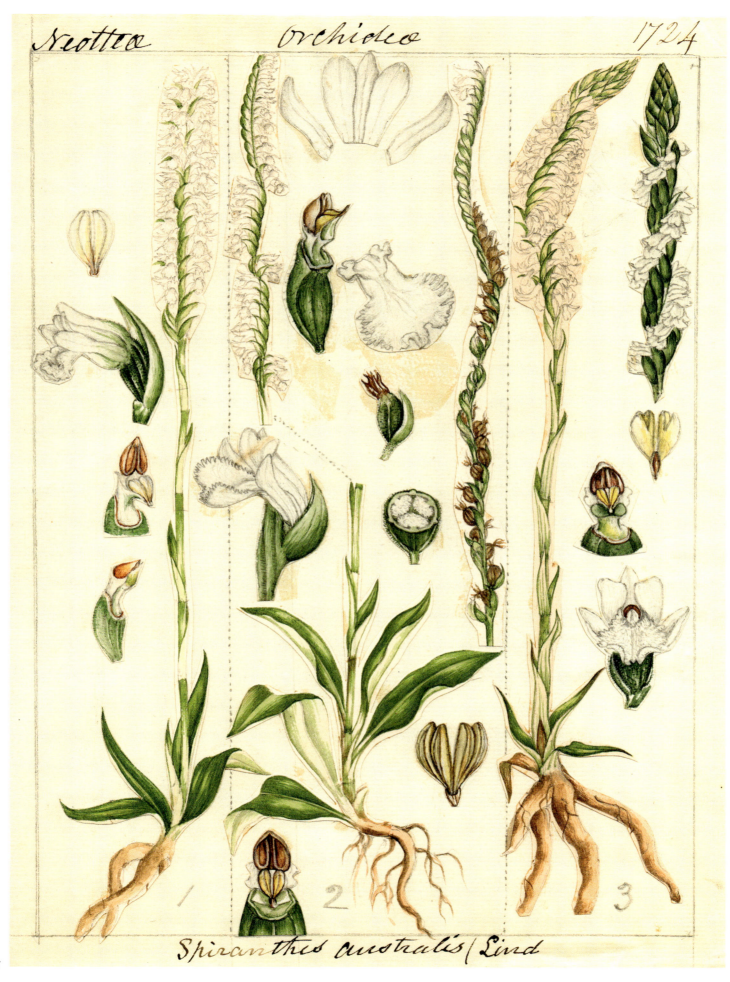

Spiranthes australis/ Lind

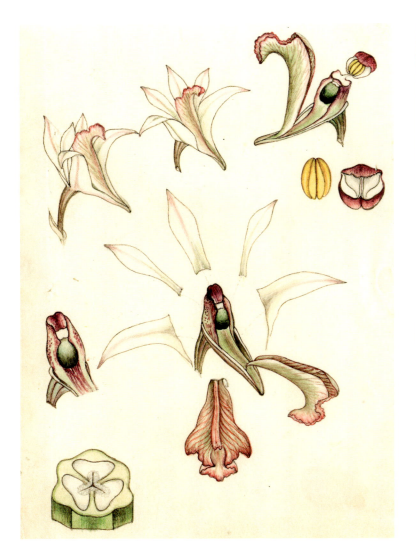

128 A & B. Dendrobium microbulbon

A. Richard

ORCHIDACEAE

Bodycolour heightened with gum arabic over traces of pencil, 205 × 276mm (299.1), 115 × 165mm (299.2). By Govindoo, *c*.1850.

Wight described this plant as *Dendrobium humile* from the Iyamally Hills near Coimbatore, and this drawing is part of the original material. It is no longer recognised as distinct from *D. microbulbon*, an epiphytic species occurring in the Western Ghats from North Kanara southwards to the Anamalai Hills in Tamil Nadu. *D. microbulbon* was described in 1841 by the Parisian botanist Achille Richard, based on specimens collected near Ootacamund by George Samuel Perrottet. Perrottet was a French botanist who worked at Pondicherry and made early collections in the Nilgiri Hills. This is another collaged drawing, on which Wight has written a note instructing the lithographer how to compose the plate for the *Icones*.

Annotations by Wight: Malaxideae Orchideae 1643, Dendrobium humile (RW) (ink, recto); bring the large figure a little down to give the small one more room (pencil, recto).

Published as plate 1643 of the *Icones* (1851), lithographed by Dumphy.

RBGE W299.1 & 2 R (SERIES E)

129 A & B. Bulbophyllum fimbriatum

(Lindley) H.G. Reichenbach

ORCHIDACEAE

Watercolour heightened with gum arabic over traces of pencil, 250 × 219mm (306.1), 111 × 122mm (306.2). By Govindoo, *c*.1850.

This orchid was discovered by the Jerdons in Coorg, flowering in January, and, from the form of the inflorescence, Mrs Jerdon dubbed it the 'umbrella orchis'. It is an epiphytic species, which occurs in the Western Ghats from Maharashtra southwards to Kerala, and was first described by John Lindley in 1839 from specimens sent to London from Bombay. In this and related species formerly placed in the genus *Cirrhopetalum*, what at first sight appears to be the lip (in this case yellow), is actually composed of the two lateral sepals that are fused and bent backwards under the lip. The dorsal sepal is the boat-shaped pink structure with marginal hairs; the lateral petals are also fringed with hairs and the lip is the small pink structure lacking marginal hairs.

Wight specifically noted that this was drawn from herbarium specimens, and it is interesting that both Rungiah and Govindoo developed this skill, normally associated with the herbarium-based tradition of Western botanical art.

Annotations by Wight: Malaxideae Orchideae 1655, Cirrhopetalum fimbriatum (RW (ink, recto).

Published as plate 1655 of the *Icones* (1851), lithographed by Dumphy.

RBGE W306.1 & 2 R (SERIES E)

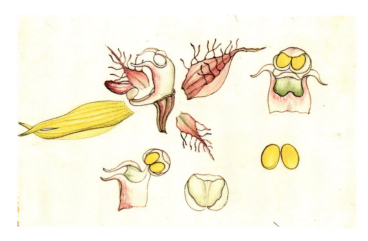

130 A & B. Eulophia spectabilis *(Dennstedt) Suresh*

ORCHIDACEAE

Watercolour heightened with gum arabic and pencil, 199 × 321mm (429.1), 102 × 125mm (429.2). By Govindoo, *c*.1845.

Watermark: [Britannia in cartouche].

A spectacular terrestrial species with flowering spikes that can reach one metre in height, and which are produced before the leaves appear. Wight described this as a new species, *Cyrtopera fusca*, from 'rocky clefts among turf in rich vegetable soil by the Kartairy Falls near Kaitie' in the Nilgiri Hills, where it flowered in May and June.

However, it is now considered to belong to a species widespread in SE Asia first described and illustrated in 1692 in van Rheede's *Hortus Malabaricus*. Rheede reported that its roots and leaves, mixed with turmeric, could be made into an ointment applied for the treatment of 'gout in the head'. This drawing is in Govindoo's earlier style, similar to that of Rungiah.

Annotations by Wight: Vandeae Orchideae 1690, Cyrtopera fusca (RW) (ink, recto 429.1).

Published as plate 1690 of the *Icones* (1851), lithographed by Dumphy.

RBGE W429.1 & 2 R (SERIES E)

Vandea Orchdea

1690 1684

cyrtopera fusca (OW.)

131 A & B. Dendrobium nutans *Lindley*

ORCHIDACEAE

Bodycolour heightened with gum arabic over traces of pencil, 220 × 250mm (300.1), 111 × 126mm (300.2). By Govindoo, *c*.1850.

Wight described this plant as *Dendrobium jerdonianum* from Coorg and the Iyamally Hills, and this drawing forms part of the original material. The flowers from the two localities were said in the original description to differ in size, but it is impossible to say which form is shown here. However, Wight's species, which commemorates T.C. Jerdon, is no longer recognised as distinct from the more widespread *D. nutans*, which was first described by Lindley from Ceylon, and also occurs throughout the Western Ghats at altitudes of between 600 and 1830 metres. In this species the lateral sepals are attached to a downward extension of the column, from the base of which arises the lip. The stems of this epiphytic species are conspicuous, with swollen internodes.

Annotations by Wight: Malaxideae Orchideae 1644, Dendrobium Jerdonianum (RW)(ink, recto).

Published as plate 1644 of the *Icones* (1851), lithographed by Dumphy.

RBGE W300.1 & 2 R (SERIES E)

Malaxidea Orchidea 1644

Dendrobium Jerdonianum (RW)

132. Bulbophyllum fuscopurpureum *Wight*

ORCHIDACEAE

Bodycolour heightened with gum arabic and pencil, 222 × 282mm. By Govindoo, *c.*1850.

An extraordinary epiphytic orchid with flowers that look like a creation of Edward Lear – the lateral petals are narrowed into linear points weighed down by swollen knobs. The plant was discovered in the Nilgiri Hills by Thomas Caverhill Jerdon, a medical colleague of Wight in the Madras Presidency, and pioneering Indian zoologist. This is a copy by Govindoo of a drawing made by Mrs Jerdon and sent by her to Wight; she called it the tongue orchid, from the shape of its lip. This species is restricted to the southern part of the Western Ghats of Kerala and Tamil Nadu, occurring from the Nilgiri Hills southwards to Periyar.

Annotations by Wight: Malaxideae Orchideae 1651, Bulbophyllum fuscopurpureum (RW)(ink, recto).

Published as plate 1651 of the *Icones* (1851), lithographed by Dumphy.

RBGE W303.1 R (SERIES E)

133. Liparis biloba *Wight*

ORCHIDACEAE

Bodycolour and pencil, 216 × 249mm. By Govindoo, *c.*1850.

Restricted to the Nilgiri Hills, this plant demonstrates the artificiality of the terrestrial/epiphytic distinction. Wight originally found the plant 'nestling among moss on the branches of trees', as shown here in Govindoo's pencil sketch, but it can also grow on the ground. Wight distinguished this species from the related *L. atropurpurea* on account of its two-lobed lip.

Although the habit is drawn with great delicacy, the floral analysis is in Govindoo's later, bolder style. This style was probably developed because the artist realised that subtle details would not be shown when the drawings were lithographed

Annotations by Wight: Malaxideae Orchideae 1633, Liparis biloba (RW)(ink, recto); dull plum colour (pencil, recto).

Published as plate 1633 of the *Icones* (1851), lithographed by Dumphy.

RBGE W292 R (SERIES E)

134 A & B. Brachycorythis iantha

(Wight) Summerhayes

ORCHIDACEAE

Bodycolour heightened with gum arabic over traces of pencil,
223 × 247mm (324.1), 102 × 159mm (324.2). By Govindoo, *c.*1850.

A typical ground orchid, showing the tubers that give the
name to the family (*orchis* being Greek for a testicle). Wight
described this species in the genus *Platanthera* (to which
the British butterfly orchids belong), but it was later
transferred to a genus described by John Lindley and
named for the short helmet-like appearance of the lateral
petals and sepals, as seen in floral detail 1. Wight knew this
species from the Nilgiri and Palni Hills, Malabar and
Courtallum, where it occurs on grassy slopes up to an
altitude of 2400 metres. The specific name refers to the
violet colour of the flowers.

Annotations by Wight: Ophrydeae Orchideae 1692, Platanthera
iantha (RW) (ink, recto).

Published as plate 1692 of the *Icones* (1851), lithographed by Dumphy.

RBGE W324.1 & 2 R (SERIES E)

135 A & B. Cymbidium aloifolium

(Linnaeus) Swartz

ORCHIDACEAE

Bodycolour and ink over traces of pencil, 295 × 445mm. By Rungiah, *c.*1830.

Watermark: J WHATMAN 1826.

An epiphytic species widespread in tropical S E Asia, which occurs up to an altitude of 2000 metres in the Himalaya. Wight knew the plant from the foot of the Nilgiri Hills, and also collected it on his brief visit to Ceylon in 1836. The species was first described by Linnaeus, based on a description and drawing in van Rheede's *Hortus Malabaricus* published in 1693. In this great illustrated work Rheede recorded the medicinal uses of plants from Ayurvedic doctors of the Malabar Coast. These doctors believed that specimens of this plant when collected from trees of *Strychnos nux-vomica* could be used, taken powdered with ginger, to cure 'old diseases, mist of the eyes, giddiness and paralysis'. However, when growing on other tree species the orchid had quite different properties, something quite contrary to Western ideas of botany or pharmacology.

RBGE W414 R + V (SERIES ?D)

Sagittaria
obtusifolia

136. Limnophyton obtusifolium

(Linnaeus) Miquel

ALISMATACEAE

Tam: neer cody (Wight), kudurai chedy; Tel: gurrapu dekka chettu

Bodycolour and ink over traces of pencil, 157 × 202mm. By Rungiah, *c.*1830.

An aquatic, usually annual, herb that grows as an emergent from shallow pools and tanks. It is widely distributed in the Old World tropics from Africa and Madagascar, eastwards through lowland India and Sri Lanka to Indonesia. Wight first collected it at Rajahmundry in November 1822, and later at Chingleput. This drawing was not published by Wight, but is one of the series accompanied by long descriptions sent to Hooker in Glasgow. It was first described by Linnaeus in the genus *Sagittaria* (to which the British 'arrow-head' belongs), based on Indian material illustrated in the works of Rheede (from Kerala) and Plukenet (from Madras). The Dutch botanist F.A.W. Miquel, who specialised in plants of Indonesia, transferred it to the genus *Limnophyton*. The flowers are of two sorts on a single plant – the ones in the upper whorls (and shown here in the analytical detail) are male. Those in the lowest whorl (uncoloured in this drawing) are bisexual, and develop into deflexed fruiting heads each composed of numerous achenes; the achenes have air chambers and are dispersed by floating in water.

Annotation: Sagittaria obtusifolia (pencil, recto).

RBGE W411 R (SERIES C/B)

137. Smilax aspera *Linnaeus*

SMILACACEAE

Tam: cody velly (Wight)

Bodycolour and ink over traces of pencil, 215 × 320mm. By Rungiah, *c.*1834.

Watermark: [RUSE & TU]RNERS.

The family has a relatively unusual growth habit for a monocotyledon being a climber ('liane') with rather woody stems. It climbs by means of prickles on the stem (not shown in this drawing) and tendrils developed from the stipules. This species has an unusual distribution occurring in the Mediterranean maquis community, and through the mountains of the Middle East and Himalaya (where it ascends to 2500 metres), with outliers in the mountains of South India (Nilgiris and Palnis) and Sri Lanka. The white flowers, in South India produced from November to May, are fragrant. This drawing was not published by Wight, though he did publish a drawing by ?Govindoo as plate 2059 of the *Icones* (under the synonym *Smilax maculata*).

Telugu annotation: (kudi vali)

RBGE W395 R (SERIES ?D)

Watermarks on papers in the Wight collections

Wove (i.e., smooth), Cream Papers of Various Weights

Series A

Possibly Rungiah's earliest drawings are on smallish (c.175 × 250) sheets of a heavy (c.184 gsm), cream paper. Most of these have no watermark (though the Kew ones of this series being mounted on opaque backing sheets cannot be examined), but the following are recorded:

Ruse & Turners 1824
RBGE 20, 21, 23, 38, 107, 129, 130, 345, 346, 390; NHM 141, 253.
Note. Made by Richard Turner and one of his partners (?Letts) at Upper Tovil Mill, Maidstone, Kent.[1]

Ruse & Turners 1828
NHM 109.1.

Ruse & Turners 1829
NHM 321, 494.

Series C

Apparently dating from pre-1831. On small (c.160 × 200) sheets of light (c.106 gsm), cream paper:

C Wilmot 1819
This is one of the most commonly used papers by Wight.
RBGE 1, 4, 7, 9, 31, 34, 39, 47, 71, 77, 79, 89, 90, 91, 92, 139, 145.1, 167, 179.1, 275.1, 383, 420.1, 431; NHM 16, 86, 160, 257, 307, 320, 350, 366, 401, 455, 462, 503.

He also used this later in larger sheets with large details (one dated 1834), and occasionally drew on this collection for the *Icones* (Series E), e.g., RBGE 275.1, with details on a supplementary sheet.

Note. Made by Charles Wilmott, Shoreham Mill, Kent.[2]

C Wilmot 1830
A single drawing on this cream, smooth paper RBGE 159.2 – details supplementing an earlier drawing.

GY Eeles 1822
A smooth cream paper very similar to 'Wilmot 1819' used in the first period on small sheets for RBGE 10, 35, 73, 137.1; and NHM 303.

J & M + Prince of Wales feathers 1823
Another paper (smooth, cream) like 'Wilmot 1819' used in small size in early period for RBGE 94, 151.1, 404; NHM 66.1, 89.
Note. Made by John Jones & John Mather, Afonwen Mill, Flintshire.[3]

Series D

Mid-period drawings with large dissections (1832–6), on larger sheets of heavy (c.162 gsm), cream paper:

II Smith
RBGE 101, 109, 111, 131, 141, 358, 382; NHM 121, 203, 227.1, 426, 457.

S & S 1829
RBGE 104, 106, 116, 127, 169, 347, 351, 354, 391, 416.1; NHM 122, 143, 201, 226, 354, 355, 487, 504, 662.

Ruse & Turners 1831
Used for supplementary details added to earlier plates: RBGE 142.2, 145.2, 147.2.

Series E

Late period, associated with the *Icones* and *Illustrations*. The majority of the habit drawings are done on light (c.90 gsm) rather poor quality machine-made papers (the earlier are rougher and have become discoloured, the later smoother and have remained whiter); they have no watermarks and are thus impossible to date. It is possible that these papers were obtained from the Fort St George Government.[4] The Superintendent of Stationery certainly supplied some of the paper for lithography of the *Illustrations* and *Icones*, and this paper is similar to that on which the prints were made. In November 1837 Wight discovered a supply of paper in the

Engineer's Office 'long since condemned as unfit' and requested 'different kinds of condemned paper … for the purposes of being subjected to experiment' 'by the application of chemical agents, resizing, &c'. This might, perhaps account for the rather poor condition of many of the original drawings for the *Icones* (Series E) in the Edinburgh collection, and gives one cause to regret Wight's parsimonious habits!

The hand-made, watermarked papers used in this period are few and far between:

Whatman 1847
RBGE 287.1; NHM 356, 514, 515.1.

J Whatman 1848
NHM 488.1.
Note. This and the previous made by William Balston at Springfield Mill, Maidstone, Kent.[5]

J Whatman Turkey Mill 1848
NHM 497, 522.1.
Note. Made by T. and J. Hollingworth, Turkey Mill, Maidstone, Kent.[6]

Grey, Laid Papers

These middling weight (c.109 gsm) papers were used for EIC records; Wight used them for notes, and Rungiah and Govindoo for supplementary floral details for Series E; also occasionally for whole drawings (e.g., some orchids, and *Pajanalia* NHM 358).

J Whatman 1826 + EIC symbol
RBGE 414; NHM 357.

JW [Script Monogram] + fleur de lys
The commonest paper used for floral details on small supplementary sheets by Rungiah & Govindoo:
RBGE 161.2, 162.2, 176.1, 203.2, 211.2, 220.2, 221.2, 232.2, 233.2, 238.2, 245.2, 247.2, 248.2, 253.2, 254.2, 255.2, 256.2, 259.2, 262.2,

263.2, 280.2, 281.2, 290.2, 315; NHM 47.2, 92.2, 172.2, 241.2.
Note. RBGE 342.1 has the same monogram, but a posthorn rather than fleur de lys.

Radway 1828 + Britannia
RBGE 429.1; notes with E 431, 432, 434, 435, 436, 437, 439, 440; NHM 66.2, 162; 665.1.

E Wise 1831 + EIC symbol
NHM 358.1, 358.2.

HARRIS & TREMLETT 1837
RBGE 207.2, 215.2, 222.2, 283.2, 289.2, 425.1; NHM 70.2, 402.2, 437.1.

C Wilmot 1840 + rampant lion
RBGE 288.1, 293.1, 321, 324.2, 334.2, 428.1; and NHM 85, 170.1496, 524.1, 525.1, 527.1, 529.1, 633.2, 650.2, 715, 723.1.

Ruse & Turners 1841
RBGE 421.1; NHM 461.

R&T [script monogram] + fleur de lys
RBGE 422.1; NHM 262.2.

C&EH [script monogram] + posthorn
RBGE 173.1, 181.1, 195 [dated 1843], 328.2; NHM 205.2, 603.
Note. Perhaps made by Clarke & Horsington.[7]

C Ansell 1849
NHM 83, 521.1.

J Bune
RBGE 179.2, 182.2.

II Smith & Son
RBGE 421.2, 422.2.

CW [script monogram] + Kent 1826
Used for notes associated with RBGE 438, 442.

KG [monogram in circle] + 1825
Used for notes associated with RBGE 438, 439, 441, 442.

Moinier's Patent 1848
A blue laid paper: NHM 94

Other artists in the Wight collections

Harmanis de Alwis Seneviratne (1792–1894)

De Alwis (as Wight gave his name) was first employed as a 'writer' in the Ceylon botanic gardens in 1818 under Alexander Moon, whom he helped in the preparation of his *Catalogue* (1824). 'Perceiving De Alwis's aptitude for drawing, Moon had him taught at his own expense',[1] and in 1823, shortly after the gardens had moved to Peradenyia, De Alwis was appointed as draftsman 'a post he continued to hold for thirty-eight years', retiring in 1861. Wight must have met De Alwis in 1836 and in 1838, when J.G. Lear had charge of the Garden, suggested that he be sent to Madras for three months to learn how to draw dissections.[2] During this period De Alwis drew the originals for 31 plates in the *Icones*.[3] He is referred to as 'Don Aluis' in a letter from J.A. Stewart-Mackenzie, Governor of Ceylon, to Wight, when he was evidently being used as a courier to take back tea plants from the Madras Agri-Horticultural Society (though he had not reached home by July 1839).[4] De Alwis was evidently highly respected and given the title 'Muhandiram' by Governor Barnes in 1831, and 'Mudaliyar' by Governor Anderson in 1854. He is the only one of the artists associated with Wight of whom we have a portrait, which has been reproduced by Desmond.[5] De Alwis continued to work under Gardner and then Thwaites, and when he retired was succeeded by his son William – in this way a large collection of botanical drawings was built up, many of which now appear to be in the Herbarium Illustrations Collection at Kew.[6] At Edinburgh is a sheet with floral dissections of two unrelated species, which from the annotations can be taken to be a drawing by De Alwis sent to Wight from Ceylon by G.H.K. Thwaites. One plant is labelled 'Alwisia zeylanica Thw. mss', but this name was never published and Thwaites must have realised before publishing the plant concerned as a new species in 1852 that it could be referred to the genus *Epicarpus*; the plate accompanying the published description of *E. zeylanicus* includes very similar floral dissections to the Edinburgh drawing. There is also a single pencil drawing by De Alwis in the NHM Wight collection.

Walter Abraham

It is not known whether Abraham was British or Anglo-Indian, though the latter seems the more likely. He worked for J.E. Stocks in Sind in 1847, having been lent to him by Walter Scott (the novelist's nephew), Superintendent of Canals and Forests.[7] Stocks sent Wight at least six of Abraham's accomplished line drawings. An unpublished one (of *Lycium edgworthii*) is in the Natural History Museum collection (NHM 383), and five were published by Wight in the *Icones* (tt.1420–bis, 1459, 1461, 1528, 1613), though the whereabouts of the originals is unknown. Abraham became superintendent of the lithographic department of the Bombay Government's Education Society Press c.1854–66 and in 1867 he was Manager of the Lithography Department of the Chief Engineer's Office.[8]

Alphonso Bertie

Bertie was an apothecary on the Madras Establishment, first appointed in 1834, and in 1840 working under the Commissioner of Mysore.[9] Nothing more is known of him though the name suggests that he was Portuguese-Indian or 'East-Indian' (i.e., Anglo-Indian).[10] Wight noted that collecting plants and making drawings was 'an accomplishment so rare among the members of his [Bertie's] branch of the service [that it] merits public commendation'.[11] By the fortunate mention in the *Illustrations* of a drawing by Bertie of *Vateria indica* with the local (Kannada) name 'dhupada mara', and the survival of this drawing at Edinburgh, it has been possible to identify a group of drawings at E and NHM as his work. These (e.g., fig.10, p.26), which, from the Kannada names, must date from his Mysore period, are simple, but competent, ink outline drawings with annotated microscopic floral analyses, doubtless modelled on the prints in the *Icones* (though one of the 'dhupada mara' drawings is partly coloured). Two plates in the *Icones* (tt.164, 241) are based on Bertie's drawings, and there are a few of his specimens, with very detailed labels, in the Edinburgh herbarium.

Gopalchunder

William Munro, when based in Agra, employed an artist called Gopalchunder. He sent two of his drawings to Wight, which were reproduced in the *Icones* (tt.1072, 1074). The whereabouts of the originals is unknown and it seems most unlikely that this is the artist of the earlier Munro Nilgiri drawings in the Wight collection at NHM.

Lakshman (Lachman, Luchman) Singh

Lakshman Singh was one of the best and longest serving of the Calcutta Garden artists. It appears that he was one of those borrowed by Royle when Wallich went on leave in 1828, as it is recorded that he also made three zoological drawings for J.F. Royle at Saharunpur.[12] What is unusual about Singh is that a documented example of his non-botanical work survives, showing another side of the work that many of the botanical artists must surely have undertaken for other patrons – a portrait of George Potter.[13] Singh later took to lithography, as shown by some fine lithographs, based on drawings of *Podostemon* by Griffith, made to illustrate a paper in *Asiatic Researches*, printed at J.B. Tassin's Oriental Lithographic Press in Calcutta in 1836 [fig.21 p.39]; Singh along with Bhogoban Chatterjee and Hurrimohun were the painters from the Calcutta Garden who worked on the illustrations for Griffith's *Posthumous Papers*.[14] Wallich sent Wight two drawings that Wight reproduced in the *Icones* (tt. 1054, 1055) in 1846, attributed to 'Lechman Singie'. The originals of these plates are unknown, but given the exceptional quality of the shaded 'tracings' of the Roxburgh Icones sent by Wallich to Wight for publication, and their similarity to the *Podostemon* plate, it seems likely that it was Singh who made these.

J. Suares

One plate in the RBGE Wight collection is initialled 'J.S.', which although indistinguishable in style from Rungiah's work, is probably by J. Suares. There is a drawing of a cotton by him at Kew that is part of the Madras School of Art series (see p.201n), and it appears that in 1856 he was working at the Government Lithographic Press, for there are two plates drawn 'on stone by J. Suares and Lithd. by J. Dumphy' in Cleghorn's 1856 paper on the sand-binding plants of the Madras beach.[15] As with Gibson's anonymous artist at Dapuri, here is another example of a Portuguese-Indian working as a botanical artist.

EUROPEANS

Further information on some of the following artists has been given in earlier publications,[16] but as a result of studying the Natural History Museum collection, several 'new' artists have come to light, not represented at Edinburgh, and additional information has become available on some of those already known.

J. Dent

When Wight was in Palamcottah (i.e., 1834–5) he was sent a freely painted watercolour (NHM 725) of a spectacular phallic fungus (*Dictyophora multicolor*), which he subsequently had copied (and improved) by Rungiah (NHM 726). The original was probably painted by (rather than for) the J [?] Dent whose name it bears, as it is rather Western in style. This is likely to be John Dent (1795–1845), who in 1830 was the Collector of Masulipatam, which is probably where this drawing was made. Dent asked 'J. Limond' (possibly Col. James Limond a Madras Artillery officer), to send the drawing to Wight by means of his 'tuppal'.

Michael Pakenham Edgeworth (1812–81)

A Bengal Civil Servant who sent numerous tracings of Himalayan plants to Wight, some dated 1838; these are in ink with only a few of the details coloured. The watermark on many of the sheets is 'J WHATMAN TURKEY MILL 1835'. These drawings have numerous analytical details, some of which must have been made with a compound microscope. Wight published only five of these in the *Icones* (tt.322–5, 1510), but 82 are at NHM and one at Kew. Kew has recently acquired a collection of more finished watercolours done by Edgeworth and various members of his family in India and Ireland.

Robert Kaye Greville (1794–1866)

Hooker must have found Rungiah's analyses of the minute floral parts on an early drawing of *Toxocarpus kleinii* (Plate 84) inadequate, and asked Greville, who often did drawings for him at this time, to provide new ones. When much later (1844–5) Wight decided to reproduce the drawing as t.886 of the *Icones*, he acknowledged Greville's unexpected contribution in the letterpress.

Flora Alexandrina Matilda Jerdon (née Macleod)

Married to T.C. Jerdon. Both were interested in plants, and they formed an illustrations collection similar to Wight's, including original drawings, and rough tracings from a variety of literature (including the *Botanical Magazine*). This was bought by Kew in 1873, which passed on about 27 'duplicate' sheets to RBGE. Mrs Jerdon drew especially orchids, and a volume of 138 of her drawings entitled 'Orchidea Jerdon' survives in the Connemara Library in Madras. Localities include Wynad, Palghat and Ceylon, and the latter suggests contacts with Mrs Walker. While clearly the work of an amateur, these are perfectly adequate scientifically. She sent some of her orchid drawings to Wight, who published two of them in vols 4 & 5 of the *Icones* (tt.1602, 1651).

Francis Newcombe Maltby (b. 1813)

A Madras Civil Servant, who, when Collector of Canara based at Mangalore, sent orchid drawings to Wight, now at NHM. These are similar in style to Mrs Jerdon's, and on blue paper.

Edward Archdall McCurdy (1797–1842)

Of the 27th Regiment Madras Native Infantry who, around 1830, published a series of topographical lithographs of the Nilgiris (e.g., Book 1 fig.27). Three watercolours of *Caralluma adscendens* at the Natural History Museum (NHM 344–6) signed with the initials EAMCC almost certainly represent his work.

Ann Maria Walker (née Paton)

A keen botanist and artist married to Colonel Walker, together they explored Ceylon when he was stationed there, and Wight met up with them in 1836. Mrs Walker made fine watercolours, but what she sent to Wight were mainly tracings of these on thin paper watermarked 'D & A COWAN 1819' [fig.8]. This probably stands for Duncan & Alexander Cowan who at this date had a Paper Warehouse at 170 Canongate, Edinburgh,[17] and the paper was probably made at one of the mills owned by various members of the Cowan family around Penicuik. Most of these were not published by Wight, and only one plate (t.932) in vol. 3 of the *Icones* is attributed to her, though the plate of *Passiflora walkeriae* in the *Illustrations* (t.108), is also based on one of her drawings [fig.7] and attributed in the text. At Edinburgh are two other drawings by her from Robert Graham's collection. The Walkers sent numerous specimens to Graham, but which, like Wight's early collections, he largely ignored, though many of them were used by Hooker and Arnott.

Robert Wight

The drawings of two of the plates in the first volume of the *Icones* (tt. 214, 215) are attributed to Wight himself; the original drawing of the latter is at Kew.

Bibliography

(For Wight's publications, and archival references see Bibliography in Book 1)

ARCHER, M. (1962). *Natural History Drawings in the India Office Library*. London: HMSO.

ARCHER, M. (1989). The Peoples of India, in *India: a Pageant of Prints*, P. Rohatgi & P. Godrej (eds), pp. 1–20. Bombay: Marg Publications.

ARCHER, M. (1992). *Company Paintings: Indian Paintings of the British Period*. London: Victoria and Albert Museum.

BAIKIE, R. (1834). *Observations on the Neilgherries* [etc.]. Calcutta: Baptist Mission Press.

BOWER, P. (1990). *Turner's Papers: a study of the manufacture, selection and use of his drawing papers 1787–1820*. London: Tate Gallery.

BOWER, P. (1999). *Turner's Later Papers: a study of the manufacture, selection and use of his drawing papers 1820–1851*. London & New Castle: Tate Publishing & Oak Knoll Press.

BUCHANAN, F. (1807). *A Journey from Madras through the countries of Mysore, Canara, and Malabar …* . London: T. Cadell & W. Davies.

CAMERON, J. (1907). *List of Botanical Drawings in Watercolours in the Collection of the State Botanical Gardens, Lal Bagh, Bangalore*. Bangalore: Higginbotham & Co.

CAREY, J. (2005). *What Good Are the Arts?* London: Faber & Faber Ltd.

[CHUBB, W.] (2006). *Fifty-One Flowers: Botanical Watercolours from Bengal*. London: Colnaghi in association with Hobhouse Ltd.

CLEGHORN, H.[F.C.] (1856). Notulae Botanicae No. I. On the Sand-binding plants of the Madras beach. *Madras Journal of Literature and Science* 1(new series): 85–90.

COOK, A.S. (1989). The beginning of lithographic map printing in Calcutta, in *India: a Pageant of Prints*, P. Rohatgi & P. Godrej (eds), pp. 125–34. Bombay: Marg Publications.

DALLAPICCOLA, A.L. (2002). *Dictionary of Hindu Lore and Legend*. London: Thames & Hudson.

DESMOND, R. (1992). *The European Discovery of the Indian Flora*. Oxford: Oxford University Press.

DESMOND, R. (1994). *Dictionary of British and Irish Botanists and Horticulturists*. London: Taylor & Francis, and Natural History Museum.

FORBES, J. (1813). *Oriental Memoirs … 4 vols*. London: White, Cochrane, and Co.

FREEDBERG, D. (2002). *The Eye of the Lynx: Galileo, his friends, and the beginnings of modern Natural History*. Chicago & London: The University of Chicago Press.

GOLD, C.(1806). *Oriental Drawings: sketched between the years of 1791 and 1798*. London: G. & W. Nicoll.

GOSWAMY, B.N. & DALLAPICCOLA, A.L. (1983). *A Place Apart: Painting in Kutch, 1720–1820*. New Delhi: Oxford University Press.

GRANT DUFF, SIR M.E. (1899). *Notes from a Diary kept chiefly in Southern India 1881–1886*. 2 vols. London: John Murray

[GRIFFITH, W.] (1850). *Palms of British East India* ed. J. M'Clelland. Calcutta: Charles A. Serrao.

GURUDEVA, M.R. (2001). *Botanical and Vernacular Names of South Indian Plants*. Bangalore: Divyachandra Prakashana.

HENDERSON, D.M. & DICKSON, J.H. (1994). *A Naturalist in the Highlands: James Robertson, his life and travels in Scotland 1767–1771*. Edinburgh: Scottish Academic Press.

HEYNE, B. (1814). *Tracts, Historical and Statistical, on India*. London: Robert Baldwin.

HILL, D.O. (1821–2). *Sketches of Scenery in Perthshire. Drawn from Nature on Stone*. Perth: Thos. Hill.

HOOKER, J.D. (1851). *The Rhododendrons of Sikkim-Himalaya* [t. 27, *R. wightii*]. London: L. Reeve & Co.

HOOKER, W.J. (1821). *Botanical Illustrations: being a series of figures designed to illustrate the terms employed in a course of lectures on botany, with descriptions*. Edinburgh: Archibald Constable & Company [Title page dated 1822, but according to TL2 issued in September 1821]. 2nd edition, Glasgow: 'unpublished' (1837).

HOOKER, W.J. (1853). Dr. Wight's return to England. *Journal of Botany & Kew Garden Miscellany* 5: 247–9

HOPKIRK, T. (1817). *Flora Anomoia. A General View of the Anomalies in the Vegetable Kingdom*. Glasgow: John Smith & Son.

[KER, J.B.] (1818). Of the three species of the natural order Orchideae, represented in Plate VI. *Journal of Science and the Arts* 4: 199–206; t. V (sic).

MABBERLEY, D.J. (1997). *The Plant-Book*. 2nd ed. Cambridge: Cambridge University Press.

MACKAY, C. & SARKAR, A.N. (2005). Kalighat pats: an examination of techniques and materials, in *Scientific Research in the Pictorial Arts of Asia: Proceedings of the Second Forbes Symposium at the Freer Gallery of Art*, pp. 135–42. P. Jett, J. Winter & B. McCarthy (eds). London: Archetype Publications.

MATHEW, M.V. (1987). *The History of the Royal Botanic Garden Library Edinburgh*. Edinburgh: HMSO.

MITTER, P. (1992). *Much Maligned Monsters: a history of European reactions to Indian art*. [Paperback edition]. Chicago & London: The University of Chicago Press.

MUTHIAH, S. (2003). A 350–year old medical heritage [newspaper article]. *The Hindu*, 12 March 2003.

NICOLSON, M. (2004) Hopkirk, Thomas (1785–1841) in *The Oxford Dictionary of National Biography* ed. H.C.G. Matthew & B. Harrison (eds) 28: 80. Oxford: Oxford University Press.

NOLTIE, H.J. (1999). *Indian Botanical Drawings 1793–1868 from the Royal Botanic Garden Edinburgh*. Edinburgh: Royal Botanic Garden Edinburgh.

NOLTIE, H.J. (2002). *The Dapuri Drawings: Alexander Gibson & the Bombay Botanic Gardens*. Edinburgh: Royal Botanic Garden Edinburgh.

NOLTIE, H.J. (2005). *The Botany of Robert Wight*. Ruggell: A.R.G. Gantner Verlag.

PRIOLKAR, A.K. (1958). *The Printing Press in India: its beginnings and early development …* Bombay: Marathi Samshodhana Mandala.

RICH, V.A. (1987). Mughal floral painting and its European sources. *Oriental Art* 33: 183–9.

SARKAR, A.N. & MACKAY, C. (2000). *Kalighat Paintings*. New Delhi: Lustre Press/Roli Books.

SCHENCK, D.H.J. (1999). *Directory of the Lithographic Printers of Scotland 1820–1870*. Edinburgh: Edinburgh Bibliographical Society.

SCHENCK, D.H.J. (2005). *Directory of the Lithographic Printers of Scotland 1820–1870: additions, corrections and revisions*. Edinburgh Bibliographical Society Transactions 6: 292–312.

Notes and References

INTRODUCTION

1 Noltie, 2002
2 Noltie, 2005; Books 1 & 3 of the present work

CHAPTER I

1 Wight, 1837l
2 Secord, 2002: 29
3 See Freedberg, 2002: 203
4 Linnaeus, *Genera Plantarum*, translated and quoted by Freedberg, 2002: 412
5 Secord, 2002
6 Note. See Book 1 Chapter 13
7 Note. Only one of these, of *Ruppia maritima*, has survived in the Hope collection at RBGE, but see Henderson & Dickson, 1994 for two contemporaneously published examples
8 Note. That this influence was more extensive is proved by the single Indian botanical drawing in the Hope collection – of the telegraph plant, *Codariocalyx motorius*, sent back to him by James Kerr from Bengal
9 Hooker, 1853
10 Note. A contemporary example of 'misuse' of a predominantly 'scientific' text is to be found in the opening of *Jane Eyre* (1847), where the heroine uses only selected parts of the letterpress (most of which she 'cared little for') of Thomas Bewick's *History of British Birds*, and the vignettes (rather than the scientifically accurate plates), to feed her romantic imagination and yearnings
11 Quoted in Secord, 2002: 31
12 Secord, 2002: 37. Note. One is reminded of the resentment that W.S. Gilbert came to feel when people in the street whistled Sullivan's tunes of the Savoy operas, but failed to remember their witty and politically pointed words
13 Wight, 1840a: ii

14 Secord, 2002: 37
15 RBGK DC 10/4, 1838
16 RBGK DC 3/59
17 RBGK DC 14/24
18 Note. 15 composite plates with material reprinted from Hooker's works see RBGK DC 3/18
19 Note. T.C. Jerdon, Alexander Gibson and William Griffith. Although none of these had doctorates, it is odd that unlike others on the list they are not denoted by their army-medical rank of 'Surgeon' or 'Assistant Surgeon' – perhaps because Wight regarded them more for their non-medical work
20 Note. Booksellers and libraries are omitted, as are multiple copies to individuals

CHAPTER 2

1 RBGK MC f. 232
2 Wight, 1853b: 36
3 See Book 1, Chapter 13
4 Arnold, 2005: 183
5 Note. No artists are given on any of Roxburgh's drawings or prints; Wallich named artists on the plates in *Plantae Asiaticae Rariores*, as did Royle on many of the plates in *Illustrations of the Botany of the Himalayan Mountains*
6 Wight, 1847a: 85
7 CBG WC pkt 19, 16 × 1835. Note. This must be Thomas Moore Lane (born 1797) who started as an Assistant Surgeon in Madras in 1822, and died there in 1844. Crawford, 1930: 310
8 Archer, 1992: 35
9 Note. He was also proud of his medical ancestry – his maternal grandfather was Sir Whitelaw Ainslie (1767–1837) who from 1788 to 1815 was a Madras surgeon. Curiously it was to provide illustrations for the plants treated in Ainslie's *Materia Medica of Hindoostan*

that was one of Wight's explicit reasons for publishing his *Icones*
10 Grant Duff, 1899 2: 200
11 Cameron, 1907
12 White, 1999
13 *Report on Public Instruction in the Madras Presidency for 1862–3* p 56. Copy seen in College. The other artists represented in the two volumes are: M. Rangaswamy Modly, P. Vijiahrangam and C. Abboy. Three drawings of cottons from this series are at Kew, and came via the India Museum – one of these is by J. Suares, who certainly worked for Cleghorn and possibly on one occasion for Wight. At this time engravings of plants were also being made in the College
14 Archer, 1992: 45
15 Rao & Sastri, 1980: 19
16 A.L. Dallapiccola, pers. comm.
17 http://www.artofindia.com/read/tanjore_art.htm, consulted 6 Feb 2006
18 For further information see Nair, 2005
19 Ibid.
20 Archer, 1962: 13–14, 89; plate 17
21 Nair, 2005: 289
22 Gold, 1806
23 Archer, 1962: 27–8, 79–80; plate 14
24 Heyne, 1814: 248
25 Robinson, 2003: 131
26 Note. Sangwan (1997) and others have written about such conflicts, and in 1832 Mary Roxburgh was still trying to extract the drawings she believed her husband had paid for from Calcutta (CBG WC pkt 18, and see Robinson 2003: 132)
27 TNA MDC vol. 847 f. 8637
28 TNA MDC vol. 848 f. 9085/6
29 Preetha Nair, pers. comm.
30 OIOC P/245/76 ff. 2415–22
31 OIOC P/246/4
32 RBGK DC 52/113
33 Nalini Persad, pers. comm. Note. The Tamil form would

have been 'Ranga' – Shashi Sen, pers. comm.
34 RBGK DC 52/108
35 RBGK DC 52/114
36 RBGK DC 52/108
37 RBGK DC 52/113
38 RBGK DC 52/112
39 RBGK DC 52/118
40 RBGK DC 52/125
41 RBGK DC 53/160
42 RBGK DC 52/114
43 RBGK DC 52/113
44 RBGK DC 53/169
45 RBGK DC 52/160
46 Griffith, 1848: v
47 Gardner, 1845: 565
48 Note. At Goethe's suggestion Runge analysed coffee, resulting in the discovery of caffeine; he also invented paper chromatography
49 Wallich, 1831
50 Griffith, 1848: liii
51 Griffith, 1850, t. 216c, 235E. This volume was issued in 'Super Royal' format at the substantial cost of Rs 50
52 Preetha Nair, pers. comm.
53 RBGK DC 54/548
54 RBGK DC 54/545
55 See Noltie, 1998, plates 59–62
56 Desmond, 1992: 119
57 Wight, 1853b: 34
58 Note. These were Wallich's *Kurremia*, and Royle's *Murdannia* (since reinstated); the third – 'Mr Thwaites' supposed new genus' is not mentioned by name, but was going to be 'Alwisia' after the Singhalese artist, but which, 'when passing through the press', was found to be a species of *Streblus*. Wight was evidently unaware of Lindley's *Alvisia* (Orchidaceae), which is now sunk into *Eria*
59 Note. This starts with plate 72, a smoother and lighter machine made paper similar to that used throughout for the *Icones*
60 OIOC E/4/952 f. 243. Note the figures added from TNA Index to PDD 1816–37
61 Jim Kay, pers. comm.

62 Cleghorn, 1873: 26
63 Buchanan, 1807, 1: 74–6 and plate 3, referring to Seringapatam artists
64 Heyne, 1814: 88–9
65 Mackay & Sarkar, 2005
66 RBGK DC 53/178
67 Cleghorn, 1873: 25

CHAPTER 3

1 Note. About 523 of Rungiah's, and 922 of Govindoo's
2 Wight, 1853b: Preface p. vi
3 Sealy, 1956. Note. Several copies of each were made by Roxburgh's artists
4 Archer, 1962: 64
5 Ibid. p. 95
6 Wight, 1838e: 87 – see Appendix 2
7 Griffith, 1848: xvi
8 Mathew, 1987: 77
9 Note. It was only in the early 1980s, with a revival of interest in the British Raj, and influential exhibitions such as Stuart Carey Welch's 'Room for Wonder' held at Asia House, New York in 1978, that this type of drawing started to fetch high prices in the international art market – earlier in the twentieth century certain museums had actually disposed of such material that they considered to be 'duplicate' (Niall Hobhouse, pers. comm.)

CHAPTER 4

1 Goswamy & Dallapiccola, 1983
2 See Millner & Manalatos Catalogue, May 2005 (also on www.millnermanalatos.com, consulted 30 October 2006) for an example of Siva-Panchanan in this Chinese style. Anna Dallapiccola (pers. comm.) has pointed out that this is an even more multi-layered example of hybridity, as the image is taken from a Kalighat painting (probably mid-nineteenth century), such as one reproduced by Sarkar & Mackay, 2000.
3 Desmond, 1992: 145
4 Rich, 1987
5 Desmond, 1992: 161
6 Noltie, 1999
7 RBGK DC 53/178. Note. This was not the first time such a

thing had been suggested and in 1774, in London, John Hill had produced a quarto edition of the first volume, but in this the 57 reduced plates were, like Rheede's, engravings
8 Cleghorn, 1873: 9
9 Note. Vol. 1: t 129 copied from t. 2028 of the *Botanical Magazine*; t. 130 copied from t. 51 of vol. 1 of *Hortus Malabaricus*; t. 255 copied from Wallich's *Tentamen Florae Napalensis*. Vol. 2: the fruit on t. 547 copied from Gaertner
10 'Notice', issued with the second part bound into the author's own copy of the *Icones*, vol. 1
11 Sealy, 1956, 1975; Desmond, 1992; Noltie, 1999; Robinson, 2002
12 Noltie, 1999
13 OIOC P/13/54
14 CBG WC pkt 47, 24 xi 1839
15 Calligraphy and content identified by Graham Shaw
16 Chubb, 2006
17 Mitter, 1992
18 Ruskin: *The Two Paths*, 1859, quoted in Mitter, 1992: 245
19 Carey, 2005: 29
20 Preetha Nair, in preparation
21 Preetha Nair, pers. comm.
22 Desmond, 1992: 82
23 See Noltie, 1999: 75–77

CHAPTER 5

1 Shaw, 1998: 89
2 Hooker, 1853
3 Schenck, 1999
4 Forbes 1813
5 Mabberley, 1985: 187
6 Ker, 1818: 206
7 RBGK DC 53/154
8 Quoted in Priolkar, 1958: 99
9 Shaw, 1998: 97
10 RBGK DC 52/113
11 RBGK DC 52/119
12 Schenck, 1999, 2005
13 Schenck, 1999: 9
14 Shaw, 1998: 102
15 Hooker, 1853: 248. The purchases evidently did not include a press
16 Schenck, 2005
17 Hopkirk, 1817
18 Schenck, 2005
19 Nicolson, 2004
20 Schenck, 1999
21 Note. David Allan went into partnership with William Ferguson in 1835, based first in Trongate, then at 57 Argyle Street, and were 'amongst the

most distinguished of the early lithographic businesses in Scotland'. Schenck, 1999
22 Scottish Book Trade Index, National Library of Scotland, consulted electronically
23 Shaw, 1998: 98
24 Cook, 1989: 131
25 Note. Forrester is not mentioned in Schenk's Directory until 1832, but was clearly active in Edinburgh a decade earlier
26 Wallich, 1820
27 Baikie, 1834
28 Note. William Monteith was Acting Chief Engineer in 1833 – *Madras Almanac*
29 OIOC P/246/3 f. 543
30 Archer, 1989: 15
31 Wight, 1835a, b
32 RBGK DC 53/178. Note. The former refers to T.F.L. Nees von Esenbeck's *Genera Plantarum Florae Germanicae*, the first 16 fascicles of which, containing plates 1–320, had been published at Bonn, 1833–7. The latter might well include the exquisite plates for the *Annales des Sciences Naturelles*, to which Wight evidently subscribed
33 OIOC F/4/1755 no. 71755 ff. 33–7. Note. This is stated in Wight's report on his economic botany work submitted to the Supreme Government, dated 1 xi 1837, and shows that Cleghorn (1873) was mistaken in saying that Wight took back a press from Britain
34 OIOC F/4/1755 no. 71755 f. 11
35 Hooker, 1853
36 Quoted in Cleghorn, 1873
37 Hooker, 1853
38 RBGK DC 53/178
39 Wight 1837l
40 RBGK DC 53/178
41 OIOC F/4/1755 no. 71755 ff. 7–9
42 Pharoah's *Madras Almanac* for 1840
43 Wheeler, 1862
44 Note on verso of drawing RBGE W174.1
45 A note to him on the Roxburgh copy of *Hedyotis ramosa* seems to refer to one of the parts of the *Icones*: 'Etterazooloo. I sent some more work enough if you have any spare to finish the part get on with them. I shall write you in a day or two sending the reprise order for pay.– RW'
46 Note. *The Athenaeum* was a

newspaper issued on Tuesday, Thursday and Saturday
47 Graham Shaw, pers. comm.
48 S. Muthiah, pers. comm.
49 Archer, 1992: 25–30
50 Dallapiccola, 2002: 21, 36, etc.
51 *Calcutta Journal of Natural History* 4(17): 534
52 Hooker, 1851

APPENDIX I

1 Bower, 1999: 87
2 Ibid. p. 55
3 Bower, 1990: 117
4 OIOC F/4/1755 no. 71755
5 Bower, 1990: 30
6 Bower, 1999: 14
7 J. Kay, pers. comm

APPENDIX II

1 Trimen 1900: 379
2 Desmond, 1992: 163
3 Note. vol. 1 tt. 92–6, 98–9, 101, 106–8, 110–1, 116–7, 119–23, 125–7, 132, 134–5, 281; vol. 2 tt. 339, 347, 380, 398
4 TNA BRP vol. 1671 ff. 577–82
5 Desmond, 1992: 82
6 Note: William (1842–1916) and his brother George also painted butterflies, some of which are at NHM
7 Noltie, 2002: 62, 84
8 Bombay Almanacs 1854–67
9 *Madras Almanac* 1840
10 Note. That apothecaries were often 'East Indians' can be shown from the fact that one of the purposes of the Medical School attached to the Madras General Hospital in 1835 was to train Anglo-Indian medical apprentices as apothecaries, and Indians as dressers (Muthiah, 2003). Both groups were taught 'diagnostic skills and aftercare'; today they would be called paramedics
11 Wight, 1838e: 87
12 Archer, 1962: 26, 89
13 Reproduced in Desmond, 1992: 82
14 OIOC P/13/54, 20 viii 1845 no. 26
15 Cleghorn, 1856
16 Desmond (1992, 1994); Noltie (2002, 2005)
17 Scottish Book Trade Index, National Library of Scotland – consulted electronically

General Index

——

Index of Botanical Names